WOMEN DOING LIFE

Women Doing Life

Gender, Punishment, and the Struggle for Identity

Lora Bex Lempert

NEW YORK UNIVERSITY PRESS

New York and London

NEW YORK UNIVERSITY PRESS
New York and London
www.nyupress.org

References to Internet websites (URLs) were accurate at the time of writing. Neither the author nor New York University Press is responsible for URLs that may have expired or changed since the manuscript was prepared.

ISBN: 978-1-4798-6603-8 (cloth)
ISBN: 978-1-4798-2705-3 (paper)

For Library of Congress Cataloging-in-Publication data, please contact the Library of Congress.

New York University Press books are printed on acid-free paper, and their binding materials are chosen for strength and durability. We strive to use environmentally responsible suppliers and materials to the greatest extent possible in publishing our books.

Manufactured in the United States of America

10 9 8 7 6 5 4 3 2 1

Also available as an ebook

This book is dedicated to

Patricia Caruso,

Michigan Department of Corrections Director,

2003–2011;

Linda,

who died in prison before the study completed

but whose words live on in these pages;

and

the 72 life-serving women who trusted me to convey

their experiences of imprisonment.

CONTENTS

It's late fall in Michigan. The skies are overcast and gray, heavily blanketed in cloud cover that blocks the sun. I hear the Canadian geese, honking loudly and defecating freely, before I see them. They populate the small pond outside of the double barbed-wire perimeter fence that surrounds the only women's prison in the state. Aside from the life at the pond, which is really an overflow basin, the prison grounds are bleak. Unlike many of the men's facilities where walkways are lined with golden yellow marigolds, purple pansies, yellow and white daisies, and black-eyed Susans, and where, after six months of clear conduct, men can request three-by-four-foot garden plots for growing their own fruits, vegetables, or flowers, the women's prison has none of the soul-soothing color and normality of those floral displays. It is the warden's choice to maintain the stark, concrete-block institution without color or contrast. Such barrenness challenges the spirit. There have been a number of "successful" suicides (and several attempts) during her two-year tenure as warden. This is the site of my research.

As I roll into the potholed obstacle course that passes as the visitor parking area, I immediately scan the other cars to see whether or not the study scribes are present and waiting. The scribes (Audrey, Danielle, Ashleigh, Sara, Brianna, and Jessica) are students that I hand-picked and trained to transcribe as much of the focus-group or interview conversations as possible. They are central to this research project because the warden has prohibited the use of any recording devices for research purposes. For "security reasons," the facility staff visually records all of our focus groups and one-on-one interviews, but they cannot make audio recordings per the Certificate of Confidentiality limitations issued by the U.S. Department of Health and Human Services. Two scribes attend and transcribe each research meeting.

If we're all present in the reception area and set to go 30 minutes before our scheduled research period, and if the prison stars align, entry procedures will go smoothly and we won't lose focus-group time. Most often, we're lucky. Seasoned officers are assigned to the reception desk. They know the procedures and they know me, so we work in tandem to have the appropriate items listed on the "in-and-out manifest," which is then delivered to the duty officer for his or her signature and authorization. When there's a newbie on the desk, everything takes three to four times as long. Freshly trained officers are never, ever willing to take suggestion from me about how to facilitate procedures.

Danielle and Ashleigh are waiting. We sign in on the visitors' log. We turn in our drivers' licenses and pick up our state ID cards. We secure our car keys, purses, scarves, and tissues in the $0.50 lockers for rent. Cell phones, prohibited in prison buildings, are left in our cars. Then we wait . . . for manifest approvals, which—if the duty officer is out on the compound—can take a very long time. Or we wait while family members and friends of the women inside are screened and delivered to the visiting room. Or we wait while the reception area officers take their breaks. But eventually we are called and can proceed.

Each time we enter, we take off our coats (no hoods allowed) and lay them on the counter for inspection. We walk through the metal detector. We take off our shoes and stockings, show the officer the bottoms of our feet, and slap our shoe soles together to demonstrate that we are not packing contraband. We are then patted down, spread eagle. We open our mouths for inspection and lift up hair that covers the backs of our ears. Finally, we list every item of jewelry each of us is wearing: earrings, rings, glasses, watches, ear/eyebrow piercings, necklaces with/without pendants, and so on. Once we are cleared for entry, the officer marks our hands with glow-in-the-dark letters of the day as though we're gaining admittance to a dance club. We're issued our garage-door-opener lookalikes, the PPDs (personal protection devices), that we must wear on our persons and that track our whereabouts on the compound. Each PPD has a grenade-like pull pin for use in emergencies. Three more sets of remote-controlled doors open and close behind us before we are on the compound and headed to the Programs Building and the deputies' conference room. This is the only room with visual, but no audio, facility recording. It is where I conduct all the focus groups and one-on-one interviews that provide the data for this study.

I have been going through these entry procedures since 1995 when my Quaker friend, Isabelle Yingling, who was the sponsor of Chapter 1014 of the National Lifers of America at the (since closed) other female facility in Michigan, asked me to come in and speak to the women about my research area, violence against women, a topic of interest to women who are often incarcerated "behind a man." That meeting changed my life. The story the women tell is that "Lora fell in love with us." I let that explanation hold because I certainly have come to love, respect, and honor many of those women and their successors. But it is also true that that meeting and my ongoing interactions with life-serving women opened a new world to me. A world that I had never considered, a world that was not in any life plan of mine, a world that I didn't know existed except peripherally and simplistically as in "people who do bad things go to prison." I had never thought about what it meant "to go to prison." Or who went to prison. Or the systemic failures that result in imprisonment. Or why the system seems so inevitable and yet simultaneously remains so invisible. Or the ways that criminal justice arguments are presented as neutral when they are not neutral at all. Or how prison can become a site for resistance. Or how gender is constructed, maintained, and contested in prison. Or how incarceration results in silencing and voicelessness.

But I learned. Over time and particularly through this research, I learned about the soul-crushing effects of life imprisonment on life-serving women themselves. I learned about its damaging consequences to families, particularly children and communities. I learned that this system, designed for protection, creates more harm and suffering than it alleviates, particularly for disadvantaged and disenfranchised communities. I learned that life-serving women who theoretically would have no reason to manifest valuable human traits like empathy, compassion, inclusion, remorse, and integrity nonetheless manifest all those values while encased in a system that daily erodes their humanity. I learned about the irony in which life-serving women, arguably the most disempowered among us, are doing the most with the least to create meaningful lives in the stark conditions of imprisonment. This research, grounded in the voices of life-serving women, grew out of those lessons. Their collective stories demystify the dangerous stereotypes of prison "monsters." They challenge cultural tropes of punishment and imprisonment. They expose fault lines in the criminal-processing system. They make the invisible and inaudible in state punishment both loud and clear. They show us the damaging consequences of mass imprisonment on our shared social fabric.

Their voices—from the extreme margin—carry important social messages. I hope they educate and contribute to the conversation on incarceration in America.

ACKNOWLEDGMENTS

Let me begin by thanking the people in the Department of Corrections. I am indebted to Patricia Caruso, its director, who made this study possible when she told the obstacle makers, "Do what you need to do to let Lora Lempert conduct this study." Without her intervention, I might still be filling out access paperwork. At the research site, data collection was facilitated by the deputies Mary Jo Pass and her successor, Kari Osterhout, and by Don Lucas, the programs coordinator. Thanks to all of them.

I am also very grateful to the University of Michigan–Dearborn for grant support, specifically a Rackham Replacement Step 2 grant and a Faculty Summer Research Grant, awarded by Drew Buchanan and the Office of Research and Sponsored Programs. I am appreciative as well for the informal support from my colleagues in the departments of sociology and women's and gender studies and for the direct support provided by Sandra Lupfer, secretary, and Ashley Fairbanks, student assistant, in transforming my hand-drawn scribbles into accessible diagrams. I also want to acknowledge Sarah Fenstermaker, the director of the Institute for Research on Women and Gender at the University of Michigan–Ann Arbor, for twice providing me with an office in which I could think and write. It was an incalculable gift.

Without the help and assistance of my research scribes in data collection—Danielle Hart, Ashleigh Hodges, Sara Czarniecki, Jessica Martin, Sarah Bassetta, Audrey Haas, Breanna McFadden—the voices of the life-serving women in this study would have been lost. I am thankful for their commitment to the research, for their careful attention to detail, for their generosity and goodwill in the hard labor of intense notetaking, and for their dedication in transcribing their notes immediately after focus groups or interviews. Special kudos to Sara Czarniecki for also managing all the endnote citations.

The lengthy Grounded Theory process of sorting, analyzing, and coding data in memos was mine alone. In presenting the integration of the abstract analyses, however, I was assisted by friends and colleagues willing to read early drafts of chapters and to offer their suggestions for improvement. Judy Wittner, Mary Lynn Stevens, Jim Gruber, Sheryl Pearson, and Fran Lyman were very helpful. My Academic Women Writer colleagues—Georgina Hickey, Carolyn Kraus, Maureen Linker, Jackie Vansant, and Pat Smith— were their awesome selves by suggesting, exploring, expanding, arguing, debating, clarifying, and challenging my written word. They aided immeasurably in the process of bringing a focused analysis to public audiences.

I was also assisted in the writing clarification process with the able editing of my old friend, Dennis Gregg, who, at several points, suggested strongly that I join a semicolon recovery group. I am very thankful, as well, for the many sessions of thoughtful commentary, particularly on use of nominalizations, which my son, Benjamin R. Lempert, offered to me. There's something quite wonderful about drawing on the intellectual expertise of one's offspring, especially when he is so gifted.

I also wish to offer heartfelt thanks to my family: my daughter and son-in-law, Naomi and Fernando Lopez; my son Benjamin Lempert and daughter-in-law, Rose Darling; and my grands, Esther and Carmen Lopez, and Caleb Darling Lempert; and my mother, Rena Bex, for their belief in me and in this project. They listened to my stories, my kvetching, and my joys as this book developed. They're still listening.

Finally, I am truly appreciative of—and honored by—the trust of the 72 women who participated in the study. Most of them attended the two sessions where I presented the developing analysis for their consideration. By commenting on the typology and by providing additional information (data), they continued to enrich the analysis and to participate in the research process. Seven study participants also read and commented on two draft chapters. All 72 women were dedicated contributors and active cheerleaders from beginning to end. I am very thankful for all of them.

Of course, thanks go to my editor, Ilene Kalish, for believing in the project and for her skilled readings and direction.

My gratitude extends to all of these men and women who assisted me along the way, particularly for their thoughtful critiques and their shared belief in the importance of the audibility of the voices of life-serving women. If there are errors, they are mine alone.

1

The Life Imprisonment of Women in America

Gender, Punishment, and Agency

We're criminals. We're not part of society. We have no rights.
Ilene Roberts

This is the lowest you can get besides death. *Royal Tee*

What I feel is not understood is that we have something to
give. Even if it is in our little communities, we have something to give our families and the free world. *Sandy*

In the last four decades, the United States has become a more punitive
society at every level of government and in all regions, supporting imprisonment without historical precedent or international parallel.[1] With 5%
of the world's population, but 25% of its imprisoned citizens, the United
States maintains the largest custodial infrastructure on the planet.[2] This
punishment American style has resulted in what criminologists Glenn
Loury and Bruce Western call a "prison leviathan" and criminal justice
policy expert Samuel Walker calls "an imprisonment orgy."[3]

One third of *all* the incarcerated women *in the world* are in U.S. prisons.[4] Although men constitute 93% of the U.S. prison population, the
number of women under state and federal correctional authority is the
fastest-growing segment of the U.S. prison population.[5] Between 1980
and 2010 the population of incarcerated women increased 646%.[6] In 2011
more than 1,400,000 women were under the supervision of the criminal-
processing system,[7] that is, on probation or parole, incarcerated, or
subject to other forms of formal justice control.[8] Race is significant in
these incarcerations, as black non-Hispanic women are incarcerated at
2–3 times the rate of white women (129 vs. 51 per 100,000) and Latina
women are incarcerated at 1.4 times the rate of white women (71 vs. 51

per 100,000), although, reflecting their higher percentage in the U.S. population, more white than black or Hispanic women are incarcerated.[9] Age is also significant: About 60% of both white and black imprisoned females are age 39 or younger, as are 67% of Hispanic females.[10] Additionally, many currently incarcerated women were single heads of households and mothers of dependent children prior to imprisonment.[11]

Prison populations, both male and female, have been increasing steadily while crime rates have fluctuated without any apparent relationship to the extensions of imprisonment.[12] Recent reported declines in prison populations are largely an effect of the May 2011 Supreme Court decision requiring the State of California to reduce its prison population to 137.5% of design capacity within two years to alleviate overcrowded conditions that resulted in constitutionally inadequate medical and mental health.[13] Because California incarcerates more people than any state except Texas, changes in California's prison population have had national statistical implications.[14]

The dramatic increases in female imprisonment, the 646% increase,[15] have not been a response to more violent female criminality as media constructions would have us believe. Women's share of violent crime has remained more or less stable since the 1980s.[16] There are, however, more female arrests now than in the past.[17]

Various scholars have offered explanations for these increases. Criminologist Barbara Owen argues that the more frequent and lengthier sentences imposed on women are a consequence of women's economic marginalization and their limited avenues for survival as well as changes in the system that have resulted in more punitive responses to women's involvement in drug-related crimes.[18] Criminal justice theorists Meda Chesney-Lind and Lisa Pasko argue that longer sentences for women reflect a criminal-processing fervor to treat men and women "equally," despite their asymmetrical involvement in criminal activity.[19] This "equality with a vengeance" accounts, in large part, for the dramatic increases in female incarcerations. Additionally, they posit that the government's War on Drugs has actually been a war on poor women of color, dramatically increasing the rates of imprisonment for women engaged in low levels of the drug trade.[20] Sentencing Project Director Marc Mauer contends that as women have always represented a small share of people committing violent crimes, their numbers in prison would not have grown so dramatically between 1980 and 2010 had it not been for changes in drug enforcement policies and practices. Criminologists Darrell Steffensmeier and Jennifer Schwartz conceptualize these changes in crime prevention protocols as "widening the net," that is, re-framing behaviors that were formerly misdemeanors and adjudicating them as felonies (e.g., shoplifting is a felony if the products are worth a particular amount and/or if the defendant has two or more prior shoplifting convictions).[21] The overcharging by police and prosecutors, which results in increased female incarcerations, is more representative of changes in policing and criminal processing than in women's violent behavior. Ashley Nellis, a criminal justice policy analyst, also argues that changes in legislation have increased the numbers of women in prison.[22] She cites specific legislative expansions of the types of offenses leading to sentences for life without parole (LWOP); the wide range of habitual offender laws that focus on the persistence of criminality over the severity of the crimes, which result in life terms without chance for parole (e.g., the "three strikes" for shoplifting convictions); and more frequent criminal-processing decisions to sentence offenders to prison terms that extend beyond life expectancy. Samuel Walker summarizes the push factors in the alarming U.S. imprisonment escalation by contending that the effects of mandatory minimum sentences, truth in sentencing laws, restrictions on good time, and a punitive public attitude have resulted in the aforementioned "imprisonment orgy" that has disproportionately affected women.[23]

In 2009, 4,694 women were serving life sentences in the United States, 28.4% of them without possibility of parole. Of the latter group, 176 were female juveniles.[24] These LWOP sentences reflect a loss of confidence in personal reformation in favor of retribution. They also reject social science, medical, and behavioral science research that clearly demonstrates that individuals—even those who commit serious crimes—mature out of criminal behavior.[25]

In Michigan in 2010, the year and site of data collection for this study, 176 women of *all* ages were incarcerated for life.[26] Seventy-two of those women participated in this study. These women—who they are and what they do to create space for resistance, agency, and meaningful lives—are the topic of this book. In this text, I seek to affect the decidedly male-oriented legislative, media, academic, and popular cultural images of prison and criminals by filling what Loïc Wacquant calls a "curious eclipse of prison ethnography in the age of mass incarceration,"[27] that is, the ethnographic gap in criminological theorizing about the neglected population of women serving life sentences. In doing so I direct analytical attention toward the ways that women incarcerated for life manage their powerless, stigmatized statuses, ultimately using guerrilla ingenuity to create self-actualized, meaningful lives behind the prison wires. I examine the ways that they develop strategies for survival in the alien environment that is prison. For some, prison becomes a place of security, a location for intellectual, emotional, and social growth free of male violence, drugs, and overwhelming responsibility.[28] For others, the challenges are constant. *Royal Tee*, like many other study participants, reports asking herself daily: "How does good come out of this? How do you not become the monster society deems us to be?"[29]

Prisoners as "Not Us"

As a consequence of what anthropologist Lorna Rhodes terms "social magic,"[30] or the out-of-sight-out-of-mind phenomenon that prisons employ in literally and metaphorically "disappearing" convicted men and women from contact with society, most Americans have confidence in a criminal-processing system that appears to them fair and just. The American public is confident in consigning lawbreakers to prison as their "just desserts" and so takes comfort in the cliché "do the crime, do the time." Social activist and scholar Angela Davis argues that this ideological platitude generates a sense of righteous separation for some, a Manichean dichotomy between "us" and "them," good and bad resulting in implicit social agreements that prisons and prisoners should be kept a world away from "us," the "good" law-abiding majority.[31] Members of the peaceable public have no reason to believe differently. For the average white citizen, prisons are abstract places, separated from their daily lives and experiences, where punishment and deterrence occur. Public opinion research presents a more complicated picture for the average African American citizen, who has historically had less trust and confidence in criminal justice institutions, especially the police, than their white counterparts.[32] Nonetheless, Americans of all distinctions take prisons for granted. Prisons, and the men and women inside them, appear as an inevitable, permanent, and uncontested, albeit often invisible, feature of our social landscape.[33]

When media exposure reveals aspects of this system as corrupt, discriminatory, or unjust, these liabilities are presented as correctible glitches, or fragments in need of tweaking, not as serious systemic failures.[34] After all, laws apply to everyone. Violators are deviants. Criminals, therefore, are not like "us," the law-abiding citizenry. They cannot be our sisters and brothers, relatives and friends, neighbors and coworkers; they are the "other," a more dangerous form of humanity.

Sociologist Erving Goffman long ago theorized that criminals deviate from the "ordinary and natural" course of life and so are deeply discredited social actors.[35] In the contemporary political landscape, crime and criminal activity have come to be understood as the moral failures of "criminals," the majority of whom are depicted in media and popular discourse as African American males lacking in conscience and morality. Criminologists and media researchers have demonstrated a pervasive American cultural propensity to link criminality with black men, such that the black male has become a media emblem of the dangerous criminal.[36] TV news, crime shows, and TV crime dramas all contribute to this racial stereotype by frequently presenting black suspects in mug shots, handcuffs, or as persons resisting arrest.[37]

Likewise, media popularly characterize criminalized women as aberrant "monsters"[38] for committing crimes (e.g., murder, assault, child abuse, substance abuse, and so on) that so violate gender norms that the purported offenders are judged to be unlike other women. Sociologist Kathryn Farr argues that "although the precise images vary—vamp, black widow, femme fatale, she-devil, monstrous-feminine—the danger evoked [in women's criminality] is in women's challenge to male authority."[39] Criminally sanctioned, life-serving women are deemed deviant by virtue of pronouncements of guilt not only for offenses against the state, but also for engaging in behaviors that challenge both conventional morality and female gender roles and expectations.[40]

Life-sentenced women are lawfully identified criminals, a decidedly male category, which typifies them as ruthless and cold-blooded. The historical trend has supported identifying female lawbreakers as "abnormal" and "worse" than their male counterparts.[41] Violating legal proscriptions has historically situated women outside the prescribed gender roles of femininity and its corollary passivity.[42] Their virtual social identities, or the imputations underlying these unladylike popular characterizations, supersede their actual social identities, or the attributes they genuinely possess.[43] Only their virtual "monster" identities are visible to the public. In the widely publicized 2001 case of Andrea Yates, the white, middle-class, Texas mother who drowned her five children during a postpartum psychosis, for example, journalists sought to reconcile actions that they found abhorrent and aberrant, not simply for the homicides, but because they also violated cultural stereotypes of women as always loving and caring, as well as societal expectations that mothers are inherently competent in care-taking tasks. In media accounts, Andrea Yates represented the antithesis of femininity, a woman who murdered her children.[44] Barbara Barnett, a writer, speaker, and author, wrote a perceptive analysis of news-story narratives about Yates, particularly those that called Yates a "bitch" and "monster," demonstrating the ways that media constructions of criminally sanctioned women reinforce notions of them as less than human and often as betrayers of their sex.[45]

Most people in the free world do not want to know, or be bothered about, the nonfictional realities of prisoners and prisons yet they simultaneously consume seemingly limitless fictionalized media images of prisons and prison life (e.g., *Orange Is the New Black*, *Lockup*, *Prison Break*, *Oz*, *Jail*, and additional fictionalized documentaries, like *MSNBC Investigates* and *MSNBC Reports*).[46] However, when citizens in the free world are personally touched by the incarceration of an acquaintance, friend, coworker, or family member, new complexities challenge the one-dimensional "do the crime, do the time" political mantra. Once people are made aware of or are personally touched by imprisonment, as I was when I spoke for the first time to Chapter 1014 of the National Lifers of America in the women's facility, they can no longer remain detached and heedless. For then incarceration involves meaningful relationships and assumed responsibilities, particularly for the friends and family members of men and women sentenced to life imprisonment. For them, the "disappeared" become visible and real.

Why Study Life-Serving Women?

Life-serving women are an understudied population, numerically small, but nonetheless a significant segment of imprisoned persons. We must learn who female lifers are, sociologically, to understand imprisonment and its gendered effects.[47] Furthermore, with notable exceptions, the literature on female inmates in general is not as robust as that of their male counterparts. The research on life-serving women in particular is very thin.[48] The early work of sociologists Rose Giallombardo, David Ward and Gene Kassebaum, and Esther Heffernan, and the more recent work of criminologist Barbara Owen, sociologists Candace Kruttschnitt and Rosemary Gartner, and U.K. feminist criminal justice theorist Mary Bosworth has provided insightful conceptual frameworks through which to apprehend the experiences of incarcerated women.[49] None, however, has focused analytical attention on life-serving women.

Also absent from contemporary work is an understanding of the personal experiences of life-imprisoned women as they consciously attempt to live meaningfully as human beings within never-ending confinement.[50] It is my intention that this book will fill that void and reduce the hyper-invisibility of these women. I aim, to borrow Goodstein's words, to "balance the scales of knowledge" by calling attention to the repeated omissions (and misrepresentations) about life-serving women in criminological theory and research.[51] Contrary to popular lore and much of the research on incarcerated women,[52] far from being passive, I find that women serving no-exit sentences are actively engaged in developing life-affirming strategies for "doing life." They value and promote images of self-control and participation. They present themselves as rational, responsible agents interacting with one another and with the officers who guard them and, therefore, as shaping their daily lives within the constraints of imprisonment. Attention to their lives is "demanded by their demonstration of the beauty and power of the human spirit under conditions of extreme oppression."[53]

The voices and stories of life-serving women also reflect what feminist philosophers call "the privilege of marginality,"[54] that is, in a system of disadvantage those who occupy the margins have unique vantage points from which to assess and critique the center. This study of life-serving women then offers another important view—from the extremities—of the criminal-processing system. Life-sentenced women suffer from the dual condition of hyper-visibility through 24-hour, 7-day-a-week, surveillance and hyper-invisibility through their removal from society.[55] Forever hidden behind barbed-wire fences, they become unnamed, nonexistent, and ultimately invisible to the general citizenry.[56] Yet feminist scholars know that all knowledge is situated knowledge, that is, knowledge reflects the position of the knower at a particular historical moment and in a particular material context. The voices of these life-serving women manifest the attendant link between experiential knowledge and criminal-processing power at this moment in time.

Their incarcerations can be understood as a function of societal definitions of deviance and conformity, gender and punishment, all of which are characterized by paradox, irony, and contradiction. Their narrative voices, I argue, enhance criminological knowledge about the behaviors, perceptions, and treatment of incarcerated women, but most particularly those women "disappeared" from societal consideration through imprisonment for life. Their accounts, delivered in focus-group participation, life-course interviews, and solicited diaries, interrupt the popular cultural narratives of life-serving women as aberrant female "monsters" and reinstate them in their humanity as women who have made serious, life-altering errors of judgment.

Fyodor Dostoevsky is widely reputed to have said that "the degree of civilization in a society can be judged by entering its prisons." If such is the case, then life-serving women have a great deal to teach us about the extraordinary rise and preeminence of the United States as the world leader in incarceration. The voices of these women expose the damage—to self, family, community, and society—resulting from a retributive criminal-processing system that is highly gendered.

Collateral Consequences

The consequences of the dramatic upsurge in female imprisonment and in LWOP sentences in real people's lives and communities are alarming. The globally unique rates of U.S. female imprisonment have collateral consequences for families and communities. As Candace Kruttschnitt notes, "Incarceration restructures families, but when mothers are incarcerated, it often devastates them."[57] Although innocent of any wrongdoing, family members and children of life-serving women often "do time"—in emotional care and concern, in severely reduced financial and social circumstances, in loss of physical contact, in truncated lives, and in shared stigmatized status—with their mothers, aunts, grandmothers, sisters, and daughters.

Between 1991 and 2007, the number of children with an imprisoned mother increased by 131%.[58] A majority of imprisoned women, 65% in state and 59% in federal custody, were single-parent heads of households with children under the age of 18 at the time of their imprisonment.[59] The children of these incarcerated mothers were either in the care of their fathers (37%), grandparents (45%), other relatives (23%) or friends (8%), or in foster care (11%).[60]

Criminologists have convincingly demonstrated that maternal incarceration is more damaging to children than the incarceration of fathers.[61] The children of incarcerated mothers feel their mothers' absence more acutely, and they experience more disruption than the children of incarcerated fathers, putting them at risk for adverse outcomes.[62] Children with imprisoned mothers suffer the shame and stigma of maternal incarceration; face particular challenges of family instability (e.g., moving to new home environments one or more times);[63] undergo disrupted attachments, not only from a mother, but also from siblings, other family members, friends, schools, and communities; experience school failures; engage in antisocial, aggressive, and delinquent behaviors;[64] and are two and a half times more likely to be incarcerated as adults than are children of incarcerated fathers.[65]

Additionally, criminologists Vernetta Young and Rebecca Reviere and Jane Siegel have demonstrated that prisons do not meet the needs of women or the hundreds of thousands of children they leave behind.[66] "Children are locked out of prisons as surely as their parents are locked in. . . . Visitation is strictly controlled by the prison, and children are dependent on adults willing to take them to visit, which can mean that children rarely see their parent."[67] The Bureau of Justice Statistics reports that 59% of parents in state facilities and 45% in federal facilities have had no personal visits with their dependent children during the periods of their incarceration.[68] The children's caretakers may believe that a criminally sanctioned woman is not a good mother and so may not make the efforts necessary to keep children connected to their mothers.[69] Caretakers may also fail to arrange ongoing mother-child visits due to the financial constraints associated with travel to distantly located prisons, employment limitations as they affect availability during prison approved days and times for visits, child-care arrangements for other children, health care issues, or taxing family problems in the extended family network.

Children of imprisoned women consigned to foster care (11%) may be subject to further disruption through adoption and removal from extended family networks. The Adoption and Safe Families Act of 1997 authorizes termination of parental rights when a child is in foster care for 15 of the previous 22 months. Life sentences for women, whose social and familial networks are so fragile that they depend on foster care, result in a loss of parental rights and any further contact with their children.[70] As Erin George, an incarcerated poet and mother, notes, such forfeiture of contact with children is a "soul killing loss" borne by both life-sentenced mothers and their children.[71]

Communities also struggle to recover from the aftermath of women's imprisonment for life. When women, who often serve as the glue holding disorganized neighborhoods together, are incarcerated, communities are further disadvantaged.[72] The quality of social life in their neighborhoods declines in their absence. Neighborhood solidarity and trust decrease when these women are lost from the daily interactions of normal life in the free world—phone calls, family news, evolving lives, the minutiae of family experience[73]—as well as the exchanges, greetings, watchful eyes, and attention to activity in their communities. Family disruptions, the consequence of the incarceration of the female heads of household, also result in decreased community control over misbehaving youth,[74] and community disorganization becomes a stimulant for further criminal activity.

The consequences are far reaching. "Mass incarceration, far from reducing the stigma associated with criminality, actually creates a deep silence in communities of color, one rooted in shame. . . . Even in church, a place where many people seek solace in times of grief and sorrow, families of prisoners often keep secret the imprisonment of their children or relatives."[75] Families make claims of extended work assignments in faraway locations, of foreign exile, even of death in order to reduce the ancillary stigmatization of having a daughter, mother, wife, aunt, or grandmother who is imprisoned for life.

Once a woman is sentenced to life without parole (LWOP), she is often erased from social forms of humanity. Although her life continues behind bars, she joins the invisible world of "forgotten women."[76] In this in-depth study, I examine the ways in which 72 women sentenced to life imprisonment in Michigan cope with the ramifications, to self and others, of the enormity of their sentences. I identify the patterns and practices embedded in the women's focus-group narratives, life-course interviews, and solicited diaries. In analyzing the processes that these women use to reflect on both their carceral lives and the pre-imprisonment choices that led to lifetimes of imprisonment, I focus particular attention on how they cope pragmatically and creatively with their endless confinement. Presenting holistic views of the means by which these life-serving women agentically construct and use prison time to actively salvage their stigmatized identities, I consider how they do so within the processes they develop as formulas for living their lifetimes behind bars. I present the strategies they developed to heal from the wounds of their pre- and postimprisonment life experiences as both victims and offenders, as well as the strategies they used to resist the erosions to body and soul that are a consequence of no-exit sentences. Additionally, I discuss the tactics they use to assert their humanity and self-determination within and against institutional constraints. With notable exceptions,[77] the efforts of life-serving women are largely, if not completely, invisible in both popular and scholarly discourse.

Detailing the processes by which life-serving women sustain identities of self-worth, agency, and power deepens conventional understandings of the meanings and roles of imprisonment in contemporary America. It further locates female lifers within broader feminist research on gendered forms of resistance and on articulations between agency and structure, and it enables a more nuanced and critical analysis of the use of power in prison.

Considerations of Gender

Although 20th-century feminist criminology and research have challenged the masculinist constructions of crime, deviance, and social control, criminal-process theorizing continues to be dominated by men and men's issues. As Canadian human rights activist Karlene Faith has said, "Maleness and masculine gender are taken for granted [in criminal processing]; they are fundamental to the enterprise; they are the unarticulated essence of (almost) every criminological paradigm."[78] Most criminal-processing books are geared toward men, as are penal codes, sentencing guidelines, and correctional programs and opportunities.[79]

Officials at every level of the criminal-processing system are over-whelmingly male.[80] And voices of imprisoned men and women, in many instances, have been forgotten, marginalized, or simply ignored with the consequence that "the prisoner voice remains largely unrecognized and relatively inaudible."[81] In this text I abandon the traditional ways of defining and viewing incarcerated women as ancillary to their male peers and I instead examine how life-serving women themselves endure and create their lives.

Historically, gender-based policies have shaped men's and women's prisons, just as violent men inspired the model for all prisons and the expectations of all prisoners.[82] Current mass imprisonment, aptly termed a "prison leviathan" by criminologists Glenn Loury and Bruce Western, has resulted in more incarcerations for longer periods of time with fewer opportunities for parole or rehabilitation for both men and women.[83] Women have been particularly affected by this trend, as was detailed earlier, and their imprisonment rates have soared. The con-tinuing focus on men has meant fewer carceral resources for increasing numbers of women, reliance on one-size-fits-all, gender-stereotyped programming, and inattention to gender-specific needs like substance abuse, HIV treatment, obstetrics and gynecology, child care, and psy-chological needs.[84] In a system designed for violent men, it is a chal-lenge to get adequate health care for women's particular physical and mental needs.[85]

Although most imprisoned men and women come from socially marginal, economically stressed, disorganized communities in which physical violence is a primary dispute resolution strategy, women's ex-periences, pre- and postincarceration, differ significantly from men's.[86] In their pre-incarceration lives, women experience higher rates of drug and alcohol abuse; report disproportionately more histories of rape, in-cest, and physical abuse; are diagnosed with higher rates of illness and mental health problems; and are the primary caretakers of dependent children.[87] The Bureau of Justice Statistics provides evidence for these claims: 57% of women in state prisons have been victims of violence in their lifetimes, 47% have experienced physical abuse, and 39% have been victims of sexual abuse. Many have experienced multiple types of abuse.[88] One-third of women in state prisons (33%) reported having been raped prior to their imprisonments.[89]

Men and women also differ in the types of crimes they commit.[90] Women's pre-imprisonment economic circumstances are more fragile than men's.[91] Most often, women's offenses are crimes generated by poverty and ensuing strategies for survival.[92] Steffensmeier and Schwartz assert, for example, that "the most striking gender difference [in the commission of a crime] is the proportionately greater involvement of females in minor property crimes and the relatively greater involvement of males in more serious person and serious property crimes."[93] Recent government research supports their contention. At the end of 2010, 25% of women in state prisons were imprisoned as a result of drug convictions, 29% for property crimes (burglary, larceny, fraud, etc.), and 26% for robbery, assault, public order offenses (drunk driving, court offenses, commercialized vice, morals, and decency offenses), and other unspecified crimes. Conversely 689,000 men and 34,100 women were held for violent crimes including the 10% of women who were imprisoned on murder charges, charges that incorporate those women sentenced in felony murder cases where someone else was the "do-er."[94]

The situational factors of violent crime are also different for men and women. Under the latest "widening the net" criminal-processing protocols,[95] women are often convicted in homicides where their male partners were the primary perpetrators. Most of the women in this study, for example, were incarcerated in relation to the death of a victim (91%), that is, these women were themselves the perpetrators (40%) or were convicted for aiding and abetting a perpetrator (60%) (i.e., on a felony murder charge). Felony murder law is a rule of criminal statutes that any death that occurs during the commission of a felony is first-degree murder, and all participants in that felony or attempted felony can be charged with and found guilty of murder as aiders and abettors.[96] For the women convicted as aiders and abettors, it was their connection to violent partners, most often male, whose violent choices, directly or indirectly, resulted in the women's sentences of life imprisonment. All but one of the women I interviewed took responsibility for complicity in the crimes for which they were incarcerated. They argued, however, that the sentences meted out to them often did not "fit" their involvement in the crimes.

Of the 72 respondents in this study, 13% participated in killing their abusive partners, sometimes as the "do-ers" and sometimes as conspirators, often after years of unrelenting assault. The act of killing is extraordinary, but most women who kill are in every other way ordinary.[97] For those women who are the primary offenders, murder is often their first and only criminal offense.[98] When the focus is on the deed, or on the woman's flaws and weaknesses, and not on the social forces that underscore the crime, women who kill become the monsters of popular lore. However, when their deeds are contextualized and the criminal actions are demystified by an understanding of the details of their lives (e.g., disorganized childhoods, inadequate educations, sexual abuse and physical trauma, limited employment opportunities, delinquent peers, violent relationships), they lose the sensational qualities and much of the onus shifts to society's failure to provide relief to women trapped in intolerable situations.[99] It is in this shift that we are able to see the social gaps in police, family, friends, clergy, shelters, child care, education, and employment structures that contribute to women's incarceration. Mass imprisonment is silently absorbing women who have been abandoned by formal and informal safety nets, and, in the process, it is destroying and demoralizing communities.[100]

Compared with their male counterparts, women also have more experience with the incarcerations of other family members, such as fathers, brothers, uncles, and so on. Moreover, they may enter prison while pregnant, requiring, but not often receiving, pregnancy and prenatal care, help in parenting skills, and child welfare issues.[101] These pre-incarceration experiences leave women more vulnerable to adverse carceral conditions. For example, women with serious health and abuse issues that lead to mental health problems are often confined to prisons that are more geographically isolated and therefore less subject to outside oversight than male facilities where they can become prey to corrupt officers.[102] With increased geographical distance, such women also have less accessibility to the children, family, and friends that serve to stabilize them.[103]

"Death by Incarceration"

Although a life sentence can result in social death for the families and communities of life-serving women, in a state like Michigan without the formality of a death penalty, a life sentence is, nonetheless, "death by incarceration."[104] *Liberty Flynn*, a study participant, asserts, "We weren't given death sentences, but we're treated like we're already dead, by society, the justice system, and MDOC [Michigan Department of Corrections]." "Death by incarceration" is an essential assumption of both life-serving women and their correctional officer keepers.

A correctional officer, for example, tells *Merrilee*, "you don't have anything to lose." From the officer's perspective, *Merrilee* is living a civil death because no further criminal-processing punishment can be inflicted on her. She already has a life sentence; the officer has no further criminal system control mechanisms to access in governing her behavior, yet the officer does retain carceral controls aimed to induce compliance. But *Merrilee* does not have to comply, conform, or amend her behavior as any further criminal punishment is ultimately meaningless.

Nevertheless, *Merrilee* does modify her behavior. She has a different, more inclusive, definition of herself: one that is in tension with the officer's definition. *Merrilee*, like the other women I interviewed, experiences herself as a person of value. She itemizes the successes that would justify her social value in the world outside the prison gates: arriving in prison with a seventh-grade education, she earned a bachelor's degree; she's enrolled in and has successfully completed several vocational training courses; she's engaged in self-help programs; she's mentored other women; she has used every opportunity available to rehabilitate herself. Although unable to confront an officer who dismisses her essential humanity and the significance of her personhood, she became irate in the focus group—"Bitch! I've got everything to lose!" She could lose her sense of self. She could succumb to the mind-numbing, routine boredom of prison schedules, or to the sometimes rampant despair, or to drug-induced painlessness. But she doesn't. Even so, *Merrilee* acknowledges that her achievements are not enough to rehabilitate her in the eyes of the officer or those with the power to free her. She knows that she "can't ever be good enough to go home." She has been legally consigned to "death by incarceration."

Women's Agency Inside

Nonetheless, life-serving women are actively engaged in interactions with the other incarcerated women who populate the prison community, and they also demand recognition of their humanity through meaningful involvement with institutional staff regarding behavior, policies, and procedures. Candace Kruttschnitt and Jeanette Hussemann argue that consideration of notions of agency in a prison context is problematic because imprisonment subjects women to either personal deconstruction or to reconfigurations of how acts of agency, or the choice to act autonomously, are understood.[105] I contend that either/or constructions of women's agency as control or resistance dichotomize their self-directed processes and reduce consideration of the complexities of their actions. Instead I argue that the behavior of life-serving women includes resistance, but their agency is enacted in the service of personal meaning-making as well as in shaping interactions with officers and other women. Their acts of agency, consequently, affect—and sometimes challenge—the institutional culture.

Imprisoned women are "independent actors whose actions help to determine the meanings and effects of punishment." Their self-determination undermines the fixity of prison as totally rational and in control and destabilizes the fiction of correctional hegemony. Individual and collective resistance challenges correctional presentations of reasonableness and organizational consistency.[106]

Agency, or the choice to act autonomously, is not always visible materially or recognizable in institutional terms. Sometimes the women's resistance and self-determination appear passive as when they work to keep their minds active through reading, developing expertise on correctional department policies, or researching their cases in the law library; sometimes women employ ruses and protests to fill an institutional gap; sometimes they form groups, write letters, or engage in confrontation.[107] Often their expressions of agency are interpreted as resistance[108] and defined by a male model as evading or overcoming the imposition of power.

In examining women's agency under the carceral conditions of coercion, surveillance, and control, I draw on Bosworth's trenchant formulations of agency among women incarcerated in U.K. prisons.[109] I develop her exposition of agency as a dialectical relationship between imprisoned women and representatives of institutional control. I examine these ongoing tensions of associations as study participants, overtly and covertly, report preserving their ability to negotiate power and to resist penal oppressions. Like Bosworth, I consider the ways that women, disempowered and vulnerable institutionally, act and negotiate power, despite their subordination and confinement. I consider women's self-actualizing behaviors, embedded in the trinity of "staying busy," companionship, and religion, as well as their self-determination in interaction with their peers.

Missing, however, from Bosworth's insightful recognition of imprisoned women's agentic behavior are the patterns and details of their self-determining processes in personal and institutional interactions. There is, I believe, an identifiable order to coping in this environment—an order that results from a series of causes and effects—giving rise to discernible patterns that can be understood and predicted by examining the sequences that produce them.

Individually and collectively, life-serving women develop coping and resistance strategies that disrupt routine prison practices and correctional ideologies. They are active in formulating ways to identify and define the problems they face, in developing strategies that contest the erosions of prison life, and in constructing vocabularies of motive to legitimate their choices.[110] Their vocabularies, or interpretations of social conduct, presented throughout the text, reflect the gendered nature of their decision making. Care-taking talk, reflected, for example, in *Elizabeth Ashley's* strategy to "go after leadership roles to protect 'my girls'" (defined as friends without any "intimate" relationship [her air quotes]), reflects the relational motivation and logic of gender roles and female responsibilities to nurture. Their vocabularies of motive appear as well in the "transformative actions women initiate to press their own claims in relation to others who discriminate against them."[111] These study participants, who are "in constant dialogue with the institution,"[112] also challenge institutional power by appealing to general notions of humanity. Although their responses are constrained by institutional policies and procedures, policies and procedures do not consistently determine their responses.

The Women in This Study

Although life-serving women, as well as women "with years" (the "short termers" of prison parlance), and women living outside of the prison gates reflect a number of different subject positions—race, class, sexual orientation, education, employment status, marital status, parental status (e.g., see table 1.1)—the central difference among them is freedom. For women "with years," Kruttschnitt argues, incarceration is temporary.[113] In contrast, life-serving women are not—*and will never be*—free. Their imprisonments are intended to last their entire lives.

Table 1.1. Study participant demographics.

Pseud-onym[a]	Race	Age at Crime	Years Served	Length of Sen-tence	# of Chil-dren	Marital Status	Employ-ment at Time of Crime
Alexan-dria	African Ameri-can	22–25	8	LWOP	1	Widowed	Employed Full Time
Alison	Cauca-sian	26–35	4	LWOP	5	Divorced	Not Employed
Anna Bell	African Ameri-can	26–35	28	Parol-able Life	1	Divorced	Employed Full Time
Anta-nashia	African Ameri-can	15–18	15	LWOP	1	Single	Employed Part Time
Azianna	Cauca-sian	26–35	6	LWOP	1	Married	Not Employed
Baby	Multira-cial	26–35	8	Parol-able Life	4	Divorced	Employed Full Time
Bella	Multira-cial	22–25	12	LWOP	0	Single	Not Employed
Bel-ladonna Momma	Cauca-sian	36–45	22	LWOP	5	Divorced	Not Employed
Brenda Olds	Cauca-sian	46–55	15	LWOP	0	Divorced	Not Employed
Cameron	Cauca-sian	36–45	17	LWOP	0	Divorced	Employed Full Time
Caren Sue	Cauca-sian	15–18	3	LWOP	0	Single	Employed Part Time + Student
Chelsie Marie	African Ameri-can	26–35	13	Parol-able Life	2	Single	Not Employed
Ciara	Cauca-sian	26–35	15	LWOP	3	Divorced	Employed Full Time

Table 1.1. Study participant demographics (*cont.*).

Ciara Blue	African American	15–18	23	LWOP	1	Single	Student
Cindy	Caucasian	19–21	5	LWOP	0	Single	Employed Full Time
David	African American	36–45	7	LWOP	1	Single	Employed Part Time
DeDe	African American	26–35	25	Parolable Life	1	N/A	Employed Part Time
Dennis the Menace	Caucasian	19–21	9	LWOP	2	Married	Employed Part Time
Destiny	Multiracial	19–21	16	LWOP	1	Divorced	Employed Part Time
DJ	Caucasian	26–35	30	LWOP	5	Single	On Welfare
Doll	Caucasian	36–45	24	LWOP	2	Widowed	Employed Full Time
Donna	Caucasian	36–45	8	LWOP	N/A	N/A	N/A
Elizabeth Ashley	Multiracial	15–18	23	LWOP	0	Single	Not Employed
Esther	Caucasian	36–45	19	Parolable Life	4	Divorced	Employed Part Time
Faith	African American	15–18	15	Parolable Life	2	Single	Employed Full Time
Floyd	Caucasian	36–45	17	LWOP	1	Widowed	Employed Full Time
Ginger	Caucasian	46–55	1	LWOP	2	Single	Not Employed
Glenda Gale	Caucasian	46–55	14	Parolable Life	2	Divorced	Employed Full Time
Grace	Caucasian	26–35	21	LWOP	2	Widowed	Not Employed
Harmony	Native American	26–35	18	Parolable Life	5	Divorced	Employed Full Time
Ilene Roberts	African American	19–21	9	LWOP	1	Single	Employed Full Time
Jane	Caucasian	26–35	18	LWOP	2	Widowed	On Welfare

Table 1.1. Study participant demographics (*cont.*).

Jannel	Caucasian	36–45	9	LWOP	2	Divorced	Employed Full Time
Jesus Lady	Caucasian	36–45	19	LWOP	0	Widowed	Not Employed
Jet	Caucasian	46–55	6	LWOP	2	Divorced	N/A
JoAnna	Caucasian	26–35	8	Parolable Life	2	Single	Employed Part Time
Journey	African American	19–21	17	LWOP	0	Single	Employed Full Time + Student
Joyce	African American	22–25	24	LWOP	1	Single	On Welfare
Juice	Multiracial	26–35	8	LWOP	5	Single	Not Employed
Kari	Caucasian	19–21	22	LWOP	0	Single	Employed Full Time
Lauryn	Multiracial	22–25	11	LWOP	1	Single	Employed Full Time + Student
Liberty Flynn	Caucasian	36–45	11	LWOP	5	Widowed	Not Employed
Linda	Caucasian	15–18	20	LWOP	1	Single	Not Employed
Lizzy	Multiracial	19–21	4	Parolable Life	2	Single	Not Employed
Lois	African American	26–35	3	LWOP	1	Single	Employed Full Time
Louise	Caucasian	36–45	16	LWOP	4	Divorced	Employed Full Time
Love Evans	African American	19–21	23	Parolable Life	3	Single	On Welfare
Lynn	Caucasian	22–25	24	LWOP	1	Single	On Welfare
Lucy Spencer	Caucasian	26–35	21	LWOP	1	Widowed	Employed Full Time
Martha	African American	19–21	9	LWOP	0	Single	Not Employed
Meme	African American	36–45	15	LWOP	2	Divorced	Employed Full Time

Table 1.1. Study participant demographics (*cont.*).

Merrilee	Caucasian	22–25	20	LWOP	0	Divorced	Employed Part Time
Monaye	African American	26–35	25	LWOP	3	Married	Employed Part Time
Pamela	African American	19–21	12	Parolable Life	1	Single	Employed Full Time
Passion	Caucasian	22–25	13	LWOP	2	Widowed	Not Employed
Pooh Bear	African American	19–21	23	LWOP	1	Single	On Welfare
Raine	Caucasian	26–35	11	LWOP	4	Single	Not Employed
Royal Tee	African American	26–35	13	Parolable Life	3	Divorced	Employed Full Time (Self)
Ruth	African American	36–45	25	LWOP	6	Widowed	Not Employed
Sandy	Caucasian	26–35	14	LWOP	2	Divorced	Employed Full Time
Sasha Lavan	African American	22–25	20	LWOP	4	Single	Not Employed
Scarlet	Caucasian	19–21	28	LWOP	1	Single	On Welfare
Sheila T.	Caucasian	46–55	11	LWOP	3	Divorced	Employed Full Time
Shemetta	African American	36–45	10	Parolable Life	0	Single	Employed Full Time
Sheri	African American	19–21	27	Parolable Life	1	Single	Not Employed
Shequetta Tasha Lynn	Multiracial	19–21	23	LWOP	2	Single	Employed Part Time + On Welfare
Simone	Caucasian	19–21	14	LWOP	1	Single	Employed Full Time
Sister	African American	22–25	36	Parolable Life	2	Single	On Welfare

Table 1.1. Study participant demographics (*cont.*).

Taylor	Cauca-sian	26–35	9	LWOP	0	Divorced	Employed Part Time + Student
Tootsie Roll	African American	26–35	5	LWOP	7	Single	Employed Full Time + On Welfare
Wink	African American	26–35	14	LWOP	6	Married	Not Employed
Yasmeen	African American	26–35	7	LWOP	1	Single	Employed Full Time

Note: Because some information provided by the women is personal, idiosyncratic, and identifiable, particularly in the focused chapters, the author has selected alternative pseudonyms. These alternate pseudonyms do not appear in this chart.

In this study, at the time of their sentencing, the women ranged in age from juveniles (age 16) to mature women (age 51), although the average age at the time of their crimes was 29 years. Twenty-two percent of these women (16) had spent more time incarcerated than they had lived as children and young women in the free world.

In some aspects these 72 respondents reflect the norm for the female prison population. That is, 36 white women participated, as did 27 African American women, eight multiracial women, and one Native American woman. Additionally at the time of their crimes, 29% reported being unemployed, 15% were engaged in part-time employment, and 12.5% were on welfare. On the other hand, 39% were employed full time. Educationally, these women report more academic success than is typical, but this is probably an artifact of the study's demographic survey in which women were asked their highest level of education. The question was not qualified as highest level of education entering prison. *Merrilee*, for example, listed a bachelor's degree as her highest level of education. She entered prison with a seventh-grade education and, when it was still possible in the State of Michigan (prior to 1993), she earned a college degree inside. Some women responded with current level of education; others with entering level of education. Four women (5%) reported having bachelors' degrees, 12 (16.6%) reported earning associates degrees, and 20 (28%) reported some college experience. Alternatively, three (4%) had less than an eighth-grade education, 10 (13.8%) had ninth- to eleventh-grade educations, 12 (16.6%) had earned high school diplomas, and nine (12.5%) had earned GEDs at some point in their adult lives.

Most of the study respondents (45, or 62.5%) had dependent children at the time of their incarcerations. Others had adult children (11, or 15.2%) and 22.2% of the women had no children, which was noted by many of them as a particularly acute and irredeemable loss of imprisonment. Thirty six women reported being single, although the data are not clear on whether or not they were single at the time of the commission of the crime, or they became single as a consequence of the crime (e.g., they divorced, or were divorced, in the aftermath of the sentence). The same is true for the 10 women reporting "widow" as a marital status as some respondents had participated in the deaths of their spouses.

The 72 women who participated in the focus groups, interviews, and/ or diaries varied in their abilities to express themselves, describe their experiences, understand the effects of their experiences, discuss their identities, and explain and interpret the meanings of life events. Consequently, I provide common anecdotes and experiences, noting that common does not equate to "the same."[114] The social worlds of female lifers are subjective experiences. I do not assume that the women, or girls, as a group behave similarly to each other; the reasons for imprisonment and the experiences of prison are many, and are affected by age, style, life experience, race, class, sexual orientation, and social capital.

Blurred Boundaries

The life stories of these women situate them within "blurred boundaries" between what both the legal system and the general public recognize as the mutually exclusive categories of "victims" and "offenders."[115] "Blurred boundaries" describes the permeability of the pre-imprisonment experiences of victimization and offending in the lives of the women in the focus groups. Most of them experienced multiple forms of individual and social oppression before their legal sentences of life imprisonment. They revealed pre-incarceration lives that were fraught with neglect, frequent physical and sexual abuse, sometimes negative educational experiences, oftentimes poverty, disorganized neighborhoods, dysfunctional families, and crime. Many had already been imprisoned in symbolic ways by the social conditions of their communities, families, and intimate relationships before their formal incarcerations.[116] They were, for the most part, victims before they became offenders. It is in these indistinct, blurred spaces between being victims and offenders that the important link between women's childhood trauma and adult criminality becomes obvious. *Louise* captures this phenomenon succinctly: "My mother was my first abuser. She prepared me for him [her violent partner]. He prepared me for here."

Feminist criminologists have clearly demonstrated that criminal behavior may follow as a consequence of such victimization and that abuse and trauma are risk factors for women's offending behaviors.[117] The socially marginalized women in this study were particularly vulnerable to both abuse and involvement in illegal activities.[118] Like *Louise*, they more closely resemble a "community of victims rather than a collection of victimizers."[119]

The social disorganization and trauma that characterize the pre-incarceration lives of life-serving women cannot be wrapped up in a neat package called "crime." Yet criminal-processing discourse and practice rely on unproblematic identities of "victims" and "perpetrators" as mutually exclusive categories and further on unchallenged assumptions of free choice actions and responsibilities.[120] These legalistic and often quite simplistic categories of victim and offender are not adequate descriptions for the messy overlap of such categories in the lives of offending women.[121] As the multiple sources of evidence cited previously indicate, imprisoned women have extensive pre-incarceration experiences of abuse and trauma, often perpetrated by intimates, where they are indeed the victims. Young and Reviere provide perhaps the most concise commentary on the simultaneity of victim/offender boundary blurring in their claim that "when women are victims of abuse, their lives are a crime scene already."[122]

The Study Site

In 2009 the Michigan Department of Corrections spent four days moving approximately 800 women in belly chains and leg irons to their current location, the only remaining correctional facility for women in the state. It is a sprawling, unadorned complex of one- and two-storied buildings that house more than 2,200 women. The 13 housing units each have different room and space configurations. Some women are double bunked in "wet cells" containing two beds, a sink, and toilet; some reside in more conventional two-person 6-by-8-foot rooms with shared toileting and shower facilities at the end of the hall. Their beds, stainless-steel sinks, and commodes are constructed so that they cannot be easily broken and are anchored to the walls or floor. All the women are constantly surveilled by 1,400 cameras dispersed throughout the compound.[123]

Cell mates, or "bunkies," are assigned by staff; two strangers share a living space the size of a conventional home bathroom. Prison personnel do not assume responsibility for problematic bunkie relationships, but they do apply sanctions for incompatibilities. Locked in place and locked in space, *Scarlet* notes pragmatically that "inside you have to work through it; outside you could just get in your car and never see them again."

The study site was originally constructed as two facilities, sometimes joined by a single administration and sometimes run by two administrations. In the most immediate past, the facility housed (in separate locations on the site) both seriously mentally disturbed men and the general population of women. The men were transferred to other sites when the general population of women was joined by their female peers from other facilities to constitute a single, multiple-security-level facility for all the imprisoned women in the state. The facility provides all reception-center processing for women and includes 13 housing units for general-population prisoners in security levels I, II, and IV, Residential Substance Abuse Treatment, and the Residential Treatment Program. It houses acute care, an infirmary and detention (aka solitary confinement). It has two perimeter security fences with electronic detection systems.[124]

In 2009 the new arrivals moved to the side of the campus that was converted from the site for mentally ill, imprisoned men. By the department's admission, the facility conversions were not on schedule and the facility was not completely ready for the transition. Research by Kruttschnitt and Gartner demonstrates clearly that different prison environments shape incarcerated women's adaptations to their environment.[125] Their findings are supported here. *Jane,* one of the women moved in 2009, described the new location as a "hell hole" where previously resolved environmental issues again became salient for the women—lack of cleanliness, being double bunked in single-bunk rooms, having open-flush toilets and sinks in their rooms, correctional officer attitudes, inadequate system functioning, tighter restrictions, and "less [freedom of] movement." She, and others, described a location lacking in essential facilities where punishment for small infractions became the norm, a place akin to "hell on earth." About the change, *Esther* noted that "you can't even count on being fed properly in here. On Thanksgiving, they ran out of food." In spite of the detailed deficits, the most intractable problem identified by all the women in the study was the new set of relations with officers.

In a focus-group discussion a full year after the move, *Anna Bell* explained the source of the problems: "You've got three sets of officers here." There were officers from the previous prison, new officers, and the officers remaining in the converted facility. Like others, *Anna Bell* claimed that "those" from the repurposed facility "hated" the women after the men left and "that caused conflict." *Jane* remarked that some officers expressed a preference for working with men. Other officers were perceived as liking the institution better when it was a medical facility and the residents "were doped up." Most women agreed that, in comparison, the officers from their former prison were "all right and know just about everyone"; however, they claimed that the officers remaining in place were used to having "their feet on the necks of the [mentally challenged] men" and they simply transferred their management styles to the women. No formal or informal gender training was provided to the officers by administration in anticipation of the conversion. In interactions with the women, officers remaining in place were said to rely on the default one-size-fits-all correctional management model that was used to discipline dangerous male prisoners.

Methodology

The diverse methods used in this study—focus groups, life-course interviews, two-week solicited diaries—reflect a process of research triangulation.[126] Triangulation refers to combining multiple methods in the same study in order to maximize the validity of the research results and the credibility of the accounts.[127] Multiple methods are likely to be more accurate because each affords particular opportunities for deepening the understanding of the research topic, covering the same areas with multiple respondents, asking additional questions, and getting corrective and/or alternative feedback. By triangulating methods, I attempted to cancel out the biases of any single method.[128]

Additionally, because the facility's warden prohibited even research use of taping equipment, I trained hand-picked students to serve as research "scribes." Two scribes attended each focus group and interview. They recorded conversations and as much exact wording as they could capture. The use of two scribes was intended to increase the reliability of the written records. Scribes transcribed the sessions immediately after they ended and then sent them to a dated and timed, encrypted dropbox. Scribes were also encouraged to include their own observations of the process or content of the discussions in personal "afterwords." The data collection, for which scribes were essential, began with focus groups.

Focus groups are a staple of qualitative research methodologies. They involve small groups of people with particular characteristics, in this case life-serving women, convened for a concentrated discussion.[129] They are principally functional for generating interactive data and for gathering individual information quickly and efficiently in a group context.[130] Because focus-group talk replicates the "natural language" of normal speech as research participants bring their collective narratives together, focus groups elicit evocative stories and in-depth explanations.[131] *Wink* articulated this personal experience: "I'm surprised how much I spoke. I don't like to talk."

The act of participation in a focus group, rather than in a one-on-one interview, occasions increased disclosure in part because participants feel relatively empowered in a group situation surrounded by peers.[132] Focus groups are also particularly useful for interrogating issues perceived as culturally sensitive.[133]

Additionally, feminist research is predicated on methodologies that reduce the hierarchical relationship between researcher and the "researched."[134] Focus groups do not completely eliminate the power disparities. They do, however, shift the discourse opportunities to an interactional experience between participants, which may be less influenced by researcher agendas and more reflective of the negotiated meanings of participation.[135] After being presented with an open-ended list of potential discussion topics, *Louise*, for example, asked, "Can we just throw it open?" They did. In this group as in others, the respondents often determined the topics of discussion and the directions of those discussions.

The usefulness of focus groups, however, is limited by multiple and overlapping conversational and relational contexts, which foster "problematic silences" (lack of disclosure) and "problematic speech" (strategic shaping of comments) in group discussions.[136] One study respondent left shortly after her arrival for a focus group, saying she just didn't feel "safe" with the other women who were invited to that group. She did not continue in the study, although she did attend the author's presentation of the research analysis to the respondents.

In a prison context, focus groups are also subject to interruption by prison personnel. One incident early in the study resulted in the reluctant participation by two respondents. Jessica, one of the day's scribes, reports the event:

> At this point in the focus group, we're once again interrupted by the officer who lets us know that Dr. Lempert has a phone call [with the deputy warden to resolve the current issue of location]. While Dr. Lempert is gone, the women stare dejectedly at the topic sheets as the officer stands by the door, watching. The women eventually begin to speak, but they do not discuss any of the topics or what we were discussing in the focus group. Instead, they discuss personal information, such as their parole board hearings. When Dr. Lempert returns, the officer leaves, and Dr. Lempert discusses with the women the options of either continuing in a room where there would be surveillance with no audio, or canceling and rescheduling the focus group.
>
> LL: We have to move. They say it is because we are too isolated here. I am leaving it up to you. We can cancel and reschedule or we can go to another room that will be surveilled but will have no audio.
>
> *Juice*: Are you sure about the audio?
>
> *Ciara*: This is just their way to control things.
>
> *Jet*: You know if you move now, they will move you again and again.
>
> The women come to the conclusion that it's best for them, and the research overall, to not give in to the bullying of the officers and

instead cancel and reschedule. They all show signs of deep agitation and disappointment.

Processes like these interfere with the value of focus groups as a singular research strategy for understanding individual feelings, experiences, and decision-making processes.

Life-course interviews are another tool for the comparative analysis of the carceral biographies of women imprisoned for life, and I employed them with 10 selected focus-group participants. Roma Stovall Hanks and Nicole Carr note that the literature on understanding life-course criminality is very thin and feminist criminologist Joanne Belknap argues that life-course research to date rarely includes women in samples and, thus far, provides no adequate assessment of childhood abuse variables; therefore, life-course interviews were a particularly appropriate methodology for this study.[137] As a theoretically grounded methodology, life-course interviews elicit participant "stories" about key life events and turning points, as defined by the participants, that convey the whole social context as well as the distinctive themes in each individual's life.[138] The interviews provide opportunities to observe the respondents' own use of language as they describe and foreground their cognitive and emotive processes.[139] When participants engage in life-course interviews, a frequent reported result for the respondents is a more active and thoughtful relationship with their past and current lives.[140]

In their histories, I invited respondents to examine their lives before incarceration to understand if and/or how problems followed them inside prison walls. I interviewed each respondent independently of the others. I provided each woman with a blank line, identified as a timeline, which began at birth. Each woman was advised to draw a line at the point at which she was incarcerated. I then instructed her to mark and label the five most relevant life experiences, from her perspective, that occurred before incarceration. I was thus soliciting the meaning of the events to the interviewee and the ways that she identified those events as relevant to her imprisonment. I then invited her to add any events after her incarceration that have also affected her.

Yasmeen's first relevant life experience was not atypical: "At one and a half, I don't remember it, but it was a major event. My feet were scalded with hot water by my mother. She was mad at my father so she put me in a tub of hot water." As a postincarceration-relevant event, *Yasmeen* said, "Since I've been down [incarcerated], I've been in groups" where the leaders were faith-based. *Yasmeen* said that a 12-week "Bridge Builders" group, which provided a workbook from which she could do daily activities, was "extremely helpful" in dealing "with how I feel" and with how others might feel. She said it also helped her "not dwell on them not forgiving me." Like *Yasmeen*, the women who participated in life-course interviews all appeared, as narrative psychologist Dan McAdams noted about others creating accounts in meaning-making processes, to "struggle to find life-narrative forms that more-or-less see them through a difficult life terrain, amidst personal setbacks, failures, frustrations, and a demanding and stubbornly un-co-operative world."[141]

Focus-group discussions and life-course interviews are both shaped by interactive social contexts directed, in part, by the researcher. The two-week solicited diary, however, is shaped by the participant as the expert of her own life and experiences.[142] Consequently, diaries, long accepted as a rich source of qualitative research data, were the third research methodology I used. I asked selected participants to keep a daily journal recording how they spend their days and evenings, including activities, events, interactions, reactions and responses, and reflections on their values.[143] The diaries were intended to provide insight into what women do as compared to what they say they do. I chose the solicited diary participants on the basis of their perceived literacy, capacity to read and write with ease, as well as the physical competencies of vision and hand coordination to write legibly.[144]

Solicited diaries have a different focus than personal diaries. Solicited diaries are written with the researcher in mind.[145] They produce rich data because they often include issues that do not arise in focus groups or life-course interviews.[146] I asked each writer, at the completion of her day, to reflect on how she spent her time, the content of and her responses to interactions with others, and her general feelings, perceptions, and understandings. Each respondent wrote with the knowledge that I would read and interpret her accounts. The diary writers acted as both observers of self and surroundings and as research informants providing a "view from within."[147]

Diaries can also be empowering because they allow participants to identify their own key concerns.[148] Some of the writers included notes to conclude that their two weeks of journaling spoke to such empowerment. *Elizabeth Ashley*, for example, wrote, "I wish the journal writing had been a month, as some days I've been in a funk and not really in a mood to write—though I've enjoyed the opportunity to express some of my thoughts, feelings, and ideas. I know one thing—it will always be my desire to be a better person than the day before and my hope is to be able to touch someone else's life in a positive way and give them the hope of a brighter tomorrow in the face of much adversity and darkness."

These multiple methods of data collection and presentation are more likely to be accurate than any single measure. As a Grounded Theorist, from my original articulation of this research interest to the specifics of the central analytic category, erosion, my work has proceeded inductively.[149] Additionally, I twice took the provisional analysis of the stages typology (detailed in chapters 3 and 5) back to the participants. I presented each stage to the participants in a small auditorium and I asked for feedback. Many women responded with questions and clarifications, some of which are now included in the text. *Doll*'s was a typical affirmative response: "I saw myself in every stage." There were no challenges to the processes I presented. Further I also sent two draft chapters each to seven active participants for comment and critique, and some of their amplifications and expansions are also included in the following chapters. *Raine*'s and *Destiny*'s narrative comments were common to others. "Overall, the two chapters are very compelling and thorough. It is nice to see in black and white, that life-serving women can be portrayed as relevant, to a world that tends to believe otherwise [*Raine*]." *Destiny*: "I believe you've correctly explained the experience of life imprisonment. It is a testament to how actively you've listened to us throughout the years. . . . They [chapters] accurately reflect the lives most of us live." Others, like *Royal Tee*, simply wrote their comments next to the text of the chapters: "trash to transformation" . . . "good analogy" . . . "correct" . . . "yes! Indeed!" . . . "you nailed it."

Additionally, as is common in feminist research,[150] the participants exerted considerable informational control over topics of discussion and related events. They chose the topics for focus-group discussions; they selectively presented their life histories; and they determined what to include and exclude from their two-week diaries. They all retained the right to reticence. Some chose not to participate.

As a feminist researcher, I recognize the inequalities and power relationships present between researcher and research respondent. I chose methodologies to reduce the disparities, and I enacted practices of engagement to minimize their effect.[151] Each of the respondents chose her own pseudonym for confidentiality and recognition purposes. Some chose male pseudonyms. Some chose only first names; some chose both first and last names. I have retained their choices throughout. I italicize their chosen names whenever I quote their precise, often colorful, language. I use their pseudonyms to consistently identify speakers in order to underscore the framework that the analysis is about individuals, not cases.[152] While my analysis highlights individual voices as emblematic of collective processes, I have "increasingly recognized that the form and content of these narratives intimately connect to the social addresses" of study participants.[153] My focus is on the social-interactional, social psychological, and cultural mechanisms of prison life, not on their individual attributes.

Although pseudonyms provide some identity protection, prisons are closed communities and women could be identified by prison personnel and other women through a descriptive story or experience. For example, outcomes of a relationship with an officer could be known to others, and the particularities of their work might identify individual women, as might the nature of their crimes. Women might also be distinguishable by unique turns of phrase typical of their communication styles. Consequently, throughout the text, I altered individual histories when it seemed that the women could be identified. I created composite respondents. I added additional pseudonyms. However, the words of the women are intact in *all* instances where they are quoted or paraphrased. I made no changes to their uses of language.

Jim Thomas argues that language is one of the few unrestricted resources that incarcerated people possess.[154] In that vein I examine both what the women specifically say and what they didn't say, or what they avoided talking about. I report their words as recorded by the trained scribes. Yet I leave it to readers to determine for themselves the veracity of these accounts. I did not, for example, ask for names of officers discussed in focus groups, so I don't know if it is one officer repeatedly behaving unprofessionally or if the behavior is characteristic of an en-

tire unit of officers, or if—in fact—any officers behaved unprofessionally. But when the repeated messaging in the focus groups supported the
women's narratives, I presented and analyzed their claims. On the other
hand, I acknowledge that the focus groups might well have encouraged
conformity. I try to reflect the tenor of interactions in the range and
complexity of the analyses.

There is no singular truth to women's meaning-making in prison,[155]
and I present no unitary truth in these pages. Women in prison share
common experiences, but not the same experience.[156] As Bosworth
notes, "The effects of imprisonment are not uniform. Rather, both the
collective and individual identities of the women are active and changing, constantly under formation and never complete."[157] Similarly, the
women may have comparable practical opportunities for agency, but
their choices and decisions to act rest on their varying degrees of social
and analytical ability.

Life inside the prison walls is characterized by complexity; it is the
range and complexity of study respondents' experience that I present in
this text. I analyze the patterns of interaction, and I do so through the
use of the women's narrative voices. My data are "the raw spoken words
of inmates."[158] Like Karlene Faith, I also "liked to visit my friends inside.
While prisons are sickening, the people in them are often uplifting. It's
inspiring to know people with gumption who are able to transcend dehumanizing circumstances."[159]

Additionally, to avoid the associations generally resulting from the
labels of "criminal," "inmate," "prisoner," and "convicted murderer/felon/
child abuser" and the like, I refer to the women in this study as "life-
serving women," "imprisoned" or "incarcerated" women, or "female lifers." Describing the women by the conditions of their lives, rather than
by stigmatizing labels, provides opportunities to consider their humanity. "Inmate," "prisoner," and "convict" are depoliticizing notions that
exclude the other significant identities that the women embrace, such as
wife, mother, coworker, or daughter. The former are terminal words that
signal an end to the processes of being and becoming.[160] Likewise, in
relations between the "kept" and their "keepers," I refer to correctional
officers (COs) or simply officers, unless the women are quoted referring
to them as "guards" or "PO-lice" or "gray and blacks" (uniform colors).

Plan of the Book

Behind prison walls, life-serving women develop lives that are meaningful, reasonable, and in many ways ordinary. They assert themselves as active agents: that is, their actions help to determine the meanings and effects of the punishment meted out to them.[161] They negotiate and exercise power, not just acquiescence, as a response to their circumstances. They sustain definitions of self that counter their organizational identities and they reconstruct themselves from the fragments of the memories of their lives and from the detritus of their carceral circumstances.[162] This text addresses both the scope and limit of human possibilities available to these women. I examine female life imprisonment through an analysis of women's agency, demonstrating simultaneously that order and control are "not impermeable"[163] and that everyday prison pressures erode the women's self-actualization processes.

In four chapters I detail as exemplars the personal stories of 5 of the 72 study participants. Choosing representative women was extremely difficult. Like the first-person speaker in Robert Frost's poem "The Road Not Taken," I am keenly aware of the 67 other stories that are not included. Nonetheless, these five women, two of them juvenile lifers, represent a spectrum of experience, both pre- and postincarceration, and they each offer particularly compelling and detailed descriptions of the ideas and experiences of life-serving women, often through layers of meaning about their complex interior lives.[164]

Chapter 2, for example, presents *Carmela*, a young African American woman sentenced to life imprisonment for a homicide. Before her incarceration, *Carmela* lived a life that is emblematic of blurred boundaries separating victims from offenders. Her experiences of abuse and neglect, disrupted education, and disregard by caretakers are common pre-imprisonment events in the biographies of many life-serving women. They were often victims before they became offenders. *Carmela*'s precarceral story establishes the context for her imprisonment, or the "train wreck right in the middle" of her 21-year-old life story. *Carmela*'s detailed story is the preamble for chapters 3 and 5. These chapters are the central scaffolding of the book.

In chapter 3, "Beginning the Prison Journey," and chapter 5, "Actively Doing Life," I present the stages of imprisonment and adjustment that life-sentenced women experience and negotiate. In chapter 3 I consider the first two stages common to *all* sentenced women: becoming a prisoner and navigating the "mix."[165] All sentenced women become prisoners, and, after release from a mandatory term in closed custody, they enter the general population, or the "mix." To minimize imprisonment's corrosive effects, the women must sort out the prison status hierarchy and their places in it; they must learn who to trust and who to avoid; and they must determine how to avoid conflict in an environment where oppressive conditions are the norm and from which there is no exit.

In chapter 4 I introduce two juvenile lifers, now middle-aged women, who were sentenced to life imprisonment in the early 1990s when they were adolescents. Their early imprisonment experiences are emblematic of the dystopia resulting from incarcerating children in adult facilities. *Ann*, a white woman, and *Crystal*, an African American woman, "were minnows in a shark tank" when they were released into the mix. Using their limited social skills, they learned how to navigate the volatile, highly sexualized prison culture. "Raising ourselves" inside, the two have been good friends for over 20 years. Their descriptions of their troubles reflect the "cruel and unusual punishment" inherent in mandatory life sentencing for juveniles.

In chapter 5, I return to the stages that life-serving women go through in the process of developing agency and identity confirmation in this deprivation environment. The framework I present is grounded in the details and realities of women's lives, in their immediate contexts, and in larger social structures. I outline the stages particular to life-serving women, which include acting at a choice point, establishing a counternarrative, developing an internal compass, and rebuilding social bonds.

Chapter 6 is another short biographical chapter in which *Desiree*, an African American woman in her late 30s, who "grew up in here" and describes herself as "a care giver by nature," illustrates her processes of self-actualization. She tries "to live my life as an example for others." Her narrative is an instance of a means of developing an internal compass, rebuilding social bonds, and self-confirming identity through empathic behavior. *Desiree* reports moving beyond the deprivations and losses in her life to a space where, as she says, "I want to change the way young black women feel about themselves growing up in a situation close to mine." Her empathy toward others in the aftermath of an institutional suicide is emblematic of the broader outreach that serves her peers and that also keeps her own hope alive. She is an example of self-actualizing in place.

Chapter 7, "Correctional Officers or 'Us' vs. 'Them,' " directs attention to life-serving women's relations with COs, interactions that are at best ambiguous and at worst hostile. COs are the criminal-processing representatives who enforce the day-to-day, minute-to-minute surveillance and control that is imprisonment. Their supervision of the women is designed with clearly defined "us" and "them" boundaries. Participants in this study reported rigid restrictions between "black and gray" and themselves, while some simultaneously declared, paradoxically, that they loved "with all my heart" particular officers. The women and the COs constantly reciprocally create, negotiate, and modify rules and norms in a "dance of power and control."[166]

In chapter 8, "Eating the Life-Sentence Elephant," I examine the particular strategies that the women use to contend with officers and to counter the social and psychological erosions of a life sentence. While there is considerable overlap in the strategic use of limited resources, most frequently the women's strategies reflect their own idiosyncrasies, talents, interests, and skills. Collectively considered, however, their coping strategies illuminate relationships between agency and structure and converge around four axes of decision making: (1) normalizing chosen activities using "as if" outside world analogues; (2) maintaining individualized action orientations generally described as "staying busy"; (3) forming affective and instrumental relationships with peers inside; and (4) developing and sustaining a self-defined spiritual center by engaging in periods of intense reflection and spiritual communion.

Chapter 9, the last biographical chapter, focuses attention on the women's oft-reported "relationship with God" as a self-defined spiritual strategy for securing calm, support, and forgiveness inside. I present the "relationship with God" experience through the individual story of *Candace*, a prayerful white woman in her 18th year of incarceration. God is omnirelevant in *Candace's* life as He "graces [her] with favor" when she is able to shower before count time, or when she is "blessed" because "God wakes me up in time to watch Joyce Meyer [a charismatic Christian minister] at 6:30 a.m." As was also reported by her life-serving peers, God's presence gives meaning to life in prison.

Chapter 10, "The Way Forward," presents the women's ideas for institutional and systemic changes. They suggest solutions for the intransigent problem of life imprisonment, focusing their attention on rehabilitative programming for life-serving women, gender training for officers in women's facilities, facilitating access to the children of imprisoned mothers, ending mandatory minimums across the board, stopping prosecutorial overcharging for everyone who "catches a case," amending felony murder statutes to focus on the do-ers, and terminating "the punishments that keep on giving" for all former felons.

2

Carmela

"Blurred Boundaries"

I'm not a bad person, but a person no one really cared about.

Music blares from a scratchy CD as *Carmela* glides into the cavernous prison gymnasium in a glittery, hyacinth pink gown, her handmade costume for tonight's entertainment. The evening has been devoted to thanking prison volunteers, most of whom are religious visitors and mentors from Alcoholics Anonymous or Narcotics Anonymous. I am in her audience. I have known *Carmela* for nearly half her lifetime. I am the coordinator and recruiter of volunteer university faculty who offer college courses in the prison. I am also a cosponsor of Chapter 1014 of the National Lifers of America (NLA) at this prison. *Carmela* has been my student; she has also been a member and officer of the NLA. She is now a voluntary study participant.

Oblivious to the surrounding clutter of metal chairs and gym equipment, *Carmela* loses herself in the music of redemption. For these few moments, she is no longer a "prisoner"; she is a danseuse. As I watch her elegant movements, I am overcome by the same questions I asked when she was sentenced 17 years ago at age 20. What is *she* doing here? How did this gentle, lovely woman come to commit the murder that led to her life sentence? After nearly two decades of interacting with women serving life sentences, these questions still plague me, though I know the answers. As Bruce Western, faculty chair of the Harvard Kennedy School Program in Criminal Justice Policy and Management, notes, "The violence people bring into the world has its roots in the violence they witnessed, or which was done to them, at very young ages."[1] *Carmela*'s imprisonment is but one example of the ways in which hurt people hurt people.

Blurred Boundaries

I present *Carmela*'s pre-incarceration biography as an illustration of blurred boundaries, the simultaneous experience of being both victim and offender, that characterize the pre-imprisonment experiences of many of the life-serving women in this study.[2] *Carmela*'s history is a stark instance of the inadequacy of the mutually exclusive, legalistic binary of victim and offender in understanding the motivations, actions, and responsibilities associated with female criminality. *Carmela* is neither the murderer featured in sensationalized headlines nor the graceful danseuse; she is at all times *both*. Nonetheless, she is required by law to live the life sentence of a "murderer."

Carmela's biography—structured by poverty, physical and emotional abuse, parental substance abuse, social marginality, racism, sexism, impoverished communities, dysfunctional family life, and more—reflects the symbolic sanctions and confinements that occurred long before her final criminal processing and imprisonment. The world she saw both in and outside her home was marked by violence. She was herself a victim of violence on more than one occasion. Her life story is a tragic example of a system that didn't work and the failures that compelled a young black woman, oppressed by poverty and victimization, to develop her own self-protection strategies. It is in the spaces of exploitation and abandonment that youthful strategizing becomes the primary link between childhood trauma and adult criminality. As criminologist Beth Richie notes of other criminalized African American women, "some women are almost destined to fail; they quite simply *cannot* succeed in the current social arrangements."[3]

Carmela as Exemplar

Carmela's life story is not exceptional in this population of life-serving women; rather, her biographical narrative is an exemplar of the combined effects of childhood and adolescent neglect, physical and emotional abandonment, sexual trauma and molestation, and abuse by family members and intimate partners in fueling female criminality and consequent incarcerations. Her particular biography reflects persistent themes in the lives of many of the women in this study.

In theorizing the "sociological imagination," C. Wright Mills asserted long ago that women and girls, like *Carmela*, experience firsthand the private troubles that arise from public issues.[4] *Carmela* and her imprisoned peers confronted sometimes horrific childhood experiences. Their "bad luck" personal difficulties occurred within the context of conditions in the broader society that also shaped their lives. Taken alone, no single experience that *Carmela* shares signals a pathway to prison; some of her experiences may even appear commonplace. Her inexorable path to prison lies in life circumstances not of her choosing, delivered by others, and lived without nurture. "They could have arrested her after she was born," one study scribe observed following *Carmela*'s life-course interview. "She never caught a break." *Carmela*'s biographical narrative demonstrates what comes before imprisonment; the text itself explores what comes after.

***

Carmela is a little bit of a woman. Five feet tall and barely 100 pounds "soaking wet," as she puts it, she wears beribboned dreads that frame her flawless café au lait skin and that bounce when she walks. She is, I think, quite beautiful. She has an elegance of movement that I envy.

Incarcerated at 20, she has served 17 years of a life sentence. Without a "Hail Mary" commutation from the governor or legislative changes in the law, *Carmela* can expect to spend another 48-plus years of her life in state confinement, the number of years actuarial tables indicate she can expect to live before her "natural life" ends.

To say that *Carmela* entered life with the odds stacked against her is to belabor the obvious: poor, black, female, born to an alcoholic mother and an incarcerated father. *Carmela* spent much of her childhood with her many siblings either homeless or shuffling back and forth between temporary housing and shelter at her grandmother's house. As an adolescent, *Carmela* was sexually violated by a neighbor, an uncle, and her male partner—a relationship that ultimately led to her incarceration. By naming these violations, I am not intending to reduce her to a pawn of her personal history; rather, my intent is to identify her experiences, track her strategies, present the contextual conditions that shaped her decisions, and provide empirical evidence that challenges the binary of victim *or* offender, a binary that collapses in *Carmela*'s biography and is representative of many others.

Father's Abandonment

"He straight out said I wasn't his kid." Her father's abandonment and denial was the first of five life experiences that *Carmela* identified in her life-course interview as leading to her self-characterization, and later incarceration, as "a person nobody really cared about. " Claiming that *Carmela's* mother had sexual relations with other men and that *Carmela* didn't look like him, her father denied paternity and any responsibility for his daughter in an apparent move to inflict harm in a marital war game. The claim was devastating to the 12-year-old struggling with pre-adolescent physical and emotional turmoil. *Carmela* experienced his repudiation not as mean-spiritedness, immaturity, or failure to consider the consequences of his words on his young daughter but as censure of her, ratifying her sense of insignificance in the family constellation. Instead of love and kindness from family members, *Carmela* says "I had so many names thrown at me" all her life that she internalized a sense of personal unworthiness. Her father's repudiation of her left *Carmela* unclaimed, unprotected, and unloved by the central male figure in her life. Her deep longing to be loved made her desire his affirmation, even as he violently verbally distanced himself from her. Having later come to accept his emotional limitations, she now observes of her younger self, "I think I just wanted a father."

Mother's Inadequacies

If her father was rejecting, *Carmela's* mother was callous. Poverty, physical and emotional impairments, schizophrenia, economic marginality, a disordered community, and substance use undermined her mother's parenting abilities. *Carmela* repeatedly notes in her "relevant experiences" that, while she was desperate for love, she was most often left without emotional support or maternal assistance. Her mother, a substance abuser when *Carmela* was a child, enjoyed pitting the children against one another in contests for her attention, and she routinely encouraged one-upmanship games: Who is prettiest? Who has the nicest hair? The significance of these mind games is not their exceptionality, it is in their ordinariness. *Carmela's* home provided no "safe haven," no acceptance, and no uncontested affirmation. Her mother's self-serving manipulations prevented the siblings from establishing trusting, meaningful relationships with one another that might have helped fill the void left by parental failures. With few social and no familial resources, *Carmela's* siblings also did not fare well. One brother is also incarcerated; her youngest brother has been remanded to a boys' home.

Through hindsight, *Carmela* laments, "I think when I was a kid I could have gotten away if I would have stopped hoping for something else." Her deep longing for an "ideal" family trapped her in the vortex of dysfunctional family interactions. *Carmela's* then 16-year-old older sister, in contrast, chose a typical social survival strategy for girls with troubled home lives. She ran away. But escape didn't end the effects of the family life she left behind. "Things still bother her from when we were little," *Carmela* observes.

"I Didn't Want to Be Like My Family"

Carmela is "smart" in all conventional understandings of that word. Even inside the prison, she wants to be recognized as "somebody who's focused on their education and learning. Or the person that loves books. I have a duffle bag full of books." Recognized by all as the family "smart kid," as a child, she sought refuge in academic success at school, her only source of affirmation and importance. "I was happy thinking I was smart." Although she took pride in her good grades, no one else noticed. "Usually people care when you get a report card." Her mother and grandmother told her she should go to school but were indifferent if she skipped. In elementary school, *Carmela* won second place in the school science fair. No family members bothered to attend the awards ceremony. "It was like winning by myself."

Being smart sustained her through some difficult challenges, but *Carmela* mentioned no school figure who provided mentoring, support, or assistance. She reported no teacher, principal, or counselor who singled her out for attention; she managed on her own. When other children taunted her because her family was poor and often homeless, or they called her names like "musty" and "nappy head," because hygiene was not a family priority, she persevered because "I was smart!" *Carmela* maintained a vague sense that somehow education would change her life. She was also developing some foresight: "I didn't want to be like my family." Nonetheless, "I ended up worse than them."

"I Didn't Know Nothin' about My Body"

Carmela was raped when she was 13 by an "older, like 20-year-old guy" who lived in the neighborhood. She was a virgin. She acknowledged liking attention from boys, but simultaneously declared: "I didn't know nothin' about my body. Didn't know about bleeding after the hymen is broken. None of that." She was a girl in a developing woman's body.

Her violator had offered her a ride to school but instead drove her to his house and "pulled into the backyard." *Carmela* questioned him about the detour; in her naiveté she was concerned about being late for school. When he demanded that she "give him a hug," she did. She had a gut reaction: "I knew I should have run, but I didn't know where to run to." As "a person no one really cared about," *Carmela* could turn to no protector, no sanctuary. She froze. He asked for "a bigger hug" and pushed her onto the car seat, pinned her, and raped her. Afterward he told her dismissively to "fix" her hair and then simply dropped her off at school.

In math class, *Carmela* heard the girls behind her laughing and realized that her clothes were stained with blood from the rape. Desperate, alone, scared, and wounded, she left school. That day "I started smoking marijuana." She self-medicated. Like the thousands upon thousands of women who experience rape and decide to handle it alone, *Carmela* did not report the assault to the police, seek medical care, or consider counseling. An adolescent without support, she turned to mindlessness through drugs, a ready antidote for pain and humiliation.

The experience of rape also catalyzed a new relationship to her body. *Carmela* began to treat her body as a sexual object without value, something she could just give away or that others could take. In time she began "to sleep around to get over it [the rape]."

Carmela did confide the assault to her mother and her mother's response—"It's your fault. You shouldn't have taken a ride. School is only three blocks away"—was a defining fracture in her life. Bewildered, blamed, and shamed, *Carmela* told no one else. She understood that in this, as in all other circumstances, she was on her own. She was the guilty offender. Later when her uncle began molesting her, groping her breasts or crotch every time he passed her in the house, *Carmela*, diligent in anticipating virtue and suppressing doubts, once again tried to secure protection and support from a female family member. Sobbing, vulnerable, and defenseless, she unburdened herself about her uncle's behavior to her grandmother, her uncle's mother, and was wounded again. Her grandmother simultaneously characterized *Carmela's* experience as trivial as she protected her son by saying, "He's just playing. He plays like that with everyone. Don't tell anyone." When *Carmela's* mother heard about her sibling's behavior, she again absolved herself of responsibility and blamed her daughter, claiming that *Carmela* had brought it on herself because she was "fast" and hanging out with her "fast cousins."

"Fast" is a code word, a frequent justification for parental indifference. "Fast" brands *Carmela* as out of control sexually; it labels her as a girl, not a woman, racing thoughtlessly into an adulthood for which she is ill prepared. "Fast" is also an accusation that *Carmela* is acting outside gender-proscribed roles. When *Carmela* is molested, the assaults are *Carmela's* "fault" because she—not the perpetrator—is "fast."

The depiction of *Carmela* as "fast" demonstrates the patriarchal values that form and shape the family network and, consequently, *Carmela's* resistance strategies.[5] In her mother's gender model, *Carmela* is the prime offender in her rape and molestation. Her crime is her failure to understand that men have a right to sex with women who are "fast," attractive, and therefore available.

The accusation also highlights the complex border zone and insecure boundaries between childhood and adulthood. The maturation process unfolds unevenly. No one is a child one day and an adult the next.[6] The distinctions between child and adult categories are in constant flux during adolescence, resulting in vulnerabilities and boundary instabilities.[7] Thirteen-year-old girls like *Carmela*, charged with behavior labeled "fast," lack adult access to the information, options, and strategies to deal with potential violations of their persons.

Yet not a single one of *Carmela's* familial role models provided her with guidance, protection, comfort, or support. The men in her life were predatory. She did not have a loving, protective father or the support and care of a kind uncle; instead, the men in her life used and abused her. Her female role models left her to her own devices and resistance strategies, then blamed her when her tactics failed. Due to youthful inexperience, early socialization to negative stereotypes of women, and injurious community and peer experiences, the strategies that *Carmela* chose were logical within her unsophisticated framework but counterproductive in outcome. She was still, after all, an inexperienced adolescent trying to survive the circumstances of her life in the best way she knew how. She ranged about for love in another direction.

He Had "a Messed-Up Life, but His Story Was Mine"

At 15, in an attempt to escape the chaos of her home life, *Carmela* chose sexuality as her route to independence. "I got with a man because I felt like everyone else in my family was abusing me." Her "man" was a 16-year-old, living on his own in an apartment in the neighborhood and making his way by selling drugs. He had "a messed-up life, but his story was mine. I could sympathize." Inadvertently running from one abusive situation to be exploited by another, she set about trying to improve her man's life by giving him "what I didn't have," specifically lots of love and affection. Her feminine devotion to her partner was a symbolic measure of the social and emotional stability she so desired for herself. She sought solace from her family's alienation in the private space of a happily-ever-after life with her "man."

But loving care and attention were not his intention. *Carmela* had watched "my father abuse my mother," and that experience provided the basic instructional lessons of womanhood in her family network. Consequently when her "man" became physically and emotionally abusive, it was no surprise. She accepted his behavior as a condition of a romantic relationship. "I told myself that he loved me because he said he didn't want me around anyone else." She interpreted his control as love and his jealousy as romance. In fairy-tale imagery, she saw herself as the Beauty who would release the Beast and restore the prince through unconditional love. *Carmela* stayed with him for five years, until the "train wreck" crime that halted her "free" life.

Immersed in their relationship, *Carmela* stopped doing well in school, although she had never previously missed a day. Her boyfriend didn't go to school and didn't care about her schooling, so she lost interest as well. Although not entirely. *Carmela* did attend summer school so that she could graduate with a diploma. She invited family members to the graduation and attempted to create her own celebration, noting that her other classmates went out with family and friends to party after the ceremony. But her boyfriend took her back to his basement apartment, which by then had become her personal prison, and left immediately to make a drug sale.

"He'd Lock Me in the House"

His apartment was her final preparation for state-sponsored confinement. "He'd lock me in the house. I'd stare at the four walls. He'd go out with his friends." *Carmela* experienced his return as déjà vu, a reenactment of her mother's criticisms and the family's name-calling. He'd see her sitting in the apartment and ask her why she "was sitting there looking so dumb." "Some women are in shock when they come to prison, but I wasn't." *Carmela* had been imprisoned, in one form or another, all of her life.

Carmela's Crime

It is here that *Carmela* parts company with other poorly parented, unloved women who grow up in poverty and experience physical and sexual violations. Most do not commit murder. Although she had no previous criminal record, *Carmela* was incarcerated for life for the murder of a drug dealer who was a rival of her "man." Her "man" initiated and planned the murder and directed *Carmela* to carry it out. He remains free; he was never charged even as an accessory.

I do not present *Carmela's* pre-incarceration biography to minimize her responsibility in the crime for which she is imprisoned. I do not offer "the abuse excuse" for *Carmela's* decision to engage in violent behavior. However, as child psychologist Bruce Perry and journalist Maia Szalavitz argue, "There are complex interactions beginning in early childhood that affect our ability to envision choices and that may later limit our ability to make the best decisions."[8] *Carmela's* resources were limited.

Yet it would be a serious mistake to define *Carmela* solely as a victim; she is also at all times a creative agent in constructing her life. *Carmela's* narrative is replete with acts of agency, of strategizing, and of resistance, as she struggles to manage the environmental forces moving her inexorably toward crime and incarceration. Hers is the narrative of a young girl turning to perceived resources to fend for herself in a dangerous, adult world. Without consideration of her agency, *Carmela* becomes a caricatured victim of circumstance. Although she suffered greatly from her life circumstances, she never identified as a victim. Throughout her chronicle, *Carmela* is a complex actor deploying the logic of an unsophisticated adolescent in the struggle to manage her environment.[9]

Carmela's life story makes clear the connections between early childhood trauma and victimization and subsequent offending in the lives of life-serving women.[10] It illustrates the multiple points at which people and institutions that might have offered support treated the serious violations of *Carmela's* person carelessly, while sanctioning her forcefully for the violence of her crime.

Victim *and* Offender

Carmela's crime is grounded in the social conditions of her life and in her role as a female within a patriarchal family and society. Criminologist Beth Richie argues that African American women, like *Carmela*, are at once victims and offenders who are "left with no good, safe way to avoid the problematic social circumstances that they find themselves in, unable to change their social position, and ultimately blamed for both."[11]

The failure of the legalistic categories of victim and offender to capture the complexities of criminal action is unambiguous in *Carmela's* life story. About criminally sentenced women, Adriani Fili, a scholar of gender and human rights, says, "Umbrella terms of either responsible agents or dependent victims assume a false universality that excludes particular kinds of experience and obscures the realities of women in prison."[12] *Carmela's* experiences are more precisely defined by "blurred boundaries," or the simultaneity of being both a victim and an offender.[13] Violence was an organizing principle in *Carmela's* life and, like other female lifers, the violence in her life contributed to her exclusion from legitimate avenues of fulfillment.[14] The frame of her life circumstances—sexual violation, adult relational violence, childhood abuse and neglect—had an unrelenting, cumulative effect that resulted in her crime and incarceration for life. Her life course is a clear demonstration of the ways in which experiences of sustaining harm are consequent to inflicting harm.[15]

***

Narrative voices, like *Carmela's*, appear throughout the following chapters as life-serving women describe their attempts to build healthy identities. To survive emotionally, *Carmela* said, "Eventually I had to separate myself [from my crime]. I committed the crime, but that was one day in my life. I'm not that person every day." Women like *Carmela* are more than the singular acts for which they are incarcerated; it is possible for them at all times to be moral and yet to have committed the socially immoral acts for which they are imprisoned. Most exist simultaneously within the blurred categorical boundaries of victim *and* offender.

3

Beginning the Prison Journey

Prison is a social world, a society. *Lauryn*

You can't just be honest. Honesty will get you nowhere in prison.
If you lie, everyone believes you. *Martha*

This place is not like Burger King—Have it your way. *Love Evans*

Imprisonment constitutes an unseen, unconsidered social world within
our "free" world where men and women are sentenced to "death by
incarceration."[1] A life sentence is a death penalty in slow motion, a
condition of social invisibility, isolation, and desolation.[2] It is a damaging experience, particularly for women, resulting from the continuous
process of erosion—the slow wearing away of self, of social value, of
autonomy, and of agency through the daily assaults of institutional policies designed as one-size-fits-all but predicated on male imprisonment.[3]

A sentence of life imprisonment is the framework for daily, long-
term, and nanosecond erosions in the tedious process of working
against "letting time do you." The processes of erosion are maintained
and amplified through institutional control practices, through the gossip and "drama" of other imprisoned women, and through the gradually
diminishing contact with friends and family in the "real" world.

Raine speaks to these consequential forces when she claims that
"something happens to people in here. They come here and get worse."
The women about whom she speaks adapt to prison in personally harm-
ful and destructive ways. For those women "the prison is the street, the
street is prison," and they continue to draw on pre-incarceration experiences and habits that don't serve them well in their new surroundings.[4]
Floyd, for example, says, "When I came in here, it was party time, making hooch, yelling at cops, going to seg [segregation]. Seg wasn't a big
thing to me. [It was] a chance to get away." *Floyd* transferred her ungov-

erned street behaviors to the carceral environment. Sanctions served as respite from the chaos of her choices, but they didn't modify her behavior. But not all life-serving women respond to incarceration like *Floyd*. For many of her peers, imprisonment is a wake-up call that demands assessments and analyses of past decisions, pre-incarceration lives, and the contexts and relationships that contributed to their lockup for life.

Stages in a Meaningful Life Framework

Once sentenced, life-imprisoned women are enmeshed in a system that doesn't support second chances; that gives lip service to rehabilitation while it warehouses mothers, daughters, sisters, girlfriends, and cousins for "natural life"; and where a single day typically stretches out for decades. [5] Life-sentenced women lose their prior social identities, adult lives in which they managed complex roles and relationships, and instead they incur the attritions inherent in the outcomes of a punishment system committed to sticks instead of carrots.

"Prison journeys" are solo journeys, but imprisonment imposes structural conditions and consequences that shape life-serving women's patterns of movement toward socially meaningful lives and identities.[6] In this chapter, I present the first two stages, common to all imprisoned women, in a typology of movement through "doing time," but I focus analytical attention on those women doing "natural life" in unnatural circumstances. I investigate the centrality of the agency of life-serving women, their self-determined ability to negotiate power, in creating meaningful lives inside prison walls.

Agency, "the sociocultural mediated capacity to act,"[7] the capacity for self-determination, that, in this particular study, arises from the social and cultural dynamics of the prison context, is central to each respondent's sense of herself as carceral-functional. Agency for these women was not static; it was not all or nothing. It was not that the women had agency or didn't have agency. Their ability to self-determine depended on their current situations, their personal processes, and the churning institutional context.[8] The women in this study discussed manifesting different levels of agency in different ways at different times in different situations.

The two initial stages that are the subjects of this chapter, becoming a prisoner and navigating the "mix," are common to *all* impris-

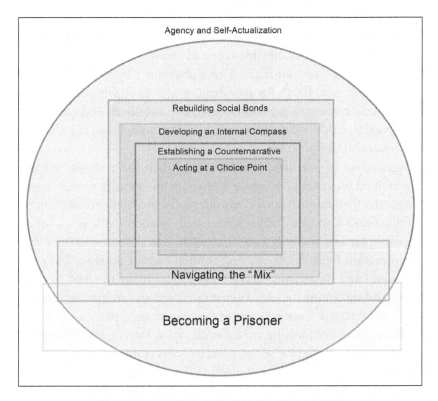

Agency and Self-Actualization

Rebuilding Social Bonds

Developing an Internal Compass

Establishing a Counternarrative

Acting at a Choice Point

Navigating the "Mix"

Becoming a Prisoner

FIGURE 3.1. THE SIX-STAGE TYPOLOGY

oned women but are amplified by the endlessness, the permanence, and the material solidity of a lifetime in confinement. Locked in, locked up, and constantly surveilled, the study respondents had limited opportunities for self-determination. But they were never completely without agency, even if the choice available to them was simply to refuse compliance with an order.[9] Their movement through the identified states of the stages presented in figure 3.1 reflected their capacities to resist the erosions inherent in the environment and to become active in their own social transformations. Sometimes they chose passive resistance; other times they actively shaped the prison culture, activated ruses, protested, formed groups, wrote letters, kept their minds and bodies active, and engaged in confrontations with other women and with officers.[10] In short, they acted with agency whenever possible.

Their self-actualizing processes are identified in the six-stage typology. Each of the stages is a constructed analytical category that reflects the women's choices as they manage and resist the conditions and attritions of their imprisonment. These phases are supple and permeable, not static and fixed. Because dealing with a life sentence expands and contracts women's personal, social, psychological, and emotional resources, all of the stages represent ongoing, sometimes circular, but continuously fluid processes.

Agency for life-sentenced women begins in the environmentally constrained process of becoming a prisoner and develops when negotiating the mix, the two stages common to all incarcerated women. As criminologist Candace Kruttschnitt noted, women "with years" often choose to lay low and wile away time as they await return to their pre-incarceration lives.[11] Life-serving women cannot do that. They are removed from those lives *forever*. They must make the best of their never-ending circumstances. They must adapt and reconstruct meanings and identities. Consequently each of the ensuing phases—acting at a choice point, establishing a counternarrative, developing an internal compass, and rebuilding social bonds—reflects the processes of life-serving women as they are involved in developing increasingly more complex agentic attitudes and behaviors. They move back and forth through these processes feeling and being less agentic in the early stages of prison acculturation than in later phases, but at all times attempting to maintain some practice of self-determination and affirmation. Their agency is at all times situated in the moment-by-moment, day-by-day, year-by-year negotiation of their daily realities as women sentenced to "natural life."

At each stage, life-serving women cope with the structural forces intrinsic to the prison policies and simultaneously with the practices that determine every aspect of their daily existence: the interactional culture of other women, the officers who surveil them, as well as their own life experiences and traumas. They actively attempt to counter the mordant effects of penal policies, sometimes through the interactional, highly sexualized "drama" of the mix, an arena characterized by criminologist Barbara Owen as "a continuation of the behavior that led to imprisonment, a life revolving around drugs, intense, volatile, and often destructive relationships, and non-rule abiding behavior."[12] They do so by dragging in their own emotional baggage, the detritus of pre-incarceration lives lived on social margins, as *Harmony's* biography reflects. Abused as a child and abused by her husband, the "abuse followed me" into prison. Some life-serving women get lost in the lure of "the mix," captivated by the intensity of unpredictable, potentially explosive interactions.[13] Still others transcend their circumstances and develop agency, self-determination, relevance, and identities of meaning and social value. Self-actualization, or the fulfillment of human potential, nonetheless, remains on lockdown in prison. *Lauryn* provides one example of the frustrations of thwarted self-actualization as she compares her experience of program outcomes to that of her civilian supervisor:

> To further this thought . . . the glass ceiling just often feels impenetrable and the opportunity for advancement is all but non-existent. I worked with (but really under) a state employee in the field of social work within a substance abuse treatment program. The structure of the program, based on the therapeutic community model, leaves little room for any staff member to not be touched by it in terms of questioning their own self-actualization and fulfillment of human potential. My co-worker (supervisor) was on one such journey simultaneously with me but as we/she began to grow and see herself differently—realizing greater potential and capacities for greater demonstrations of our/her higher self (ves) she was able to make the decision to take a better paying job that would benefit more people and I had to watch her go while I remain stuck in the consequences of decisions I made 15 years ago.

Although actively committed to self-actualization, *Lauryn's* agency is inhibited by the never-ending conditions of her confinement. Literally caged, she consequently moves back and forth through the analytical stages, sometimes falling back into the mix, at which time she will seek out "weed and the girl with my favorite pills," sometimes self-actualizing when she will "take whatever [programming] I can get." Self-actualization inside is not static and fixed; it is fluid and responsive to circumstance.

Hence demarcation between the six stages is indefinite and permeable. The stages are analytical processes, not material locations. Only the becoming a prisoner stage is ever completely finished. "Doing time" is

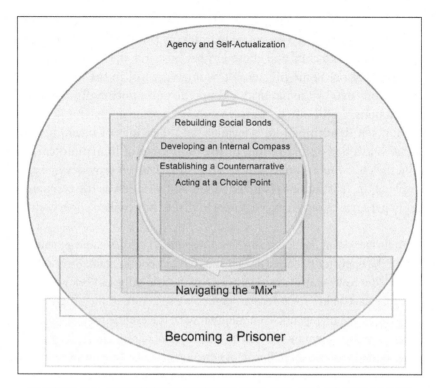

FIGURE 3.2. MOVEMENT WITHIN THE SIX-STAGE TYPOLOGY

never just one adjustment or one acceptance or one rule. Women incarcerated for life experience constant demands to re-adjust, to respond to changing institutional personnel or circumstances, to negotiate power relations with correctional officers and with other women, and to find ways to define themselves within and against the definitions implied in this deprivation environment.

The processes are sometimes overlapping and at other times discrete. For example, one might develop a stable, consistent counternarrative but, as a consequence of the newly initiated narrative, may need to re-negotiate relationships and participation in the mix. This overlap is represented in figure 3.2.

Not all women move through all six stages. Some women become stuck in place, enmeshed in the erosions resulting from prison policies and practices, from the allure of the mix and from their own maladaptive problem-solving choices.[14] Others move through the stages in circular processes of to-ing and fro-ing as they develop self-actualizing perspectives and then revisit earlier understandings of themselves that then require further reflection and additional changes.

Not all women move through all the stages sequentially. As Owen found in her study of women in the general prison population, some women "dip into" the mix at the beginning of their terms but begin to avoid it when they start to participate in programming. As life-serving women have more "time down" (years of imprisonment) and have established their own interactional niches, they report spending less time navigating the mix.[15]

Reflecting the fluidity of the phases in the framework, both *Raine* and *Meme* advise constant vigilance, perhaps because both were convicted of aiding and abetting. *Meme* clarifies: "I was blind-sided 17 years ago, not anymore." In attempting to maintain the moral prescriptions of her own internal compass, she is continuously attentive to her surroundings and to "what everyone around me is doing." She offers the example of the many opportunities for "transactions" in her prison job where she is responsible for collecting, washing, drying, and delivering laundry. She could hide contraband, move contraband, and deliver contraband, but she is not approached for these opportunities. Other women know "I don't mess with things like that." Her reputation precludes invitations for these "transactions." She has established her niche and her counternarrative; she isn't into the mix. Her deliberate decisions to avoid transactions reflect her self-affirming choices, albeit limited, and her strategic planning abilities.

Grace is more analytical about her peers, the other female lifers, as she hypothesizes a bifurcation between "some of us" and another group that "doesn't care" about themselves or others and so keep the mix active. Those women do not engage in the meaningful activities that diminish their losses. *Kari* highlights the agentic proclivities for criminality of this group stuck in the mix:[16] "People do whatever they want to do in here. If you want to steal your whole bit, you steal your whole bit. If you want to fight your whole bit, you fight your whole bit [the bit of time reflected in one's sentence]."

Grace's other group, "some of us," have "taken advantage of the opportunities" presented in prison programming, prisoner-initiated groups,

Bible study, religious education, Alcoholics Anonymous and Narcotics Anonymous groups, and GED and other educational possibilities. They "help other people." These are the women whom *Grace* identifies as having transcended the circumstances of permanent lockdown, as having left the mix behind, as choosing to self-determine in place. The stories of particular women who exemplify these prison journeys[17] are considered in the discussions of other, more agentic stages in chapter 5.

Most life-serving women do not fall into the either/or of *Grace's* categorization schema. They report repeated movements back and forth in and through the various stages, sometimes occupying more than one at a time. Women who enter prison with well-defined personal, analytical, educational, and/or social skills (e.g., women with professional or managerial backgrounds) seem better able to resist its corrosive effects, to move more quickly through the early stages, to skip processes, or to be able to simply tweak their internal compasses to survive in context. But they may simultaneously have fewer life experiences to enable them to respond effectively to the deference required of their "prisoner" status.[18] Having had some measure of social prestige and privilege on the outside, their life sentences immediately render them powerless on the inside.

For the women whose pre-imprisonment lives included few social or personal resources, or whose lives were derailed by experiences of incest, rape, and/or battering that often precede offending, time can be hard and its effects destructive.[19] They arrive, as *Destiny* notes, already diminished: "We come in here with many wounds. Our wings have been clipped." They are the marginalized women whom *Raine* described earlier who have "lived at the edge spatially, educationally, and economically" and whose adaptations, like their pre-incarceration lives, produce counterproductive results.[20]

Individual personalities, pre-prison experiences, and prison conditions are all associated with how women respond to prison.[21] It is a paradox of their many forms of adaptation that the outlets for resistance within the system may simultaneously provide means of reinforcing it.[22] For women with counterproductive coping strategies, their adaptations continue the too-familiar cycles of violation and punishment.

The First Two Stages

All women sentenced to prison, for the short or long term, begin their "prison journeys" within the first two stages.[23] These are the avalanche stages of the attrition processes. They are the only stages not voluntarily assumed; they are imposed as a consequence of sentencing where women become socially and legally defined as criminals and are remanded to prison.

Women, agentic in the free world, become "prisoners" in prison.[24] They must learn to be "inmates" and to live in a culture and environment that is defined by others. Although becoming a prisoner is not a choice, as they do in all the ensuing stages of the continuum, life-serving women respond to their new circumstances with some measure of self-determination, albeit through actions that are constrained by the structural conditions of imprisonment. Confinement doesn't end agency. All the stages, including becoming a prisoner and navigating the mix, reflect study participants' autonomous processes. Their agentic choices are imbricated with the strategies and tactics that they innovate and develop, both collectively and idiosyncratically, to ward off the corrosive effects of a sentence of life imprisonment.

A primary task of the first stage is learning official prison rules, norms, and culture, as well as adopting a deferent demeanor. Once taught the formal expectations of the institution, women are then assigned to the general population, or the less-restricted community of other incarcerated women. In this stage they must access personal skills to navigate the mix,[25] or, in the argot of this facility, "the prison thing." Using the social world understandings developed out of their previous life experiences, they have to thread their ways through the highly sexualized environment of gossip, intimate relationships, power struggles, and daily "drama," in short, the informal norms of their new lives.

Becoming a "Prisoner"

As a consequence of sentencing, processes of carceral erosion and labeling are set in motion. The women in this study have been remanded to prison and hence have become "prisoners" of the state . . . for *life*. "Prisoner" is not an identity of choice, nor is prison a circumstance of choice.

The label and the assumption of the identity of "prisoner," "inmate," "felon," or "criminal" is thrust upon them in the reality of their initial carceral experiences, that is, in the highly secured environment of closed custody. Closed custody is the 22-to-23-hour lockdown that begins any woman's orientation to prison. Confinement in closed custody lasts for months and may sometimes last for years. It is the site for the coercive control strategies that orient new arrivals, whatever their sentence length, to the expectations of the correctional system.[26]

The primary goal of this institutional orientation is to socialize the sentenced women into the routines of the institution and into their new identities, or, as French philosopher Michel Foucault argues, to use the institutional "machinery of power" to create "docile bodies."[27] For many women, social ties with their friendship and family support networks are ruptured by the custodial confinement. Upon arrival, the newly sentenced woman is immediately stripped of her sense of herself; as *Cindy* affirms, "When I got here . . . I lost who I was." Criminologist Bryn Herrschaft and her colleagues note that "when women perceive or experience a disruption in their intimate connections, it is not simply a loss of the relationship, but rather a loss of identity and self."[28] Prevented from access to the outside, *Cindy* was forced into what Erving Goffman identifies as role dispossession, that is, the total break with past roles and locations that occurs through imposed processes (like compulsory uniforms, the isolation of closed custody, and the prohibitions on visits from outsiders).[29] Institutional standardization increases consistency at the expense of humanity.[30] For *David* the experience "was all kind of surreal. I couldn't really believe it." Prison life was confusing and perplexing; there was always someone telling her what to do, where to go, how to go. Previously accustomed to making her own decisions, she laments: "I was all turned around."

Along with the disorienting prison orientation processes, women, like *Ginger*, who are unfamiliar with the patterns and values of differentially raced and classed women who populate prisons, experience their daily lives unfolding in an alien, anonymous, and abrasive environment. A key aspect of total institutions is the destabilization of most divisions in the free world.[31] In prison, life-sentenced women are consigned to a community of strangers. *Ginger* describes her re-orientation process during the "nine months and a day" that she spent in closed custody sharing a 6-by-10-foot space with another newly sentenced woman: "There's a lot of drama. It's intense. You're on lockdown 22 hours per day. In the outside world, you don't deal with people like that. It's a struggle every day."

She had to share space and coexist with others with whom she would not associate on the outside. She also had to manage the resulting interactional disequilibrium on her own.[32] Yet, as Goffman noted, the apparent stability of the system conceals latent possibilities for transgressive use of that time, as *Lauryn* demonstrated in her claim that there's "a lot" one can do in an hour.[33] Through prioritizing and managing her time, while in closed custody she could "make a meal, iron, wash my hair, and have sex."

Transgressive sexual activity, particularly in early stages of imprisonment, is met with a range of carceral sanctions. *Elizabeth Ashley* details the penalties for the array of nonconforming behaviors women can and do enact: "There's seg [segregation], harassment, pack ups, shakedowns, getting your stuff taken, daily summaries, and loss of privileges," any of which could be initiated for recalcitrant behaviors like "not having your shirt tucked in." All of these sanctions *Elizabeth Ashley* characterizes as "just vicious and hateful stuff" dominating an environment that has sanctions for every possible interaction and where every staff person can impose them.[34] When a woman is a "prisoner" for life, she must learn to navigate this organizational terrain with minimal destruction to self.

At its most basic level, the process of becoming a prisoner appears simple. Once incarcerated, the woman is a "prisoner" of the state, a one-dimensional identity, an indisputable fact. Yet, as Canadian human rights activist Karlene Faith argues, "It [labeling] ignores processes of criminalization, namely the ways by which 'criminals' are socially constructed and processed by the criminal justice system, within a dynamic of power relations which determine sanctions against specific, selected behaviours and populations. It implies a false and generally class-based dichotomy of good people (non-criminals) and bad people (criminals)."[35]

The learning curve for the newly labeled "prisoners" is knotty and steep, particularly so for women who are never intended to leave its definitional frame. "Prisoner" is a structural placement and a social construction; it is not an immutable identity. As *Joyce* aptly noted, her imprisonment for life is "what I am, not who I am." In warding off the unyielding consequences of the label, she establishes a clear distinction between her sentence and the institutional terms defining her. As does *Elizabeth Ashley*, who is "really offended" when an officer calls her an "inmate" or "prisoner": "I am a resident. If you call me something other than my name, I am a resident. . . . Correctional officers say 'prisoner' like you're a sack of crap or something. . . . I am a woman. I am Elizabeth Ashley."

Reminiscent of the "ain't I a woman?" cry of Sojourner Truth, *Elizabeth Ashley* demands an acknowledgment of her gendered humanity and her individuality. Her "resident" assertion calls forth a demand for recognition of her moral character and lays claim to treatment as a particular kind of rational and responsible person on the basis of her human dignity.[36]

Women like *Joyce* and *Elizabeth Ashley* resist the social meanings of the label "prisoner" (bad, immoral, dangerous, menacing, and untrustworthy) by refusing to internalize them and by complicating the premise that the stigma relies on: bad people who do bad things end up in prison.[37] *Kari* articulates the perspective of others when she says "a lot of people think we're just crap to society. It's not like it used to be, anyone can come to prison! You can just be in the wrong place at the wrong time." Good people, they all affirm, do end up in prison.

Nonetheless, for reasons of control and management, correctional systems work to ensure that placement in prison is coexistent with the identity "prisoner." Admission procedures convert a person into an object, "inmate," that is subject to administrative routines, like replacing a woman's name, a significant identity indicator, with a number, which also marks her as belonging to the institution, or by replacing her distinctive personal clothing with mandatory uniforms designed for men.[38] Skirts and dresses are not allowed for female prisoners. Their uniforms, identical to those of their male counterparts, are blue pants and shirts with orange stripes down the sides. They are the overt designations of imprisoned men and women as property of the State of Michigan, a social location and an assessment reportedly supported by Michigan Department of Corrections policies. *Lauryn* claims, for example, that if women are caught tattooing themselves or others, they receive sanctions for "destruction of state property." Imprisoned women are shaped and coded by procedures like these that turn them into genderless, bureau-cratic objects.

In spite of the recognized extraordinarily high level of sexual abuse histories in the lives of offending women, as property of the state in-carcerated women are given little control over their bodies in prison.[39] They are searched, fingerprinted, photographed, showered, and issued two (often worn) uniforms with their new identity numbers emblazoned across the shoulders and down the pant legs. They lose their personal possessions and are subject to physical nakedness and the loss of a sense of personal safety.

Goffman describes the consequence of these processes as personal defacement, or the loss of an "identity kit," those features of their pre-incarceration lives that they presented to self and the world as identity markers.[40] Prison orientation processes remove their "identity kits" and attempt to substitute new personas (i.e., "prisoner," "criminal," or "inmate"). The relabeling, resocialization process is at the center of institutional social control because an essential feature of managing inmates, of transforming and rehabilitating criminal errants, is defin-ing them as persons in need of control. The crimes for which they have been sentenced are evidence of the necessity for surveillance and monitoring. This stripping away of identity dissolves the conventional frameworks of normality that give meaning to common existence.[41] The process is not always successful. *Martha*, for example, agonizes over this social metamorphosis: "I don't know how to transition from being a person to being property." In the throes of the carceral pro-cess, *Martha* has been involuntarily transformed from a person with autonomy to an object to be managed, monitored, surveilled, and controlled.

Lauryn's resistance to this deferential position is embedded in her characterization of the identity challenge as "psychological warfare." *Lauryn* believes, and Goffman theorizes,[42] that prison personnel try to reprogram the thinking of the women. For *Lauryn* these efforts are subtle coercions to enforce conformity and to have women "accept your fate." Imprisonment suppresses choices and imposes organizational identities, and women are expected to become what the environment dictates.[43] As "prisoners," they "have to 'learn' to live in a regime gov-erned by strict controls within which each has to survive."[44]

"THE REST OF YOUR LIFE": EROSION AVALANCHE

While incarceration itself is a difficult personal struggle, receipt of a life sentence is yet another avalanche of erosions in which life-serving women are forced to face "the confused uncertainty of a life of confinement."[45] It took *Sheila T.* "five or six years" to work through the stages that were "just like grieving for me to come to terms" and accept the reality of a life sentence in real time. The meaning of a "life sentence" is even more difficult to grasp for adolescent women (see chapter 4 for an example of the personal journeys of juvenile lifers), who, as *Sandy* notes, "haven't even grown up yet, let alone learned how to survive in here."

Juveniles incarcerated for life face triple jeopardy: imprisonment, immaturity, and a corrosive environment. Sentenced to prison at 17, *Linda*, now 42, has already spent one and a half more lifetimes inside than she lived as a child before her incarceration. Nonetheless, she retains a strong sense of self. Her agency is defined by outreach; she makes "a special effort to educate [newly sentenced juveniles]. I don't think they understand the gravity of the situation—that a life sentence means *the rest of your life*" (the emphasis is *Linda*'s). It's a difficult concept to comprehend. Comprehension may be even more difficult for the children of life-serving women. *Lauryn* shared this experience of her adolescent daughter's dawning awareness of the significance of her mother's sentence: "Imagine having to explain what 'the rest of your life' means to your child that you left when she was five and finds the courage to ask what it means at 18. 'It means that I will one day leave here in a box, honey.' The piercing sobs that echoed through and silenced the visiting room still haunt me. She's 21 now."

Most people don't think in terms of the full extent of their lives. They dream. They have expectations of a future that will have possibilities and opportunities, perhaps limited, but not repetitiously so. They don't consider the future as being the same as the present over and over. *Cindy*, herself a recently sentenced adolescent, remarks about some freshly adjudicated juveniles who "think this is a game." She wants to shake them and say: "Wake the hell up! You have a life bit."

It's the meaning of "a life bit" that takes time to grasp. Life means until you die. At 16, 17, or even 18 years old, death is not an immediate future consideration. For most adolescents, realistically it is 60–70 years away—that is more than four juvenile lifetimes—too much for young women to grasp cognitively and emotionally. Yet they must come to understand that their lives, as traditionally understood, are over. They have been decisively removed from conventional maturation and growth; from developing job skills; from love, marriage, and family building; from dancing, singing, and hanging out with friends; from voting; from learning to cook, garden, or paint; from walks in the woods or walks through the mall; from the sights and smells of daily living; and from all the social discourses that construct public lives. "In general, we think it constitutive of a person having *a life* that he or she claims some authority over saying what is happening in it."[46] *Life* imprisonment challenges this expectation; it results in the loss of autonomy, privilege, personal security, liberty, and privacy, and it requires diverse and complex strategies for survival, especially so for adolescent women.[47]

"The symbolic message of the [life] sentence" in the public arena is that life-serving men and women are living lives that lack social worth.[48] As social outcasts, imprisoned men and women are stigmatized, demonized, and accused of draining "the system" of resources. Sentenced to life imprisonment, study participants have been "institutionally erased from the category of human beings."[49]

Dispossessed of pre-incarceration roles (e.g., woman, mother, worker, sister) that they could previously shape and discard, the life-sentenced women's master statuses now become "inmate," "prisoner," and "criminal."[50] Women can and do create roles within that context. They pose. They withdraw. They reconstruct themselves with salvaged pieces of their outside lives and with foraged resources from their new locations.

But removal from the social and cultural networks within which their previous identities were embedded is often traumatic.[51] Dislocation, shock, insensibility, grief, and inability to deal with the consequences of, as *Ginger* said, being "slammed with my verdict," may result in feelings of powerlessness and apathy in the face of the highly personal disaster of a sentence of life imprisonment.[52] While most study participants reported being "numb" when they were remanded to prison, *Cindy* says she "didn't care." "My whole life was taken away like that [snaps fingers], but I decided I gotta do something otherwise I'm gonna lose my mind. On the other hand, if I lose my mind, who will care? I'm in prison." *Cindy* recounts both the personal and social transformation of a life "taken away" in a snap. She recognizes that, in a life-altering instant in time, her adolescent self offended and, in another "snap" of time, she became a "prisoner." Now identified as part of the throwaway citizenry, those lacking in social value, those not missed in the wider society, she became a member of the society of invisible women incarcerated for life.[53]

Some women faced with the same transition attempt to hold on to identities that they no longer possess. They assume that old skills will work with the problems that now threaten them. They look for familiar markers to orient themselves to this environment, but, confronted with a strange world that challenges their assumptions and creates an instability from which there is no retreat, they are forced to tackle the learning curve associated with becoming a "prisoner."[54] They develop awareness that prison not only fails to protect individual identity, it crushes individuality by enforcing collective compliance and discipline.

Prisons function by disrupting those activities that in civil society indicate that an incarcerated woman is a person with self-determination and some command over her world. Disruption is a rationale for the challenges to self that are bound to occur in managing the daily activities of a large number of people in a restricted space at limited expense. Prison is a place where the basic conditions for the individual reflect institutional arrangements that, by definition, are designed to limit opposition and to homogenize opportunities.[55] Faced with these challenges to their identities, some women opt to define their imprisonment from the perspective of an outside, transient visitor.[56] *Alexandria,* for example, "wouldn't take a footlocker" because she "wasn't staying." The implied permanence of a footlocker was a symbol of her acceptance of confinement for life. Imprisonment is her reality, but she was resistant emotionally and psychologically to the endlessness of the "lifer" identity that a footlocker implied.

In each stage of the typology, the study respondents generated multiple forms of resistance to the acceptance of a "prisoner" identity. However, eventually, given that there were few collective resources available to resist assimilation into prison culture and given the grinding routine where every day was basically like the day before, some women chose the ease of becoming "prisoners" in their identities.[57] In *Glenda Gale's* words, "they wear the hat they were given." They chose what sociologist Allan Johnson calls "the paths of least resistance"[58] and they accepted the "prisoner," "inmate," and "felon" definitions of them.

In becoming "prisoners," all of the women had to adapt to institutional rules for dress codes, eating, working, sleeping, and surveillance. In the gradual process of wearing away, they internalized the norms of formal prison life. Those choosing "the path of least resistance" manifest what *Tootsie Roll* describes disdainfully as getting "all caught up . . . you're making this your home." These women become comfortable in prison, finding warmth and (pseudo) family relationships, and ultimately succumbing to and embracing "prisoner" identities. Others adopt a rueful pragmatism in managing institutional power and, given the prison's capacity to punish nonconformity, they adapt to the rules. Acclimatization to organizational norms of behavior is a social survival skill in prison, but many continued to resist the imposed identity.[59]

Navigating the Mix

Institutional rules for becoming a prisoner, while enforced idiosyncratically, are learned in the hothouse of closed custody. In their first step out of that hyper-controlled environment, life-serving women learn that the next stage, navigating the mix begins with assignment to "general pop [population]."[60] Women who enter this arena of eased security restrictions start navigating the new context by paying careful attention to what's close at hand and immediate. The hyper-sexualized prison culture, the drugs, the loud talking, the profanity, the double-bunking, the "drama" of relationships played out in public, and the perceived institutional "disorder" can be, as *Shequetta Tasha Lynn* claims, "a shock to your system."

Interactionally, the women must sort out the cultural status hierarchy and their places in it; they must learn who to trust and who to avoid; and they must determine how to avoid trouble in what *Jane* has previously described as a "hell hole," an environment where oppressive conditions are the norm and from which there is no exit.[61] Some women report spending "a lot" of time continually assessing and reassessing this new world, using observations of interactions with others to make informed judgments about the safety of their own circumstances and that of other women.

These respondents, like *Jannel*, recounted their initial fearfulness: "I was terrified of inmates because I only knew what I'd seen on TV." Yet, in

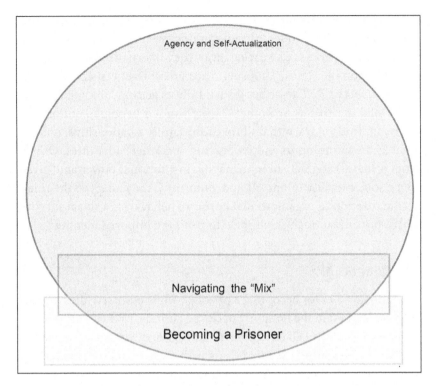

FIGURE 3.3. THE TWO STAGES THAT ARE EXPERIENCED
BY ALL INCARCERATED WOMEN

a courtroom moment, she was transformed into the "inmate" of her own terror, instantly changed from "being respected to being someone people wanted to spit upon." *Joyce* also reported drawing on media images and was more specific in her worry about becoming a "bull dyke's bitch or ironing clothes because I was someone's woman." Other women in this study also identified their early fears, their assumptions of popular cultural definitions of incarcerated females as predatory, as their motivations for initial isolation and avoidance. Implicit in these apprehensions is the cognitive dissonance of "I am here, but I am not like them."

Continuing to clutch the mantles of their now-irrelevant outside identities, these women see themselves as different from their life-serving peers and, although not claiming innocence of their crimes, as not "belonging" in prison.[62] They claim a moral distance between themselves and the others, the "criminals," that they view as tainted. Simultaneously harboring two inconsistent understandings—of a self as a "good person" who erred but also of a self as an "inmate" with its attendant social definitions—they must either give up the idea that they are "good" or alter their popular cultural notions about "prisoners." Because this dissonance is uncomfortable and because being imprisoned for life is not likely to change quickly, they struggle to find ways to adjust their "prisoner" cognitions to make the two more consonant.[63]

They observe and come to understand the roles and statuses, responsibilities and mores, of the context. They learn the gendered cultural rules inside: They limit self-revelations, establish boundaries in sharing histories of abuse and victimization, learn to read the subtexts of verbal exchanges, and ascertain who is a safe associate.[64] Eventually the oscillations in movement between "me" and "them" stabilize as the women, like *Joyce*, learn that other incarcerated women are "not as scary" as expected and are, in fact, "women just like me, who had made bad decisions."

As reported, *Joyce* and many of her peers recognized these commonalities. As an example of these shared experiences, many study participants spoke of coming into prison "behind a man," that is, they had been manipulated by men, abused by men, been "gullible" and "stupid" in the service of men, aided and abetted violent men, or had murdered their brutal male partners. Recognizing both their analogous circumstances and a, sometimes lengthy, reluctance to acknowledge community, *Harmony* points out that "why you are here is important to everyone else," but all of the women inside have been convicted, "so get over it." In support of the obvious, *Sasha Lavan* also notes, "We all have six digits [Michigan Department of Corrections inmate numbers]." In the prison environment, their six digits are the presumed equalizers of unequal sentences, free world capital, race hierarchies, and personal resources.

While having six digits and wearing "the same pants with the orange stripe" (*Destiny*) marks immediate status and creates a form of carceral leveling, for some women it does not result in acceptance of institutional demands for deference and submission. *Sheri* says, "[I] was mentored by dope addicts. The first thing they taught me was how to go on a visit and get a package," that is, how to bring dope/drugs inside the facility. When others ask *Alison* "what have you learned from prison?" She responds forthrightly: "How to become a criminal."

"YOU HEAR, BUT YOU DON'T HEAR": CODES OF CONDUCT INSIDE

Cultural norms guide behavior inside the women's facility and form the beliefs, values, behaviors, and even the material goods that constitute a way of life for these incarcerated women. One life-sentenced woman in this study, for example, noted the contrast between the material activities and cultural environments of male and female prisoners. "Men make weapons; women make dildoes." Male prisons are characterized by both latent and enacted violence; women's prisons can be characterized by their cultures of hyper-sexuality,[65] described in this prison by *Sasha Lavan's* terse characterization: "they flippin' like patties in here." *Ciara Blue* reflects both the culture and the tension between the women's sexual activity and the correctional officers' attempts to eliminate it: "I have lots of sex. But I don't get emotionally attached. I've been here since I was 17 and I'm *going to* have sex! Go ahead, move me, I'm going to have sex" (emphasis is *Ciara Blue's*). As Erin George, an author and life-imprisoned woman, notes: "To deny the possibility of bona fide sexual relationships is to deny what little autonomy the prisoners feel they have."[66]

Women's prison culture, like cultures everywhere, is governed by a formal control structure, in this instance it is the Michigan Department of Corrections, and by the informal norms developed by the women in response to the conditions of imprisonment. *Martha* sums up her prison lessons with a sigh: "You have to do wrong to get respect in here." Respect between and among the women is closely tied to observance of the informal norms of conduct.

Men are said to have an "inmate code" that standardizes the inmate culture.[67] The code may be more of an ideal type than a description of everyone's behavior at all times. The code's primary rules and values are embedded in the following maxims: do not snitch (e.g., do not report the malfeasance of others, do not trust staff), do your own time (e.g., mind your own business, look out for yourself), and do not appear weak (e.g., act tough, appear dangerous). Criminal justice theorist Joycelyn Pollock argues that women enact an uneven adherence to the men's code and they do not develop a code of their own.[68] This study identified gender consensus in the code of not reporting fights to officers for, as *Anna Bell* notes, "we don't need to be locked up inside," an inclination supported by criminologist Rebecca Trammell's study of prison culture from the perspective of formerly incarcerated men and women.[69] Trammell found that both men and women inside refused to report "a good deal of violence," preferring to handle the problems outside the confines of institutional sanctions.

With regard to other identified male inmate code guidelines,[70] respondents in this study reported agreement. *Sheri*, for example, learned "fast" that whatever you hear, you shouldn't repeat. Also referred to as "penitentiary slick," the norm succinctly holds that "you don't repeat what you hear or report what you see." *Louise* elaborates, "You hear, but you don't hear. You see, but you don't see. You take care of you. You don't go to the officers."

Nonetheless, Pollock finds a number of ways that imprisoned women deviate from the value system of incarcerated men.[71] "Do your own time," a basic tenet of the men's code and one given lip service by the women in this study, for example, is regularly transgressed in the steady flow of gossip about relationships and breakups, participation in the "drama," and their interventions in others' disputes. Prison culture reflects "meanings that are manufactured, imposed, negotiated, altered, and highly structured, yet permeable and amorphous" and, in the oft-quoted words of the symbolic interactionist theorists W. I. and Dorothy Thomas, "if situations are perceived as real, they are real in their consequences."[72] The meanings developed in the social worlds of these women provide them with informally sanctioned behavioral codes and standards of conduct.

Like the legends of the thin blue line in police work, or the male inmate's code of conduct, life-serving women also have informal rules that govern interactions, but they are less collective than the male examples and the rules are often more observed in their violations.[73] Women, for example, trust officers more than their imprisoned male counterparts do.[74] *Alexandria* notes that some lifers are "at the officer's desk all day" purportedly telling them "everything that everyone else is doing." Acknowledging the behavior, *Kari* wonders about the pointlessness of the motivations: "What's the purpose? You're not gonna get parole for that."

Although viewed suspiciously by their peers, life-sentenced women may talk to the officers for any number of personal reasons. *Lauryn* says, for example,

> When I am interacting with the officers at the desk . . . I am either identi-
> fying with their identities as free people working in a job: allowing them
> and me to see I am no different from them . . . or I am attempting to get
> them to see us [incarcerated women] differently and their relations to us
> differently. We are not just property. They do not work at GM [General
> Motors] with machinery. They work in a warehouse with real people with
> real feelings.

But *Lauryn* also agrees that "these things do have an impact on my
interactions with other women" who assume that any lifer at the desk
in conversation with an officer is there to ingratiate herself by reporting on the malfeasance of others. Erin George alleges that snitching in
prison is pervasive and indiscriminate and that everyone knows who
the snitches are.[75] If women are seen "at the officer's desk all day," others assume they are snitches and they may be sanctioned by isolation,
avoidance, gossip, or infrequently even violence.[76] As a proactive strategy, other life-serving women, like *Grace*, refuse to snitch or to associate
with people who do. So much of the culture around the mix concerns
notions of reality, definitions of reality, ownership of reality, and the
dead-endedness of reality that *Simone* asserts, even with snitches, "we
have to let everything roll off our backs in here."

While many female lifers identify the ideal of never snitching as part
of the informal norms of cooperation, they also simultaneously report going to the correctional officers themselves about problems with
bunkies, to "conversate" and receive informal therapy, and to share their
personal triumphs. As she's spent more time inside, *Louise* says, "I've felt
bolder to step out and go against what they're [snitches] saying," but she
continues to maintain that "you don't go to the officers" to resolve issues
or to report on behavior. Being a "snitch" is a stigmatized identity, with
or without informal sanctions.

With few options for positive engagement, life-serving women report
that the oppressive policies, rules, and idiosyncratic enactment of institutional sanctions require that they manipulate the system. Supporting *Kari's* claim that "that's really the only way to get what you want in
prison," they resort to behaviors that they would not have considered
on the outside like over-exaggerations, outright duplicity, and "making
things up." In interactions with ill-mannered peers, *Grace* claims, "If I'm

not calling you a name, it doesn't get through. Look, little girl, you really need to back up off me. I'm, like, all right, I've got your attention now, bitch." She feels compelled to use language and discourse patterns that don't reflect the ways that she experiences herself in order to be heard and understood.

Sociologist Rik Scarce, in describing his process of "becoming an inmate" (for refusing to release research data) and the "slow shedding of my old self," noted that his metamorphosis, like the women's, included using language that he rarely used on the street, adopting attitudes that would have been unthinkable prior to imprisonment, and violating rules.[77] His narrative is an illustration of the ubiquity of these corrosive carceral outcomes.

The single, informal, inviolate rule identified by the women in this study, although noted more in its multiple breaches by "short termers," or women "with years" (women with delineated minimum and maximum sentences and, therefore, "with years"), is never throwing a woman's time in her face, never calling her "a life-doing bitch." It's an insult that demands response.[78] Most focus-group participants claimed that their life sentences are thrown at them *"all the time"* (their own emphases) by "short termers." It's salt in their wounds. Female lifers have expectations of respect from other women—respect for their time served, their ages, their knowledge of prison culture and policies, their personal conduct—and it is in this perceived disrespect that the epithet is most profound. *Joyce*, for example, is called a "life-doing bitch" by "short termers" but gets her retribution when "I see them coming back," doing what *Elizabeth Ashley* calls "life on the installment plan." *Shequetta Tasha Lynn* suffers both insult and upset when people "throw your case" in your face, but especially so when the epithet includes additional commentary like "you're just going to die here."

The cruelty is intentional, the aim is to hurt, to strike an emotional blow, as *Yasmeen* notes: "They [short termers] know it's hurtful, so they pull that card." The verbal assault is vicious and unpredictable. A simple disagreement over microwave use can precipitate the spiteful sobriquet, as *Kari* laments. "Stick to the issue. It goes from the phone or microwave to my time. They come botherin' you and now you're a life-doin' bitch."

The verbal malice has real consequences. *Alexandria* begins to cry as she explains its meaning for her. "At first I had a visit every day. I see my daughter once a month now. That's what I think of when people say 'life-doin' bitch.'" "Short termers" experience significant social and material losses through imprisonment, but are eventually reinstated to civic life. Women with life sentences face permanent losses as well as the additional emotional burden of these unexpected verbal assaults.

"PINK BITCHES" AND COLOR-BLINDNESS: RACE IN "THE MIX"

Although, as *Liberty Flynn* notes, "the dynamics of a unit change almost on a daily basis, due to staff changes or prisoners moving in or out, or from room to room because of bunkie problems," some changes are also precipitated by women's exchanges in the barbed use of disparaging verbal assaults, like "life-doing bitches," or in outright racial taunts. The shared circumstance of imprisonment plunges life-serving women into involuntary contact with incarcerated peers of races and ethnicities different than their own. Their coerced confinement together often engenders more interracial contact and conflict than was common in their pre-incarceration lives. A number of life-serving women reported experiencing racial culture shock as a consequence of their release from closed custody into the mélange of "general pop." *Lynn*, a white life-sentenced woman, claimed, for example, "When I came to prison there was not a lot of Caucasian women here. For every ten blacks, there was one [white woman]. You learned to fight or you got run over."[79] Although *Lynn's* statement appears to imply otherwise, Pollock argues that informal racial integration is the norm in women's prisons.[80] Sociologist Juanita Diaz-Cotto additionally claims that, prior to incarceration, women may have been divided by racial/ethnic loyalties, residential segregation, and the hyper-segregation of American social life, but once imprisoned and confronted with alien others, they are forced to set aside their prejudices to survive, cope, and thrive.[81] In this study, *Merrilee's* experiences support Pollock's and Diaz-Cotto's contentions.[82] She says, "It's [acceptance of racial difference] because we don't choose where we live. [pause] I might live on a wing that's the 'hood. [pause] We're interacting daily." *Merrilee* is white and living "in the 'hood,'" a coded word choice that clearly signals her experience of minority status in a residential unit she identifies as black space. An unintended consequence of *Merrilee's* physical location is her incipient awareness of previously unnoticed discriminatory treatment of her peers of color.

Merrilee describes a race "epiphany" she underwent after interaction with a correctional officer, who "treats me well" but who verbally abuses her African American peer, *Pooh Bear*. "You can't be OK with me and dog *Pooh Bear* out. That's where my epiphany came." Although *Merrilee* had expectations of equalized disparaging treatment from officers in the one-size-fits-all prison context, she was confronted with undeniable evidence to the contrary. *Merrilee's* "epiphany" is in her recognition that her whiteness gives her some privilege in interactions with officers. She has come to understand that indignities inherent in being "dogged out" are part of the daily existence of her peers of color. Her small measure of race privilege, being treated well by an officer and not being "dogged out," occurs at their expense. *Merrilee* has made the analytical connection between *Pooh Bear's* disadvantage and her own racial privilege.[83]

Diaz-Cotto's and Pollock's claims are in part borne out in this study, but the race picture inside is not quite as unproblematic as they assert. Instead, this study data indicate that race is a central social organizing factor among these life-serving women, and, as a result, the trait of race frequently overwhelms all their other perceptions. For example, to ward off the verbal assaults of others and to engage in informal boundary marking, many women employ race-based name-calling—a simplistic verbal assault used to categorize and locate others in the prison hierarchy. *Sandy* recalls her first experience with a racial taunt inside. "I remember when I first came in and someone called me a 'cracker.' I was just confused. I had no idea that it was a racial term." She learned quickly that race-labeling and name-calling are integral to the drama of the mix,[84] locating women in the cultural pecking order, as well as establishing the informal boundaries for their interactions. So unavoidable are the race labels that *Dennis the Menace* claims, "I've only been called a 'pink bitch' four times in my whole bit, but it's because they were mad heated." Based, as the "pink bitch" slurs were, in the passion of anger, *Dennis the Menace* shoulders the gibes and excuses them. In the process, she unwittingly accepts the use of racial epithets as an informal cultural exchange.

There is no escape in prison from the toxicity of race-based name-calling. It influences interracial interactions inside and shapes the lives of life-serving women. All focus-group participants claimed a wide range of practices and outcomes for racial gibes. They reported a number of verbal exchanges where "pink bitch/cracker" and/or "black bitch/n-word" were used as colloquial designations. The terms used—either by the participants themselves or by others as descriptions of them—were sometimes casual affinity markers of in-group status. The in-group status vernacular became an issue of contention when it was used by an out-group member and/or when officer sanctions were perceived to be applied unequally. One focus-group participant claimed, for example, "There was an incident where a white girl called a black girl the n-word, and she got sent to seg [segregation] over it. But a black girl could call a [white] girl a 'cracker' all day long and nothing would happen." In other instances, the terms were intentionally directed slurs thrown in anger at a particular individual or group. Those gibes reportedly elicited quick responses.

Life-serving women's interpretations of the racial taunts—their own applications and those directed against them—depend on the ways they identify racially. In focus-group discussions, it was clear that most female lifers saw what they expected to see in others based on their identities as white women or as black women. *Sandy*, for example, speaks the stance echoed by other white study participants: "You get in big trouble for calling a black woman a name, but nothing happens if you say something about a white woman. They can say 'pink bitch' all day long, but if I called someone a 'black bitch,' there could be a race war." White women repeatedly reported experiencing institutional processes that they defined as favoring the interests of their black peers. Alternatively, *Lauryn*, a multiracial study participant, claims that "if a white person goes [to an officer] and says someone black did something, they will act on it. But if a black person says a white did something to her, there will be an investigation into it." Black women tended to report experiencing institutional processes that replicated American racial hierarchies and that disadvantaged them. Whether life-serving women's perceptions were accurate or not, their interpretations followed the logic of their race imputations.

Alexandria, a black life-serving woman, gives voice to the stereotypical race tropes that she, and others, claim define interactions inside prison walls. "Racism is everywhere . . . like if a white girl has too much soul" then she's characterized as "trying to be black" and "if a black girl is intelligent" then she's "trying to be white." These applications of race labels to behavior, like race-based name-calling, drive expectations of appropriate behavior, narrow opportunities for cross-race engagement, and act as informal means of social control. In discussions of interracial romantic liaisons, for example, the consensus among both black and white focus-group participants took the form of a reinscription of troublesome, archetypal racial stereotypes. When two women of different races "get together," others see the black woman as "using" her white partner for "commissary" (prison store food and/or personal items). *Lauryn* explicates the narrative. "Black people period see white people as docile and submissive. I have seen black people be on the prowl, I'm not saying all of them. It is very calculated. They watch who they can get and what they can get. If it's between a black or a white with money, they'll always pick the white. [With] the black, they will have to work way too hard." Yet race-based "using," participants also agreed, works both ways. *Merrilee* says, for example, that the gossip narrative about an interracial relationship is that "a tough black girl" is necessary to "protect" a weaker white one. *Lauryn* correspondingly argues that "white women can be very cunning. They tell [their black partners] 'you do what I want because you want this' [commissary or other support]." In focus-group conversations, interracial romantic liaisons were not portrayed simply as loving relationships. They were continuously subjected to imputations of stereotypical, dichotomized black or white racial narratives.

Yet there are also exceptions to the dominant race themes. For some life-serving women, the opportunity to be friends with women from other races was an unexpected prison "positive." *Chelsie Marie*, for example, an African American female, raised in a residentially segregated African American community, and educated in residentially segregated urban schools, describes the origins of her first friendship with a white woman:

> She was a Christian and I was not. I was by myself a lot. One day she came and sat and said, 'I think we should be friends.' I asked, "You gay?" She said, no, that she's a Christian. She came back every day. . . . After a while, she wore me down. Even after I would give her crap, she would stay. She said, "I refuse to let you scare me." She would say, "Why you lookin' so mean?" She would carry a mirror to show me. That white girl was crazy. But we are friends now.

Chelsie Marie expresses both appreciation and admiration for "that white girl" who showed initiative and persistence in crossing informal racial boundaries to engage with her. She also delights in the novelty of her first interracial friendship.

Sandy, another white study participant, offers a different, but significant, account of the institution's enforced integration. She speaks of her initial expectations and later realizations about race inside:

> *Sandy:* When I got in [to prison], white was the minority. I was really scared because I didn't know anything about black people. I didn't grow up in a diverse environment, so I was really nervous.
>
> LL: What was the reason for that fear?
>
> *Sandy:* I just didn't know better. . . . All I knew of blacks was what I heard came out of Benton Harbor, drug dealers, murderers, rapists . . . and black women can be very intimidating. . . . They are very strong and assertive, stronger than white women both emotionally and mentally. . . . I learned quickly that black women deserve respect, not fear. One thing that stood out to me was how black women can get into a big fight and make up and still be friends. White women can't do that; we hold grudges.

Starting in a fearful place where the only interpretive frames she had access to were race-based stereotypes, imprisonment afforded *Sandy* opportunities to overcome her pre-incarceration racial biases and begin to appreciate both the differences and the humanity of other life-serving women. Nevertheless, her interpretive frame remained locked in race-based explanations of behavior.

Life-serving black women also reported initiating sociable contact with life-sentenced white women. Sometimes these voluntary outreach activities simultaneously upset entrenched relations and reinforced stereotypes. *Meme*, for example, has "time down" (years of incarceration), so she knows the formal and informal culture of the prison. A middle-aged African American woman, *Meme* represents herself as a protector of white women, who she says are "not strong" compared to black women and who lack "street sense." She wants to "do right" and pay forward the advice and concern she received from others as a newly sentenced woman, so she befriends and advises white women. Although well intentioned and no doubt helpful, *Meme's* motivations, like *Sandy's* race observations, contribute to the reinscription of the classic race stereotypes of black women as strong, assertive, and aggressive and white women as frail, passive, dependent, and in need of protection. It's a narrative that then structures their interracial interactions with other life-serving women. Additionally, *Meme* pays social costs for her cross-race caretaking. Because she "hangs around" with white women, other black women accuse her of not recognizing her own blackness. Similarly her white bunkie claims that other white women dislike *Meme* because "she speaks her mind," a classic depiction of the behavior of the "angry black woman" of cultural lore. For *Meme's* observers from both races, it is her race—and theirs—that influences and dominates their interpretations of her behavior.

Although African American and white life-serving women unintentionally support and perpetuate these race narratives, they also lay claim to personal color-blindness, an attitude toward race that they considered to be the apex in antiracist thought. In so doing, they assert vigorously that context overwhelms race. Study participants individually and collectively argue that their status as "prisoners" overrides divisions of race, class, sexual orientation, and so on. "We all have six digits," *Sasha Lavan* says. All the life-serving women in this study used color-blind affirmations to deny the influence of race on their perceptions and on the quality of their lives. White women said, for example,

"My niece is black. I've been color-blind all my life."
"I have black friends that are like sisters."
"I don't see race."

In this environment of presumed equality, where everyone has "six digits," a good many African American women also made color-blind claims that echoed those of their white peers:

"I've never been a racist. I don't see color."
"It ain't no black/white thing with me."
"How am I racist? My best friend is white."

Indeed, while imputations of race structure many of their interactions, they deny the importance of their race ideologies.

Many of these life-serving women, black and white, fervently believe that color-blindness is a positive paradigm for thought and action,[85] a way to announce their postracial identities. They do not recognize that their claims are a way to evade race as a topic of conversation and reflection, of analysis and action. They seem unaware of their uses of color-blindness to close off rather than open up opportunities for discussion. Once their claims of color-blindness are made, "I don't see race," there's no further room for dialogue or debate because race no longer exists as a system of advantage for some and disadvantage for others. Race remains paradoxically concealed and central to their interactions.

This construction of their circumstances supports an argument made by antiracist educator Tim Wise that implicit racial biases can coexist with outwardly nonracist demeanors.[86] Many life-serving women, like *Simone*, assert with confidence that "race doesn't become an issue because we have something in common." Their shared pariah status, she argues, draws women together across racial divides. However, these same women then proceed to relate stories about discourteous behavior (e.g., letting friends go first in the shower line, letting someone cut into the microwave line, and/or taking requests out of order), and they make race-based attributions for the behavior.

Hair care is one example of the ways in which life-serving women code impolite behavior as raced. White women claim that black women dominate the "grooming room" and essentially lock them out. Prison policy states that combing and braiding another women's hair, defined by correctional personnel as an intimate activity, must take place in the public grooming room. It takes hours for a head of hair to be braided. While the combing and braiding are occurring, other women are required by policy to "stand back" and are not allowed to use the room for their own hair fashions. Black women's hairstyling is consequently read by white women as intentionally denying them equal opportunity access to the grooming room. Conversely, *DJ*, a white study participant, complains, "You can't try to be a white girl with long hair. They [black women] hate that. They say it stinks and it looks greasy. They hate white hair. They say that we shed."

Although they race-code behavior, many life-serving women continue to deny the importance of race in the culture of the prison and continue to claim a personal color-blindness. As evidence of the claim, they all assert a close personal relationship with a woman of a race different than their own. Yet they continue to define impolite action by the race of the women engaged in it. When they complain about repeated discourteous behaviors, they employ race as their primary category of explanation.

Although self-identifying as unprejudiced race allies, some white life-serving women also reported experiencing reverse racism when they were unexpectedly cast as minorities in prison.[87] *Elizabeth Ashley* says, for example, "Prison was the first time I encountered racism . . . racism for being white." Prior to her imprisonment, *Elizabeth Ashley* had lived a life where she could be unaware of the benefits of race privilege. Incarceration brought her face-to-face with women disadvantaged in a system of racial stratification from which she benefited, but from which they experienced personal adversity and damage to their communities. *Lauryn,* a mixed-race participant, spoke up to provide some support for *Elizabeth Ashley's* perception of reverse racism in the prison confines. "The [American stratification] system is more lenient on white people. It is predominantly black people that work here. Because the black people run the show on the inside, they make it harder on the white people . . . because the system was so easy on them." *Lauryn's* explanation draws on conventional stereotypes and is challenged by *Merrilee's* previous account of her racial "epiphany" when the presumed race advantage was reversed. Their interpretations depend profoundly on their own racial identifications. Both women's perceptions might be seen as correct, *if* the disparity in treatment that they describe is the result of the individual behaviors of particular officers, rather than the consequence of discriminatory treatment that is institutionalized.[88] In either case, both women assume that race is a master status in the reported interactions. Neither woman offers consideration of other potentially mitigating factors, like physical and linguistic presentation style, personal reputation, initiation of the interaction, domination of the discussion, implied physicality, and events surrounding the interactions (shift change, chow, count, and so on). Both assume racial profiling that elicits "racist" behavior directed toward an identified "other."

In spite of their unintentionally raced accounts, most study participants, black and white, as noted earlier, claimed a personal color-blindness, an attitude toward race that they assumed situated them at the pinnacle of antiracist thought. In his insightful text *Racism without Racists: Color-Blind Racism and the Persistence of Racial Inequality in America,* Eduardo Bonilla-Silva argues that while color-blindness is often claimed by those who espouse it to be the antithesis of racism, it is, in fact, a white race ideology.[89] Under the façade of color-blindness, white people can refuse to acknowledge the reality of racism, their own racism and the racism that is embedded in societal institutions. The banner of color-blindness also allows them to avoid consideration of how their white race identities provide them with privileges denied to people of color. This willful heedlessness results in failures of critical thinking, of inclusivity, of democratic overtures, and of opportunities to experience race epiphanies like *Merrilee's.*

The color-blind claims of life-serving women in this study unwittingly support Bonilla-Silva's theoretical formulation of color-blindness as a white race ideology.[90] As both black and white women appropriate the language of color-blindness, they also illustrate its theoretical importance through their denials of the significance of race in spite of the many ways that it structures their lives. They define color-blindness as the diffusion through (even prison) culture of a postracial society. They present themselves as women for whom race has ceased to have meaning. As "pink bitches" with "black bitch" friends or as "n-words" with "cracker" friends, life-serving women claim personal identities as color-blind interactants. They trust that their claims identify them as antiracists in their own iteration of postracialism. These color-blind denials of race allow them to actively avoid engaging with the destructive consequences, to self and other, of their racial narratives. The carceral circumstances of forced interracial engagement provide them with unprecedented opportunities to challenge race stereotypes and to bridge gaps in racial understandings. In laying claim to color-blindness, they miss these opportunities and instead portray themselves as being in the vanguard of a societal transition to postracialism, even as they inadvertently re-entrench toxic racial stereotypes in their interactions and in their explanations of behavior.

"DON'T BLEED UNDER THAT DOOR": BOUNDARY MAINTENANCE

The experiences of self-worth for many life-serving women are linked to these internal exchanges, especially to the camaraderie of racial/ethnic and cultural understandings but also to the external valuations communicated to them by others. Verbal cues and name-calling, encouraging or discouraging remarks, all shape how women think of themselves in this deprivation environment. Prison, by definition, already has pervasive control of the labels for their identities. In interactions with officers, life-sentenced women are defined as inmates, prisoners, and/or felons, and they are consequently reduced from whole persons to "tainted, discounted ones" with extensive discrediting effects.[91] Other imprisoned women label them with race-based descriptors, sometimes offensively, sometimes as affinity tributes in informal encounters.

As a result navigating exchanges in "the prison thing" can be challenging and women must learn to establish contextually appropriate boundaries. *Elizabeth Ashley* displays penitentiary pragmatism when she notes that prison is a society and, as in the "real" world, there will always be "people who try to use you or trick you." Conning is part of a spectrum of errors in prison, "but you have to keep trying" and make sure that when help is proffered that the provider can "set healthy boundaries." She is both sanguine and mindful—there will be people who run cons, but she refuses to have those "bad apples" define her or the context. She notes the necessity to "keep trying" to positively affect living conditions as she also counsels protection through watchful attention to "healthy boundaries."

Esther's boundary maintenance strategies move in the opposite direction. Where *Elizabeth Ashley* advises cautious engagement, *Esther* recommends avoidance. She says, "When I'm in the [residential] unit, there's no peace," but she can "tune it out" by establishing her engagement boundary: "Throw each other over the rail for all I care, but don't bleed under that door [focus-group laughter]." Enacting the inmate code of do your own time, *Esther* does not make the "drama" in public space her business unless others involve her by metaphorically "bleeding" under her door and making their business her business. *Meme's* boundaries echo *Esther's* when she attempts to limit the gossip and engagement of her self-reported busybody bunkie with a rhetorical question: "Do we live in the hallway?" In these ways, the social environment over which the women have some measure of control is defined by the parameters of their cells. They adopt a "live and let live" attitude, maintain social space, and create safe zones in their rooms.[92] Housed two or sometimes three or more to a room, engagement with the "drama" in the "hallway" brings the mix and its attendant discord into their personal space.[93]

"I WENT WITH WHAT I KNEW": METHODS OF ADAPTATION

In seeking to thread their way through the terrain of the mix with minimal damage to self, women's agency is present in their choices to participate or not.[94] Some do. Some do for a while. Some, like *Esther* and *Meme*, avoid it entirely. A significant portion of respondents report engaging in trial-and-error methods of adaptation. *Lauryn's* account is illustrative of these narrations. When she first arrived, like others, she wanted "acceptance." In steering her way through informal prison hierarchies, she identified two possible matrices of location. The first, with external controls, was race solidarity; the second, with internal controls, was crime solidarity. As a multiracial woman, she was not easily categorized, so she was not readily absorbed into existent racial networks. She also "did not identify . . . with the murderers." *Lauryn's* resolution of the ambiguity of her location was action, that is, in the hyper-sexualized environment: "I went with what I knew. Sex. I got me a girlfriend and had as much sex as I could."

Lauryn's narrative supports the theoretical argument of the importation model of prison culture that posits prison as a microcosm of the street subculture. In this model, prison is hypothesized as a completely closed system, where *Lauryn's* adjustment choices are shaped by predetermined norms and values originating in and sustained by subcultures outside of prison.[95] When faced with the ambiguities arising in her new context, *Lauryn* relied on sex—attracting it, enacting it, flaunting it—as her self-described, pre-imprisonment, problem-solving methodology. Importation theory argues that *Lauryn's* choice is shaped by her precarceral life where "the prison is the street, the street is prison" and not by her own reading of prison culture itself as a hyper-sexualized amalgam where norms, values, and beliefs imported from the "free" world are enacted in the isolated, segregated society behind the wire.[96] While importation theory may be a viable explanation, it is also the case that life-sentenced women bring in personal traits and behaviors that also influence prison culture.

Lauryn's behavior, counterproductive in the prison environment, resulted "in so much trouble" that she was issued "a lot of tickets" (prison misconduct citations, often with penalties that can affect parole/commutation considerations). Incarcerated women who are seen as a threat to the social order are frequently reassigned to highly secure units, and *Lauryn* was transferred back to closed-custody security and isolation for almost a year.[97] She found it "difficult to be by myself" but became proactive in a get-out-of-jail strategy. She sent for law books and devoted her extensive time in lockdown to working on her case, which became her "mission." She developed petitions, motions, and appeals. That learning taught *Lauryn* that it takes "a little bit of time to get caught in the system, but forever to get out of it." Here her story is more reflective of the situational theoretical model of prison culture, where *Lauryn* draws on contextual sources in the initiation and direction of her behavior.[98]

Eventually everyone finds her niche in the churning of the mix.[99] They all come to realize functional locations of objects, resources, and people that provide them with a modicum of rest, the relaxation of stress, and "the realization of required ends."[100] In this relative safety, many life-serving women begin to reassess their lives and their behavior, and they begin to contemplate different futures.

Conclusion

All newly sentenced women experience the first two stages of the self-actualization framework, that is, they all become prisoners and they must all navigate "the mix" by learning the folkways and mores of engagement in the general population of imprisoned women. To do so, they develop the guerrilla cunning of the oppressed. They make decisions about how to creatively and selectively engage with other women and with their keepers in this controlled environment. In a world managed at every level by correctional officers, they adopt individual strategies to cope with their new circumstances. They make choices. They report either first isolating themselves to observe both informal and formal rules of engagement, or the codes of conduct, in this alien environment or they use their "street sense" to jump right into the volatility of the mix. They learn from their choices. Life imprisonment requires that they all begin to strategize and to adapt in order to survive.

4

Ann and *Crystal*

Juvenile Lifers as "Minnows in a Shark Tank"

It was truly horrifying, the things I went through. Kids don't
end up in prison for no reason. *Ann*

I'm not mature enough to make the decision to smoke but
you'll take my whole life away from me???? It's always so
hard for me because I'm mature enough to serve natural life
but not enough to make decisions. It's the contradiction.
Crystal

In June 2012 the U.S. Supreme Court ruled in a combined judgment for
Miller v. Alabama and *Jackson v. Hobbs* that mandatory life sentences for
juveniles (children under age 18) violate the Eighth Amendment's provi-
sions against "cruel and unusual punishment."[1] The court found that, for
sentencing purposes, children are constitutionally different from adults.
Justice Elena Kagan, writing for the majority, stated explicitly that "their
lack of maturity and their underdeveloped sense of responsibility lead
to recklessness, impulsivity, and heedless risk-taking." Because juveniles have diminished culpability and greater prospects for reform than
adults, the court found that mandatory life sentences applied to teen-
aged offenders are unconstitutional. The court opinion halted current
and future mandatory charges but left open the question of retroactivity,
that is, what happens to juveniles sentenced prior to 2012?

Twenty-eight states have interpreted the Supreme Court's ruling
as applying to all mandatorily sentenced juveniles. In those states, attorney generals have started the necessary processes to gather the
stakeholders—police, prosecutors, defense attorneys, witnesses, family
members, and so on—to hold resentencing hearings for those juveniles
sentenced to life imprisonment on mandatory minimums. In Michigan,

however, Attorney General Bill Schuette has resisted that interpretation. He has consistently argued that families who went through the sentencing hearings once should not be subjected to the same trauma a second time. He has appealed lower court decisions supporting a retroactive interpretation. In July 2014 the Michigan Supreme Court found that the U.S. Supreme Court's decision did not apply retroactively. Michigan's juvenile lifers, sentenced prior to June 2012, are currently not eligible for reconsideration and they will not be granted new hearings. Until the U.S. Supreme Court revisits their decision and clarifies the way forward, *Ann* and *Crystal*, and over 300 other juvenile lifers in the state, remain imprisoned without the possibility of parole.

***

Ann was 16 when she was sentenced to life imprisonment for murder. She was not the killer. Her boyfriend murdered a man in a burglary that went disastrously wrong. But *Ann* aided and abetted him in the crime that resulted in the man's death. Consequently, under the felony murder statutes, she was sentenced to life imprisonment.[2]

At the time of the crime, *Ann* was admittedly a "wild" adolescent, immature, afraid and unable to see any options other than following her boyfriend's directions. About that time *Ann* says, "When you're younger, you don't have the [decision-making] capacity and it's been scientifically proven [that the brain of an adolescent does not resemble that of an adult until 20 years old]. When you don't have anything else, you know how you feel and you go by that." Responding to her "gut," *Ann* did what her boyfriend told her to do. She helped him plan the burglary that went dreadfully wrong and then, after he killed the victim, she helped him hide the body.

Crystal was 17 when she was also sentenced on a felony murder charge. She readily acknowledges her role in the death: "I am responsible for this man's life. . . . I didn't want to be associated with that word—'murderer'—I'm not a murderer. I wasn't physically there; I didn't [participate in the crime] in the house. But I was responsible [for helping to plan the crime that resulted in a man's death]." She, too, describes her adolescent self: "I was reckless. . . . I was scared." Both juveniles were sentenced to life imprisonment on felony murder charges as aiders and abettors. They have both already been imprisoned for more years than they had lived free as children.

Ann is a round-faced, hazel-eyed, very pale white woman with straight, shoulder-length brown hair. She radiates the strength and physicality of a yoga practitioner. *Crystal* is a full-bodied, dark-skinned African American woman with close-cropped, salt and pepper gray hair, a gold side tooth, and a deep throaty laugh. As with many other interracial friendships inside, there is easiness between the two women, most evident in their focus-group banter. The two have literally grown up together. With a wink and a grin, *Crystal* claims "I've always been an assistant to *Ann* [*Crystal* shrugs her shoulders]; legally I don't get it but there it is." *Ann* shakes her head and snickers her disagreement. She's choosing her verbal battles with *Crystal*, who is very quick-witted. Their humor, race-based teasing, and sarcasm at one another's expense all reflect the safety rooted in their generous feelings for one another. Together they have grown up and come to middle-aged maturity inside the prison walls. They are friends, but they are not intimates. The two find "drugs and sex are a distraction from life" and they admittedly "do plenty of both," just not with each other. They have become important to one another through their shared experiences of imprisonment, resistance, and personal growth.

"You Are Never Going Home": Cold Consequences

Although both girls were "basically numb for a long time" when they entered the prison gates in the early 1990s, *Crystal* had an additional burden. "I had to go through defense mode because I was pregnant. I went into mother mode, protection mode." Like the children of other life-serving women lucky enough to have vestiges of family support, *Crystal's* son has been raised by her mother. Although *Crystal* claims, "My baby is my world even though I've never been with him," she also acknowledges that she cannot relate to a lot of other imprisoned mothers because "I've never taken my kid to school." She was required to release him to her mother's care almost immediately after his birth.

Ann is childless (another ancillary consequence of life imprisonment for women). She has watched with interest as the children of her friends have "grown up in the visitors' room." About *Crystal's* son, *Ann* says, "Here's another phenomenon." *Crystal* delivered her son a few months after she was imprisoned. Measured in short-term visits to his mother,

Ann has noted the physical changes as *Crystal's* baby boy has grown to manhood. She smiles ruefully as she describes "watching him come in with his first beard whiskers: it makes you feel old."

Crystal sighs remembering how she would tell herself "I'll be home before he goes to school. . . . I'll be home before he turns 10." Then one day she was comparing paperwork with another woman and the length of the numbers next to the letters was different. *Crystal's* was missing numbers. She queried the unit officer who replied offhandedly, "That's because you are never going home." It was in that consequential moment that "the actual known that it's a possibility that I could spend my life here" happened for *Crystal*. At the "actual known" she had two choices: "you can give up or you can fight the hardest you've ever fought" to get out. Yet even in the retelling, the horror of the reality and the cruelty in the delivery left *Crystal* shaken. Consideration of "doing a lifetime" is too overwhelming to contemplate all at once. It can annihilate the spirit so she avoided acknowledging the meaning of "incarceration for life." Almost 25 years after sentencing, the pain of life imprisonment remains raw.

Perhaps the rawness doesn't heal because it is continually poked and prodded by a "bunkie with a three-year bit" who calls *Crystal* "a miserable bitch" and tells her that's why she's "been in here for over two decades." Short of "throwing your case in your face," this gratuitous cruelty is a constant reminder of her vulnerable circumstances. "She's been making my life a living hell. . . . It hurts." It is intended to hurt, but there is "nothing you really can do but tolerate it." With a life sentence, *Crystal* is locked in place.

"I Raised Her Right": "Perfect Storm" Families

Children facing adult charges need support. They need emotional support to cope with the sudden changes in their lives and to withstand the adversarial legal process. They need interpretive support to understand and participate in the court procedures. Mostly though, they need to know they are not alone and that they are loved and cared for even while they are held in the alien environment that is the criminal-processing system. Yet too often their family networks fail young women. The family systems of juvenile lifers are frequently too fragile to support the weight of the criminal charges and their unanticipated consequences. Many life-sentenced juvenile women report pre-incarceration family life experiences that were "perfect storms" for tragic outcomes—neglect, physical and sexual abuse, homelessness, food insufficiency, juvenile and parental drug use—sometimes accompanied by negative educational experiences, poverty, disorganized neighborhoods, and familial criminal activity. Many female juvenile lifers were victims in these perfect storm families before they became offenders.[3]

Families are conventionally expected to be children's advocates in the world. Even in economically stressed working-class or poor families, parents, siblings, and extended kin are the people who are supposed to "have your back," to be your "rock," and to support you in times of need. These expectations are especially significant for juveniles charged with criminal offenses and, even more particularly, for female adolescents charged with life-sentencing crimes. Social science, educational, psychological, and parenting literature is replete with data, stories, studies, and analyses that demonstrate focused, controlled supervision and care-taking directed toward adolescent females by families, friends, and regulatory agencies (e.g., educational resources, health care, employment, police, social welfare, and so on). Yet of the support she received from her family as a criminally charged, pregnant 17-year-old, *Crystal* says, "My family was so disappointed [in me]. They didn't care about anything [like my codefendant or the fact that I wasn't at the scene of the crime]." Her family's concerns were focused on *Crystal's* deficiencies, on her ruinous decision making, and on the many ways that her crime reflected negatively on the quality of her "home training" and on the larger African American community.

Ann's mother was also concerned with negative evaluations of her parenting as a consequence of her daughter's felony murder charge. *Ann* was raised by a single mother for whom *Ann's* trial "was more about how she looked [as a parent]. She was saying 'I raised her right' and things like that when she should have been being honest." *Ann* contends, "The life I had at home was shit. . . . It was truly horrifying, the things I went through"; however, *Ann's* mother assumed no responsibility in her daughter's unfortunate decision-making processes. Instead, she defensively experienced *Ann's* crime as an indictment of her parenting and absolved herself of all responsibility, claiming that "I raised her right."

She shifted the entire burden of the charge and its consequences to her 16-year-old daughter to bear alone.

Both *Ann* and *Crystal* were emotionally abandoned by their families at the worst moments of their young lives. They were left with over-burdened public defenders to represent them on their felony murder charges, and they were left to their own devices in dealing with the ensuing incarcerations.

"The [Male] Guards Were Like Predators": Navigating "the Mix"

"First of all," *Ann* says, "there's a great difference between when we [*Crystal* and I] came in [the early 1990s] and now. They basically just threw us in with everybody." In the back-and-forth, fill-in-the-blanks exchanges that characterized *Ann* and *Crystal's* focus-group conversations, *Crystal* interrupts to provide descriptive commentary: "We were minnows in a shark tank." Ann continues, "It was the standard then. We had to do 10 years in closed custody [before assignment to a lower security level and release into the mix]. It's better for them [newly sentenced juveniles] now because of the work we've put in since then." For girls and women sentenced to life imprisonment, the former institutional protocol mandated that the first 10 years of a life sentence be spent in the 22-to-23-hour lockdown of closed custody; the current standard is six months and a day. After the initial 10 years, the girls/women were allowed to mix with the general prison population. For these juvenile lifers, 10 years was more than half their childhood lives. During those 10 years, they received no training and had no opportunities to make the kinds of decisions that lead to maturation. They aged physically while they were emotionally locked in time. Then they were released to the mix, the general prison population of older, wiser, and sometimes predatory women. Of this period, *Crystal* says, "*Ann* and I had to raise ourselves."

They did so within a "Hunger Games" arena where there was little protection. They were released, without resources, into a potentially dangerous environment after 10 years of single-cell confinement and limited social interaction. Indeed, they were "minnows in a shark tank." The greatest difficulty for *Ann* came from the officers, not the other women. There was a "hostile sexual climate . . . when we came in. Most of us had already had our hearts broken by other men. The [male] guards were like predators. They didn't think I was a kid. They were trying to have sex with me." Some officers did take advantage of the hopeless situation of these young girls who faced the triple jeopardy of imprisonment, immaturity, and a hostile environment. With state-appointed guardians who were sexual predators, the girls had no protection at all. As parties to a class-action lawsuit brought by more than 900 women incarcerated in Michigan, *Neal v. Michigan Department of Corrections*, *Ann* and *Crystal* made public the wide-spread and systemic sexual abuse they experienced from some male officers that spanned more than 20 years and several facility administrations. After 10 years of litigation, in 2006 the Department of Corrections settled the suit with the imprisoned plaintiffs for $100 million and agreed to injunctive relief, including removing male officers from residence units and swiftly conducting sexual harassment investigations and follow-ups. In drawing *a* comparison between her entry and the entry of young women now, *Ann* says, "It was two different time zones between then and now." Although juvenile lifers now think they have "the short end of the stick," *Ann* and *Crystal* have witnessed hard-won changes in correctional sexual harassment policies.

Other prison arenas either remain contentious or have deteriorated. For *Crystal*, "The quality of life I had then and now is different. . . . They [facility administrators] have taken away so much, I can see why people are giving up" and "checking out of the game" (suicide). "There's too many of my sisters who are doing it [committing suicide]. I ask myself, 'Could I have done more?' . . . Five years ago . . . someone would have noticed that I didn't shop and I would have had a bag of supplies [shampoo, toothpaste, tampons, etc.] in my room, no questions asked. Now somebody can be in an area hanging for long enough to kill themselves and nobody notices. . . . I hold responsibility as a whole because we are in this together. I don't want to be in this type of world anymore where no one gives a rat's ass about anybody anymore." *Crystal* is deeply troubled by the institutional policies of denial and deprivation that catalyze contemporary suicide attempts and by the disinterest—from both officers and other women—that permits their completion. Her ruminations reflect the powerlessness that she, and others, feel about the conditions of their existence and the despair that can ensue.

In the to-ing and fro-ing of their conversational styles, *Ann* speaks to *Crystal's* observations: "I've been severely traumatized in my life, but I've never been so depressed. . . . For me, this life isn't worth living." The coping skills of these two juvenile lifers, who have been incarcerated for twice as many years as they were children in their families and communities, are stressed to their maximum. The effects of their lifetime imprisonment are so corrosive that they have both, at different points in their prison careers, contemplated suicide. About these assessments, *Ann* says, "I don't have any fond memories to look back on and whatever is in front will be hard. I'm in prison for murder."

In spite of *Ann's* stark vision of her future, few other life-serving women report experiencing their situations as all good or all bad, although at particular moments of despair they can certainly seem totally negative. Yet there are some encouraging moments inside. *Crystal,* for instance, celebrates having been a "lawsuit participant," saying "I've been blessed."

Laughter of the "gallows humor" variety also permeates many of their inside interactions. Humor is a resistance strategy that life-serving women utilize to transform power relations. "I just laugh. There's nothing else to do [when faced with adversity inside]." *Ann* and *Crystal* use wordplay and sarcastic retorts to reconstruct situations and to divest them of the power to do harm. They employ laughter as an antidote to depression and despair. They laugh about their helpless plight and their droll irreverence loosens boundaries and provides them with some emotional relief. *Crystal* says she laughs a lot. "I think I've laughed a whole lot. Probably at other people the most." *Ann* notes that, as a juvenile lifer, "you learn not to be surprised by anything. Everything happens here" and so everything can be a source of humor or despair.

Both *Ann* and *Crystal* are cognizant of some personal benefits that have resulted from their imprisonments. For example, *Crystal* says, "People look at me like I'm crazy when I say I'm glad I came to prison. . . . I wouldn't be the person I am. I believe I'd be dead, abused, or a welfare mom. . . . I didn't know the value of life until I started doing life." Her removal from the street may have saved her life; she believes that her imprisonment also had a positive effect on other family members. "My mistake shaped a lot of people's lives." Although her life sentence initially sent shock waves through her family, with time they "[have been] able to grab positive aspects out of it." *Crystal* explains how her lengthy incarceration "shaped my brother and the way he values family." "My sister is a big competitor with me in here," and her sister's desire to "do good" has spurred her into getting a GED and a para-professional teaching certificate as a response to *Crystal*'s incarceration. "My son thinks about where his mother and father have been when he makes a decision."

Ann's prison positives are also relational, but not familial. Her positives, few though they are, are confined to her relationships inside. She appreciates the role models she has had in prison. "I couldn't have gotten that at home. I've grown to be my own person. I had [a mentor]. She inspired me to go to school. I had different people for different things that were significant. They've built me into the woman I am today because they got me when I was younger." Adrift as a teen in the "shark tank," this "minnow" found protectors, role models, and advisors, often mature women of other races, to assist her. She did not find a single woman with the nurturing skills, interest, and gentle touch of the conventional parent model, so she had to piecemeal her way through her adolescence inside by finding women who could help her in some areas of maturation, but not in others. By combining bits and pieces from a number of mentors, *Ann* achieved a kind of personal and identity coherence as she now declares, "I've grown to be my own person."

In her process of becoming, *Ann* celebrates a particular mentor who "always stayed true to herself." The mentor maintained her own definitions of institutional situations and acted accordingly; she did not attempt to conform to expectations of the mix,[4] or succumb to peer pressure. She established an inner compass and used her own moral principles as her guide. *Ann* tries to do the same: "Whether that self is good or bad, I'm always honest about it." Indeed, in a discussion of drug use inside, *Ann* does not equivocate about her involvement: "I take pills to comfort myself."

"If You're Going to Have Bad Actions, They Should Only Affect You": Remorse

Ann and *Crystal* have also experienced personal change in their years of incarceration. They have matured. They have come to understand the impact of their crimes, not just on themselves, but on their victims' families and on their own families. Of her life now, *Ann* says, "The hardest thing for me is how what I've done has affected other people." Unlike her mother, *Ann* assumes some responsibility for her younger sister's troubled life. After *Ann's* incarceration, her little sister sought solace in drugs. Too young and too naive to moderate her drug use, her life spiraled out of control. The sister is now a woman in her mid-30s, who "still can't do it on her own" after her descent into drugs.

Ann's remorse and regret are also directed to the family of the man whose home she agreed to burglarize and who became a murder victim. "[I am] equally as sad about the victim's family. He had two kids. I wonder how they've grown up." She laments that "our actions affect so many people." The outcome of unintended consequences is a difficult concept for an adolescent to grasp: "if you're going to have bad actions, they should only affect you." The many effects of disastrous decision making become clear in the hindsight afforded by maturity and adulthood.

"In the last 13 years I've grown in leaps and bounds, but the first 10 years I think I regressed back further from the point I was at when I came in," says *Crystal*. "I was in a haze for a while. . . . I tried to commit suicide [during her adjustment to becoming a prisoner]. . . . I saw no way out [of personal pain as 'a horrible person' and of life imprisonment]." In "desperation" she returned to her religious roots in the black church. "I'm drowning in my mess and there's only one Savior that can help me. I'm at my wit's end. . . . Who can better fix me besides the person that made me? We *need* God in our life. Not just prisoners, but everyone" (emphasis is *Crystal's*). Through her return to religious engagement, through therapy, and through the support of her friends, *Crystal* came to understand that to survive a life sentence she would have to embrace the totality of her person, not just the worst, discrete act of her life. She worked diligently to "accept myself as a whole . . . to search my soul." While it was still possible in prison in Michigan, *Crystal also* enrolled in a degree-granting college program. "I wanted to learn how people worked, how the mind worked, in order to shape myself." Although she has spent many more years incarcerated than she spent as a child in the free world, and although she has worked conscientiously to rehabilitate herself, "I just had my commutation denied [in 2011] that I've been fighting for since '07." The parole board responded with a simple "no interest" in her petition.

Conclusion

If a "life sentence" is computed by age at the time of sentencing, then *Ann* and *Crystal* have already served their life sentences. Both women were incarcerated when they were still adolescents with an estimated 60–70 additional years to live. They were children when they were confined in an adult facility. Court authorities and criminal-processing personnel left them to fend for themselves in the volatility of the mix, with its drugs, sex, unstable and often explosive relationships, and its non–rule abiding behavior.[5] They found ways to cope and they survived. As juvenile life-serving women, *Ann* and *Crystal* have grown to maturity in prison. They have used their periods of incarceration to create lives of dignity and worth in the environment in which they came to adulthood. Both have spent prison time in reflection on the reasons for their incarcerations, on the contexts and motivations for their earlier choices, and on ways to reconstruct their lives with integrity within the confines of the present environment. Both women have made productive use of their time in prison to create futures different than their pasts. They have each developed committed outside support, that is, people who will support them—financially, emotionally, and educationally—in their transitions to productive citizenry on the outside. Yet, in spite of the "cruel and unusual punishment" of mandatory life sentences for juveniles, *Ann* and *Crystal* remain imprisoned for life.

5

Actively Doing Life

I had to do it myself. They threw us to the wolves. *Ciara Blue*

I have natural life. I decided if this is my life, even in this environment, I'm going to have a good life. *Sandy*

I knew this wasn't the person I was or wanted to be. *Royal Tee*

Time and life are four-letter words that reflect the profanity of American cultural slang terms, as well as the social disrespect and disdain inherent in the mass incarceration and permanent removal of marginalized populations from civil society. Time, configured in a sentence of life imprisonment, is a death penalty by erosion. A sentence of "natural life," or life without parole (LWOP), emphatically designates the current circumstances of life-serving women as the sum total of all possible existences. The parameters of their lives are not going to change; they are not going anywhere else. *Ever. Bella*'s life-sentence fatalism is evident in her rhetorical Q and A: "What are they going to do to me? I'm already in prison. The worst they could do is bury me under the prison."

In abstract quantifications prison sentences are computed in terms of time with the consequence that "time in prison stands still."[1] "Natural life" obliterates time as it is conventionally lived, experienced, and understood. Life-sentenced women are literally "captives to time."[2] *Doll*, a 26-year veteran of imprisonment, notes "it's like I've lost all concept of time in here." Their time becomes endless, repetitive, and, paradoxically, malleable. *Glenda Gale* asserts, "I do everything repetitiously. That's how my time goes. I don't know how to explain it. It's like time goes faster, but slower." *Scarlet* explains the anomaly: "It's like we're robots. You're going to dinner and you forgot what you had for lunch. You get so emotionally drained some days. Some days I feel like I'm shoved up against the wall."

For life-imprisoned women, time is "the measure of power."[3] All carceral erosions occur within and are structured by time because time is something being done to them, rather than something they do something with. *Doll* describes this prison experience of time: "My time is still their time [correctional officers'] because they can take it, change it, and affect it. It's never really mine."

Having a life of time is of little value to women who have no time of their own, whose days are structured by institutional formulas for counts, commissary, chow, gym, library, yard, work details, and occasional visits from family and friends. As sociologist Rik Scarce contends: "In professional worlds time needs to be constructed to ensure success, fame, and an increase in social status. In inmate culture time is constructed for survival."[4] In the processes of survival, personal development, and agency, life-serving women innovate to negotiate and transgress time frames that are interminable.[5]

To make this unnatural time palatable, life-sentenced women "do time" so that "time doesn't do them." The women in this study struggled to take life "one day at a time." As *Ciara Blue* notes, "It [a life sentence] can kill you. You can't do it all at one time. You have to take it in bits and pieces." Those bits and pieces of daily living combined with the scraps and remnants of their pre-imprisonment lives are fodder for the self-determination that life serving women develop in prison.

In *Discipline and Punish: The Birth of the Prison,* French philosopher and social theorist Michel Foucault argued that prison "discipline produces subjected and practiced bodies, 'docile bodies,' " through a combination of routine, punishment, and knowledge.[6] Many of these study participants would agree, but they might also argue that Foucault's argument does not recognize their agency and resistance, for as criminologist Mary Bosworth notes and these study respondents attest, power in prison is relational, negotiated, and mutable.[7] It is "not impermeable."[8] *Glenda Gale* suggests, for example, that after being down (imprisoned) for some time, and having seen the system in action, lifers know how it works and so can make "informed decisions" and "find ways around things." They remain cognizant that they're "not gonna beat the system just because you're right. It's [cooperation's] a compromise that you have to make to survive." Some women choose not to compromise. *Bella* resists and is forthright in her opposition: "I don't let them push me around. I'm not passive." All the women in this study report assuming and enacting various forms of autonomy, but they are constantly constrained by the institution, as *Shequetta Tasha Lynn* reflects: "I can't go back to yesterday and I can't jump to tomorrow. . . . Whatever I plan, they're gonna find some way to nip it in the bud." Nonetheless, these women resist docility and erosions of self by both overt and covert means (see chapter 8 for their strategies).

Having survived becoming a prisoner and navigating the mix, those women who want more than a roboticized, vicarious existence, "drama," and the erosions inherent in the endlessness of prison monotony begin the explorations of the opportunities that can lead to agency, affirmation, and worthy lives behind the wire fences. This chapter presents the ensuing four stages in the typology of establishing meaningful lives inside. The stages are a consequence of both their sentences and the determination of life-serving women to create consequential lives in this modern American prison. Those women, who choose to actively affect the way they live, create a fabric of life that, within structural confines, they determine.[9]

The Four Stages

Reportedly six or seven years "into their bit," a time that roughly corresponds with final denials in the appeal process, and sparked by circumstances requiring active self-inquiry, many life-serving women find themselves at the next stage, that is, acting at a choice point.[10] In the radically altered circumstances of life imprisonment, these women have years of unscripted time to think about how to act and what to do.[11] This stage, acting at a choice point, marks the moment when they choose to become deliberately proactive, through self-reflection and resistance, in response to their imprisonment and its personal and social attritions. As the women search for new definitions and solutions, they begin to create a counternarrative, speaking their truth to the power of the institution as well as to the "prisoner," "inmate," and "criminal" labels identifying them. They detail the cascade of emotions and experiences that impel them to claim identities separate from their "prisoner" identities.[12] The process of stabilizing a counternarrative overlaps and intersects with the next analytical stage, developing an internal compass, the route to

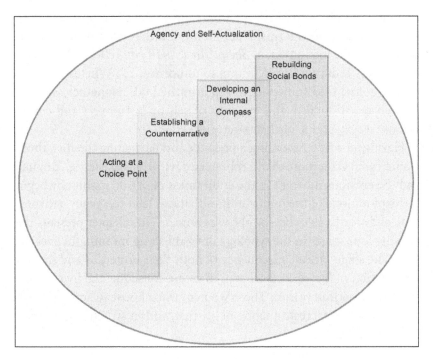

FIGURE 5.1. THE FOUR ADDITIONAL STAGES THAT
LIFE-SERVING WOMEN NEGOTIATE IN CREATING
CONSEQUENTIAL LIVES INSIDE

self-discovery in this hidden world.[13] As a condition for developing an internal compass, the women must feel safe enough inside to think beyond the present moment.[14]

Throughout these formative stages, female lifers report being on their own in creating life skills, handling emotional responses, and generating intellectual interests, as they are both part and not part of prison life. *Martha*, for example, says, "My hardest thing is whether I have to be here forever or not. I try not to focus on it. I try to keep myself busy so I don't think about it." *Yasmeen* reiterates the oft-reported message of diligent self-sufficiency in handling no exit time: "I do what I have to do by myself. I pretty much keep to myself. I have what I need to be all right on my own." Many women describe the importance of work in prison, crafts, TV, music, family visits, spiritual connection, and friendships in their coping strategies.

Often not permitted by prison personnel to enroll in programs designed for women returning to the "outside" or the "real" world, life-serving women have been warehoused and so implicitly defined as socially irrelevant.[15] Nonetheless, they are all in the same total institution, and, in the rebuilding social bonds stage, those women who have wrestled through the earlier processes now define their own relevance, forgive themselves and those who have harmed them, develop the tolerance essential inside, and establish the conditions under which they can promote trust as well as the empathy necessary to move beyond a focus on self to a sense of collective efficacy.[16] This forgiving of self and others is difficult work; the women struggle continuously to reconcile competing emotions of anger, hurt, and compassion.[17] Although remaining tethered to the mechanics of confinement,[18] most of the respondents in this study describe embracing themselves and their life-serving peers as women with social value, who make contributions to individual and social welfare, and whose lives have meaning as these three focus-group participants attest:

LL: Are there women inside that you admire?
Simone: Everyone.
Destiny: All of them.
Cameron: Yep.
Destiny: There's something that they have that can get you through. Everybody.

Acting at a Choice Point

Crime, sentence, unstructured time, boredom, and relational outreach to family, friends, and religious visitors can all serve as prompts for life-serving women to begin to engage in the private, reflexive processes of assessment and analysis that are necessary for identity growth and agentic self-determination. Using the insights gained in developing their own strategies for adapting to the mix, many study participants, like *Lauryn*, reported beginning deliberate journeys of self-discovery, autonomy, and resistance to the erosion inherent in this hidden world. "A shift occurred in me about six to seven years into my bit." She quit smoking, stopped getting high, began to work out "like a maniac," and started "a relationship with God." *Lauryn* also developed a political analysis of the injustices around her and began "having conversations about situations." Committed to the lifer mantra "I'm gonna do this time, not let this time do me," *Lauryn* began to work collectively for change, noting that "when I changed the conversation changed."

Women, like *Lauryn*, who engage in these difficult processes come to envision a "replacement self" that supplants the "spoiled identity" of felon, criminal, inmate, or prisoner.[19] As Bosworth noted in her study of the identity processes of women serving time in U.K. prisons, incarcerated women attempt to transcend their stigmatized identities and to regard themselves as individuals with rights and abilities.[20] The life-serving women in this study also experienced themselves as individuals with social value. *Alexandria* claims, for example, "I'm beautiful on the inside." *Merrilee* characterizes the "generous, kind women" she has met in prison, who are also some of the best women she has known "in the real world," further claiming their presence in her life is "a beautiful thing."

The women resist attritions of self sometimes by demanding respect for their essential humanity from officers who may be reluctant to acknowledge it. The absence of presumed respect is evident in the numbers of women, who, like *Kari*, categorically define a "good officer" in similar terms: "What really makes a good officer is when they treat us like human beings." *Lynn* bristles in interactions with disrespectful officers. "You've got these officers; they talk to you any kind of way. I'm older than a lot of them. I want to rip their heads off." Through vivid language, she articulates the frustration of the powerless when faced with disrespect in a context where there is no cultural norm of regard for the humanity, or experiential wisdom, of the imprisoned. *Bella* contends that officers "want you to be unkempt, miserable, and passive." Part of her resistance is "to carry myself" differently and to be both positive and collected. *Bella* refuses to let them "break me down." When the women begin to assert themselves, their self-esteem changes. They make conscious decisions to "do something" with their lives. *Azianna* provides an example of her altered awareness when she says: "I came in thinking I have nothing to live for and now I fight [against prison erosions] every day."

After years of dealing with trauma and abuse, often attended by economic and social marginalization, and further intensified by imprisonment, a woman's sense of her value in the world, her humanity, can be temporarily lost. Many women, like *Scarlet*, categorized those dystopian periods with dispassion: "I was numb." Passivity, apathy, and acquiescence characterized their encounters with prison life. The numbness began to dissipate when the women started to resist erosions of body and soul by making decisions. *Scarlet* reports her "aha moment" as "Wow. I have to survive." Shortly thereafter, she faced her choice point: It was a "matter of being constructive or destructive." Many women in this study, like *Scarlet*, rejected the reactive responses that characterized their pre-imprisonment lives as well as the passivity generated by their current circumstances. They tenaciously exercised proactive, although tightly circumscribed, choices. *Doll* provides a telling example of these histories and their particular outcomes. In her physically, sexually, and emotionally abusive marriage, *Doll's* husband's control was encompassing and included every moment, every decision, every action of hers. "I feel more free in prison than I did in marriage. I have choices in prison that I never had in life." *Doll* exemplifies the paradox, identified by some study participants, of a chink in the structure of imprisonment that allows them to develop personal resources and to grow more confident.

Doll is aware of the irony that "people don't usually associate prison and being able to make choices," but she declares that she can choose her own friends and choose whether or not to obey the rules, knowing that there are sanctions if she doesn't, and "that [recognition of choice] was liberating." Now "I get to choose how I do my time." Like many others, *Doll* has agentically used systemic fissures to create space for her personal choices. In these small ways, women's resistance is an assertion of agency, humanity, and self-worth.

"IT'S BEEN A LONG WAY . . .": SERIAL DECISION MAKING
Acting at a choice point is essentially a series of decision-making acts, not a one-time, all-inclusive, determination to change. The action process is conscious, deliberate, and continuous. To actively construct meaningful, self-affirming lives, women must move beyond desire for recognition of their humanity; they must experience themselves as proactive agents, not as reactive victims.

Readiness to change is an essential, but not sufficient, condition for actual, substantial change to occur.[21] *Tootsie Roll* sadly recounts the long time she spent struggling after her decision to change: "When I thought about it, I realized how much I really wanted to get out [of prison], and that if I wanted to get out, I'd have to change. . . . It's been a long way from the bad [woman] to the good [woman]." Her realization of the depth of her desire to be free catalyzed her decision-making process. Yet even with her good intentions and positive commitment, in reconstructing her identity and developing her own resistance strategies, "it's been a long way . . ." Resocialization is never an easy, or a short, process.[22]

Tootsie Roll's decision making and ultimate compliance with prison rules were not based on her acceptance of the legitimacy of the power and control vested in prison policies and procedures. She expresses disdain for her peers who get "all caught up in" the mix. "You're making this your home." *Tootsie Roll* conformed because a commutation appeal, her only viable exit strategy, always includes evidence of a change in behavior and remorse for the crime. *Tootsie Roll* wanted to get out. She had personal, practical, and pragmatic concerns and the institution had the ultimate power in their resolution. She agentically chose compliance and conformity as a means to her own ends.

With natural life sentences, study respondents have time to think about who and what they are and to assess how factors in their preincarceration lives led to their imprisonments.[23] Their deliberative choices to examine their pre- and postincarceration lives result in sometimes very painful examinations of their biographies. Their hoped-for outcome is change through agentic decision making that will positively affect their futures. As reflected in the words opening this chapter, *Sandy* illustrated the considered nature of these choices when she said "I have natural life. I decided if this is my life, even in this environment, I'm going to have a good life." Criminologist Peggy Giordano and her colleagues describe similar cognitive shifts among seriously delinquent adolescent females, in which the young women made initial moves out of delinquency, then worked diligently to craft positive lives and to sustain more positive identities and life directions.[24]

"MY POSITIVE CHANGES I MADE ON MY OWN": SOLO JOURNEYS

For all these study respondents, acting at a choice point was the initiation of a solo journey of self-reform. Most, like *Sheri*, claim that the institutional structures provided little to no support: "My positive changes I made on my own." The change for each was sparked by idio-syncratic circumstances requiring active self-inquiry[25] like *Ciara Blue's*: "You hit rock bottom. I can't stand who I've become." Her condition for change, unlike *Tootsie Roll's*, was the extreme discomfort of being alien to herself. A juvenile lifer when she started doing time, *Ciara Blue* describes her adolescent self as "reckless . . . scared . . . basically made a lot of mistakes." She didn't have many positive role models coming in to prison and didn't know how to find them inside. Her choice point came when "I got tired of sanctions and seg [segregation]. I started searching for something different." Fatigued by doing the same thing over and over and getting the same negative results, *Ciara Blue* chose change and self-discipline and became proactive in her own interests.

Ignoring the structural constraints imposed by prison counseling, a process that Jill McCorkel identifies as "responsibilization"[26] or the shift in responsibility from the state to the individual that compels the woman to "do it yourself" and self-regulate, *Ciara Blue* was encouraged to embrace the carceral message of personal responsibility and account-ability: "They [prison counselors] told me I had the power to change it [her despair], but they didn't tell me how. I had to figure that out on my own. . . . You realize that you're the one really in control of your life." Sharing the responding focus-group mirth that suggests foolhardiness, *Sheila T.* declares: "Prisoners don't ever have no power. If they think they do, they're crazy [laughter from focus-group members]." Prison person-nel expect life-serving women to take ownership of their problems and to resolve them by learning how to make the "right" choices even when, in many cases, the situations they find themselves in are not the out-come of choice.[27]

In their study of delinquent female adolescents who engaged in cog-nitive shifts, Giordano and colleagues found that pro-social features of the young women's environments, or "hooks," served as catalysts for change.[28] In this study a few women, like *Esther*, described being moti-vated by such "hooks" in the facility. For example, she named therapy, education, friends and mentors inside, and "every program that was available to lifers." For some women, programming, like *DJ's* efforts in the Assaultive Offender Program, "helped me to learn how to keep my hands off people" and thus provided invaluable life-skills training. Yet institutional opportunities were insufficient to their needs. *Esther* laments that "they don't let lifers take what they need" to improve themselves. *Elizabeth Ashley* explains why, saying that some correctional officers will "come right out" and say "why would you need that program anyway? You're never leaving here. You're going to die here." Such gratuitous verbal violence authoritatively defines these female lifers as socially worthless and consequently not meriting institutional investment in programming. Life-serving women valiantly resist the demeaning institutional definitions.

Criminologist Bryn Herrschaft and her colleagues, in examining a sample of men and women with variously stigmatized identities, including ex-felon status, provide a gendered challenge to the Giordano study about theoretical "hooks."[29] Herrschaft and colleagues found that socially beneficial environmental features, the hypothesized hooks, are most relevant for imprisoned men, whose catalysts for change tended to be status-related factors, whereas imprisoned women responded to relationship-related factors, that is, family, friends, peers, therapies, spiritual connectedness, and helping others.[30] For most respondents in this study, however, it was not the pro-social aspects of the prison environment or their relational concerns that kindled their readiness to self-determine. Like *Ciara Blue's* "rock bottom," it was despair. *Royal Tee* articulates the hopelessness that, for some, catalyzed decision making: "I've never experienced darkness like this before. You can cut it with a knife." The women's conscious decisions to become self-determining developed more as a result of the ambient culture than as a consequence of specific programs or teachings.

Jannel explains: "When you're faced with something so devastating . . . I realized I needed to make a conscious decision." In choosing to engage change, women have to come to terms with raw, sometimes harrowing, events in their lives. They must assume accountability for their offending behaviors, but they must also recognize and grieve their own experiences in the "blurred boundary" areas where they were also victims.

"EVERY DAY IS A NEW START": ALTERNATE PATHS

In their study of two female prisons in California, criminologists Candace Kruttschnitt and Rosemary Gartner found that women's resistance in prison is individual rather than collective.[31] Likewise in this study, relying on personal fortitude, much of the women's resistance was focused on managing and resisting environmental erosions. Many women sought to maintain a "fight-back" attitude that protected hope. *Joyce*, for example, resists acceptance of the permanence of her sentence by claiming "every day is a new start, I won't accept that this is it."

In a response that reconceptualizes and reframes what is commonly thought of as resistance,[32] *Esther*, like many others, embarked on a self-improvement program, proactively reading self-help books for practical suggestions about how to alter her own habits and behaviors. "I had to choose to be a better person." *Esther's* search for personal betterment is also an implicit acceptance that her imprisonment is a consequence of her individual failures rather than the shared failure of systems to educate, protect, and administer justice. It is a sentiment echoed by *Martha*, who notes, "even though we have limitations and restrictions, you have the choice of how you want to do your time" and "even if there are not enough programs, or programs at all for lifers, you can still get that book and teach yourself." *Martha's* search for new solutions is predicated on a realistic assessment of institutional opportunities for life-serving women and an ensuing commitment to self-rehabilitation. She refuses to be defined by the limits of the institutional structures. *Destiny* shares her sentiments: "We're living our regular lives inside. At home, we wouldn't be out running the streets all the time, so we don't do that inside." They would reportedly be spending time cooking or with their families, so "that's what we do here"; they reconstruct their lives inside in the absence of traditional frames of support and resources.[33]

Many study participants reported gleaning instructive life-skills lessons during interactions with other women who had also made life-altering mistakes. "We grab strength from that person" (*Scarlet*) and tailor it to fit their personalities and circumstances. They pay attention to the ways of working, ways of learning, and skills for coping that their peer role models utilize. Those women without the emotional and psychological resources required to choose a disciplined way of life, to cling to survival, and to create a fabric of life do "hard" time, as *Love Evans* notes. "It seemed like I was doing my time harder than the next person . . . so I dug deeper." They despair. Some attempt suicide as an ultimate act of agency, an individual "fuck you," that signals to the institution and the world that she, not the prison, has the final control over her own life.

Other women are indirectly motivated to change by relational support or by extraction (through imprisonment) from abusive relationships. *Harmony*, for example, reports having had to be arrested and imprisoned before she could escape from her abusive marriage. "I was really messed up when I came to prison." It took *Harmony* seven to eight years of imprisonment to "find" herself. In navigating the mix, *Harmony* made a few true friends who didn't judge her. She said, "I had never had that before [she chokes up, cries]. I started taking my power back from that." Friends inside offered her a positive image that did not exist in her repertoire of definitions of herself. Although she says that she has to tell herself every morning "this is where I am," after 18 years of imprisonment, *Harmony* has come to accept that "what other people think of me is none of my business." She has established an internal definition of herself as a valuable person.

Another route to active decision making is the relative poverty inside that makes life behind bars even more severe for women with few material resources. Deprivation in a deprivation environment encourages hustling and conning, particularly when, like *Sandy*, "conning" had been a way of life pre- and postincarceration, and her perceived need was great. As her navigation of the mix centered on "getting over" on others, *Sandy* began to see herself in "a lot" of different people. "I *so* didn't wanna be that person. I didn't like what I was looking at" (emphasis is *Sandy's*). In the looking-glass reflection of herself, *Sandy* stepped outside herself to see herself.[34] She didn't like the view. She purposefully began to shed her identity as a "con artist" and move toward her own, more positive, definition of herself. "I decided to have integrity. . . . Once I discovered my integrity, I didn't want to risk it." She signals both the importance and the permanence of her new persona in a reflective comment: "What could be so important that you'd give that [integrity] up?"

At the proverbial fork in the road, where some women take the "path of least resistance"[35] and choose "drugs, entertainment, whatever" and some few choose to "check out" through suicide, many others choose self-reflection and actions that "make it OK to live in this situation." Facing the realities of her life sentence, *Royal Tee* made a choice: "I refused to live the rest of my life in regret." *Liberty Flynn* also noted how time spent "living in captivity"[36] can precipitate active decision making: "You wake up and think, 'I can do this.'" Both *Royal Tee* and *Liberty Flynn* reported moving away from the world of their sentences into the personal knowledge that they can "do time." They acknowledged their personal resolves to survive the endlessness of limited space and stultifying routines and so, like the other women in this study, they developed strategies to resist time's erosions and to make their lives meaningful.

The process of rediscovering and redefining themselves did not engage all women, nor did it engage most of the women at all times. Some women worked out their own navigational maps for the mix and stopped there. Unable or uninterested in agentic activity, or emotionally exhausted by years of corrosive control and the drama of "the prison thing," they create a niche and are content to remain suspended there.

Others, like *Lizzy*, are temporarily resistant to the responsibilities inherent in self-actualization. Young, recently incarcerated, she is presented with new and confusing responsibilities. She acknowledges, "I still struggle because I have a problem with authority. I don't want to be forced to grow up and to take full responsibility yet." *Lizzy* wants the choice to mature in her own time, but the reality is that she's a young woman imprisoned for life. She has been tried and judged as an adult. Her resistance struggle inheres in continuing to want the agency and autonomy of choice, while she is simultaneously locked into the authority that defines the prison experience. A condition for ending her adjustment struggle is maturity, self-defined as acceptance of responsibility for her crime and acquiescence to authority. She is remorseful but she isn't "ready" to acquiesce. "I really am trying to mature." She wants to develop in her own time frame, to work out how to define herself and the pace at which she'll do that. She aims to construct a new, self-actualized identity while she is forced to submit to the authority and control of the penal system.[37] Her environment is incompatible with her continued deviation, yet her role in the choice-point process highlights her actively chosen, cognitive decisions.[38] She is responsive to her own version of recalcitrant autonomy.

The women who act at a choice point recognize that they can change themselves and their responses to imprisonment, if not the structural conditions of their incarceration. They can use their life sentences as opportunities to build more caring, inclusive identities. They believe that they can also change the larger world through the wisdom of their sorrows. Under these conditions, life-serving women engage in deep explorations of their pre-imprisonment lives and use those experiences to move toward transcendence of place and toward self-determination.

Creating a Counternarrative

In *The White Album*, author Joan Didion claims that "we tell ourselves stories in order to live."[39] Female lifers use available resources—life experiences, other women, prison programs, media, family, soap operas, TV evangelists, reading materials, personal analyses—to create alternative story lines and to tell themselves and others stories of resistance, forgiveness, and circumscribed culpability. They create counternarratives to survive in an environment that imposes constraints on the content and legitimacy of personal accounts that challenge conventional understandings of "prisoner."[40] The women's stories counter the daily attritions of their lives and sustain them in profound personal struggles for self-acceptance and moral credibility.[41] Joyce, for example, clearly challenges the labels associated with her imprisoned location, when she claims that "my sentence is what I am, not who I am."

Deeply discredited,[42] they cannot minimize the consequences of this stigma by passing, or selectively disclosing, because prison is the observable location of their stigmatization. They must establish counternarratives to destigmatize themselves in a social context that sociologist Lisa Brush describes:

> Hegemonic ideas about social problems and social change are often based on stereotypes, focused on deficits or pathologies, and rooted in moralistic judgments. When that is the case, marginalized or subordinated speakers and writers find it next to impossible to repair their stigmatized identities, overcome the explicit or implicit indictment of their character by expert and mainstream discourse, and win the thoughtful attention of service providers, mainstream media, and policy makers.[43]

It is against these dominant tropes that women sentenced to life imprisonment struggle to develop personal narratives that challenge the basis and permanence of their disgrace and shame.[44] Prison constraints and contradictions make these processes difficult.[45]

The narratives that the women construct are fluid and dynamic and responsive to personal, community, and institutional changes; they are not stagnant creations.[46] Some study respondents, for example, construct themselves as wiser women for whom it would be incongruous to commit "something like that."[47] *Joyce* exemplifies this frame in her succinct, 14-word counternarrative: "The woman I am today mourns the girl I was when I did this." She presents herself as having matured beyond the angry young woman in the throes of "graveyard love," a love about which her mother warned her, "One of you is going to end up dead." Twenty-four years later, *Joyce* characterizes herself as a responsible woman who prays for what anthropologist Lorna Rhodes eloquently describes as "the possibility that the damage haunting the present can somehow redeem it."[48]

In these counternarratives, one day, one hour, one irremediable act is not the sum total of a woman's personhood. *Sheila T.* asks rhetorically if it is fair to judge someone on "a five- to ten-minute period out of 80 years of their life?" For all intents and purposes that "five- to ten-minute period" has become the defining measure of her life, but it is not the totality of how she perceives and experiences herself, or how she wants others to see her. *Sheila T.* has a holistic view that depends on seeing her "whole" self, not just the worst discrete act of her life. *Ciara Blue's* counternarrative also articulates this embrace of self. She claims that in reconstructing an identity "you have to accept everything about you. Accept yourself as a whole. Search your soul." Such reconstructions make the totality of their lives understandable and their transformations predictable.[49]

In addition to diminishing the effects of stigma, the stories that life-serving women tell themselves about themselves and their transformative journeys also mend the fragmented persons that they were. The narratives heal those damaged women who committed (or aided and abetted) sometimes heinous crimes. As such, their stories reflect individual, personal theories of reality.[50] *Royal Tee*, for example, begins her narrative reconstruction with her acting at a choice point decision: "I've been looking at life through rose-colored glasses; it's time to take the glasses off." She initially denied responsibility for the crime for which she was imprisoned. "I was very angry . . . blamed a lot of people . . . in denial . . . couldn't accept responsibility. . . . I was angry with myself, I think disassociation was my way to cope. . . . It took me a long time to really accept responsibility for the part I had in it." *Royal Tee's* crime was the unintended consequence of an action over which she lost control. Several people died in the aftermath of her decision. She reports suffering guilt for setting events in motion that she couldn't regulate and that had tragic outcomes. Her original intent, while not harmless, was controlled. The outcome was not. "It was hard because those weren't my intentions, but I *did* this, regardless of my intentions" (emphasis is *Royal Tee's*). She was not present at the commission of the crime, she was not a participant, but she was the catalyst for its consequences. "I had to learn to forgive myself. I had to work through the pain." Without accepting responsibility for her actions, she "couldn't deal with the pain." *Royal Tee* said, "I had to get to the root of where my anger was coming from. I knew there were some ugly things I had to face. It's a daily process."

As a subjective account, the narrative highlights her changed priorities, transformed perspectives, identity work, fears, and decisive action from a choice point. Accepting responsibility for her crime and forgiving herself are ongoing processes in establishing her counternarrative. As narrative psychologist Dan McAdams notes, stories, like *Royal Tee's*, "combine a person's selective reconstruction of the past with his/her imagined anticipation of the personal future to produce a story with plot and characters to explain who I am, how I came to be, and where my life is going in the future."[51] Through the continuing process of constructing her counternarrative, *Royal Tee* has also established her agency in situ: "I can determine what I get out of it [prison]. This situation, I can choose how to do it."

The devaluing context of prison defines female lifers to the outside world, to the prison staff, and sometimes to the other imprisoned women as deviants from "ordinary and natural" societal expectations for women. The narratives they develop aim to counter the pervasive social and carceral images of life-serving women as malicious, dangerous, vicious, corrupt, and deceitful. Women use these personal narratives to reconstruct their identities and to thwart the mundane and corrosive aspects of prison life.

"THEY CAN TEAR YOU DOWN": NARRATIVE OBSTACLES

The context of imprisonment imposes authoritative master narratives about the danger and deceit, manipulations and evil intent, of women incarcerated for life. The emotional and psychological damage that women incur through incarceration is sometimes magnified in negative interactions with correctional officers (see chapter 7 for a fuller discussion) who have the institutional power to control the environment and who, therefore, control the definitions of the situations and of the women. *Scarlet* speaks to the potential for institutional harm represented by some correctional officers when she claims "they can tear you down." Like many of the women's former abusive partners, officers claim the authority to define the women in this restrictive context, so even if women self-determine and choose not to engage, they must interact with officers on a daily basis and consequently cannot slough off negativity directed toward them, as in this example provided by *Esther*: "They scream at you like you're a dog and they're training you."

There are no institutional resources that women can access to challenge these reported assaults to their senses of self. Prisons operate on the assumption that prisoners need constant control and surveillance to prohibit further offending because, by their original offenses, they have demonstrated their inability to monitor themselves. The institution controls definitions inside and their imprisoned status defines the women as criminals to the outside world.

Nonetheless, these women demand respect for unconditional human dignity. Correctional officers, on the other hand, focus on individual women while simultaneously insisting on the collective deference and respect predicated on an asymmetric status norm. In the context of a focus-group discussion that turned to officers who demean and denigrate the women inside, *Merrilee* challenges the asymmetric assumption. She asks a rhetorical question that underscores her perception of a false dichotomy between the keepers and the kept also identified by Goffman, Miller, Britton, and others.[52] *Merrilee* asks: "Where do you think we come from?" And she answers her own question: "We're your sisters and your neighbors." *Merrilee* claims a universal respect for human value as well as the familiarity bred of shared humanity. *Lynn's* adroit response to the rhetorical query, however, captures her experience of the "us and them" institutional definitions against which women labor to construct their narratives: "They think we're all crackheads and hoes." *Lynn's* "we're all" speaks to the perceived failure of officers to see the women as individuals with hopes, dreams, and personalities. Seen by officers as a stigmatized collective, the women are disqualified from social citizenship.[53]

It is against these powerful carceral definitions, both structural and individual, that the women toil to establish their counternarratives of forgiveness, resistance, change, and, in some cases, diminished culpability. With Sisyphean perseverance, they self-examine and reconstruct, and, by arranging episodes of their lives into stories that illustrate essential truths about themselves, they impose some coherence on their scattered and confusing experiences.[54] As *Royal Tee's* narrative demonstrated, their stories are less about facts and more about meanings, both subjective and constructed. They are constructing not simply what happened in "a five- to ten-minute period" that changed their lives forever, but how they felt about what happened, how they shouldered responsibility for unintended consequences, and how they feel about the events now.[55] *Floyd*, for example, demonstrates her ongoing acceptance of responsibility and remorse for the crime that resulted in her life sentence.

> *Floyd*: I never did file my 6500 motions [motion for relief from judgment]. I never tried.
> LL: Why is that?
> *Floyd*: I didn't feel like I deserved to after what I did, or was part of.

Floyd's remorse has resulted in her acceptance without argument of the state's judgment of her culpability, as an aider and abettor, for the murder for which she has been sentenced to life imprisonment.

Without establishing counternarratives, "the cloud over that building" (the correctional facility) is more than some women can handle. A sure road to depression and despair inside was the women's acceptance of institutional and popular definitions of them as deviants and monsters. The extreme consequence of life imprisonment and its corollary, stigmatized identities, is suicide. Suicide was a frequent conversational topic in focus groups. *Valerie's* comments are representative of others: "For the first time in 15 years [of incarceration], I thought about killing myself last year." For *Valerie*, imprisonment's erosion had taken its toll.

"I don't pray for my freedom every day. I'm sick of it. . . . Maybe my physical freedom isn't in the cards." *Valerie's* legal appeals have been denied. "The constant denials from court will drive you crazy." For *Valerie*, the prison doors have, thus far, remain closed. Despair is the disadvantaged clone of hope unfulfilled.

By developing their counternarratives, life-serving women mine their life stories so that their pasts can unravel their present circumstances and hopefully positively affect their futures. Nonetheless, it is authoritative institutional narratives that have the greatest effect on their self-actualization processes. Institutional narratives of dangerous prisoners serve a generalized symbolic value in defining the women, with the consequence that, as *Martha* notes, "You have to act like a prisoner. You can't act like a good citizen."

"I'M IMPORTANT TO MY FAMILY": BEING LOVED AND LOVING
Isolated behind the wire, many life-serving women seek and receive personal validation by being loved in other places. Family members in particular hold more holistic, more generous definitions of who they are, unaffected by their crimes, sentences, and incarceration.[56] The alternative definitions proffered by the people who love them confirm the women's importance, ease their isolation, remind them that they are emotionally and psychologically located in caring constellations, and demonstrate that they are valued and valuable. In these caring arenas, the women are not socially irrelevant. They matter, as *Grace* notes: "Regardless that I'm here, I'm important. I'm important to my family."

Grace's reference group is her family, not the generalized other of society or the particularized other of the prison. Her words "I'm important" echo the oft-heard refrain that prison is only "where I am, not who I am." Through grit, conscious decision making, and perseverance, *Grace* and her peers counter penal and social definitions and redefine themselves as women with significance in the world. As criminologist Barbara Owen notes, "Personal relationships with other prisoners, both emotionally and physically intimate, connections to family and loved ones in the free community (or, 'on the street' in the language of the prison) and commitments to pre-prison identities continue to shape the core of the prison culture among women."[57]

Grace redefines herself through the gendered trope of motherhood. Her children were toddlers when she was sentenced. As is typical of incarcerated women whose families have the resources necessary to provide support, her mother, the children's grandmother, assumed responsibility for their care. "My mom would come to the prison in tears" and ask *Grace* to call her home daily to help raise her children. *Grace* has a consequential social role as mother to children with whom she has had ongoing mail, phone, and visit contact despite her incarceration. "Every week since I've been incarcerated, my kids get mail from me." She provides what material comfort she can access and afford: "Hershey bars go into an envelope as well." *Grace's* counternarrative refashions her identity in a way that aligns with conventional gender assumptions of femaleness and motherhood. She centers her significance as occurring within traditionally gendered maternal responsibilities. Like many other incarcerated mothers, she does what she is able to do.

Women without close emotive relationships outside, or surrogate social networks inside, must define themselves and establish their identities on their own. They do so without the structuring obligations and responsibilities of their suspended social roles as mothers, daughters, sisters, coworkers, and so on. Under these conditions, they often define themselves through interactions with other women,[58] often in very gendered ways. As a consequence of imprisonment, *Joyce*, for example, acknowledges "I flunked raising my kid." Imprisoned, she gets a second chance with someone else's child. She can redeem her past and reassert responsible motherhood through her present care and concern for troubled young women who enter the prison system.

Joyce describes one trajectory in her adaptive parenting model, that is, "beautiful girls come in here" and "they end up bald. They think they're like boys." Some young women enter prison and intentionally develop male personas as protective off-putting guises as well as a means of gaining control over decision making in sexual encounters. *Joyce* offers parenting care and advice to four of these young women, whom she claims as her "four sons" and whom she further identifies as "kids who have never known unconditional love before." In such parental loving and care-taking, *Joyce* can make amends in small measure for "flunking out" with her own son. She can become a responsible mother to someone else's child.

By developing counternarratives of action and value, these life-serving women push back against the slow gnawing away of personal identity. They reappropriate the power to define themselves, albeit often in conventionally gendered ways. Those who persevere, who reconstruct themselves from the fragments of the memories of their lives, eventually establish narrative identities that provide their lives with some degree of unity and purpose.[59]

New identities are premised in their "whole" selves, not just the worst discrete acts of their lives. As in other contexts, women with social capital, that is, with networks of personal, economic, and social advantage, are more proficient at establishing alternative identities than women with limited social, psychological, or educational resources. Nonetheless, all the women in this study confronted their stigmatized identities as social deviants and recast their experiences in their own, more conventional terms. They did not accept their social identifications as "prisoners" as immutable. They reflected upon and contextualized their past selves and refashioned and reaffirmed more compassionate identities that were more consonant with their "remembered past[s], perceived present[s], and anticipated future[s]."[60] Through their counternarratives they agentically refashioned social and personal identities in opposition to the pervasive stigmatizing representations associated with female life imprisonment.

Developing an Internal Compass

Life-serving women build on their counternarratives to develop an internal compass, a core moral identity, that is both authentic for them and compatible with prison culture. To do so, they cultivate structures that guide their interactions and resist time's erosions. Some structures are formally imposed by institutional requirements. For example, the strictures of disciplinary time and the lack of choice compel some women to innovate in order to negotiate and resist the structuring principles of their carceral lives. Other structures develop situationally and are culturally context bound. Still others reflect the women's informal practices enacted to resist the attritions of time, place, and generalized hopelessness. At the nexus of these sometimes conflicting structures, women formulate useful moral rules and beliefs that they define as authentic for the context. These perspectives are profoundly subjective and reflect the preeminence of the distinctiveness of "prison rules" over more conventional moral codes. Their internal compasses incorporate past lessons, current experiences, spiritual awakenings, and pragmatic assessments, as well as the specific values and beliefs necessary to retain a sense of dignity and self-respect in prison.[61]

"IT'S NOT STEALING": FORMING PERSONAL ETHICS

In the process of cultivating moral centers, many women report developing what feminist philosophers refer to as an "ethic of care," or the dynamic of moral decision making nested within both cooperation and community.[62] For example, as her "personal, ethical belief," *Sheri* says, "As long as what you're doing isn't hurting someone, or coming back to hurt me," then she won't report the behavior to officers. She provides the example of stealing food from the chow hall, which she would not report, and stealing valuables from mail-order purchases, which she would report. A chow-hall theft is absorbed by the institution; a mail-order theft is the personal violation of a peer. *Sheri's* "personal, ethical belief" unknowingly builds on the legacy of feminist philosophy scholars of ethics and is consistent with life as it is lived in a woman's correctional facility.[63] Her internal compass reflects an ethic of care in contrast to the ethic of justice that is conventionally associated with males and male-authorized institutions.

An ethic of justice is foundational to criminal-processing systems, and it enshrines abstract standards of right and wrong that are detached from particularities of context and person. An ethic of justice stresses universal applicability, one-size-fits-all, over particularized context and individualized need. An ethic of care, however, emphasizes relationships and responsibilities, empathic concerns, and interpersonal consequences instead of abstract rules, laws, and punishment.[64] Using an ethic of justice standard, stealing food from the chow hall is equally as deviant as theft from mail-order purchases. But *Sheri* rejects that standard as incomplete. It does not account for variation in outcomes nor does it reflect in situ understandings of women seeking small nutritional comforts from a coercive system. Her "personal, ethical belief" is empathic and relational.

Sheri's ethical positioning was validated by most of the study respondents during my presentation of this analysis to the participants. One audience participant's support was stated thusly: "I don't consider it stealing when they already give it to you on your tray." Reflecting the particular conditions under which women decided to "steal" food from the chow hall, another woman said, "If I don't have enough time to finish my food because an officer is behind me saying in my ear 'hurry and finish up, it's time to go' and I take food that I hadn't had time to finish . . . it's not stealing." The women recognized the unauthorized removal of food from the chow hall as the violation of an institutional rule. Correctional officers may charge women with stealing for taking food from the chow hall without authorization. The women's moral positioning is responsive to their own versions of ethical behavior;[65] the officers' position is responsive to an abstract ethic of justice where violations of rules result in sanctions.

"IF YOU HAVE NO MIND AND NO SPINE, YOU'RE EASILY LED": ESTABLISHING A SECURE SELF-IDENTITY

For life-serving women the process of developing an internal compass is linked to establishing a secure identity that reduces susceptibility to seeking external validations of self-worth from others. As *Sasha Lavan* notes of those women who don't develop an internal compass: "if you have no mind and no spine, you're easily led." *DJ's* teary "aha moment" serves as such a negative exemplar: "I look for value from other people." When *DJ* is close to others, she says, "I tend to cling to them." *Esther* acknowledges *DJ's* behavior and, in the forthrightness of genuine exchange, declares, "You are your own worst enemy."

DJ has clearly not developed her own compass. She has remained focused on external evaluations, on how she is treated by others, and she reports consistently seeking to reaffirm her identity through the approval of others. Unlike *DJ,* other women report rejecting such external judgments in the process of crafting their own moral centers. For example, *Joyce* claims to ignore the "characterizations of others." U.K. criminologist Michelle Butler argues that imprisoned women so fortified are less likely to experience disrespect, threats, or challenges to their identities from their peers.[66]

Women may develop internal compasses, but without social shields they are without protections. Women characterized as "baby killers" (women whose crimes included the death of a child), for example, live on the social margins of prison culture. Their marginality diminishes protective affiliations with individuals and groups; they have no allies who will help protect them, no safe spaces, no buffers, no power, no respect, and no influence. Reflecting broad social patterns outside, other imprisoned women stigmatize them inside as the following exchange illustrates:

> *Passion*: Sometimes if you're with others in jail [during trial and before sentencing] and then they get to prison before you do, they've already started talking about your crime and what you did. The worst are the baby killers and child molesters. These women often get a hard time for their crimes.
> *Taylor*: Everybody knows my case. But I didn't kill my children. This is why I am how I am now (points to physical deformities). I was a dancer. For three years I was abused. My children are my life. I go every day to the law library [to work on her appeal].
> LL: Who was assaulting you with names?
> *Taylor*: Everyone.
> LL: Everyone, including officers?
> *Taylor*: Everyone.
> LL: Everyone, including other women?
> *Taylor*: Everyone, officers and inmates.

"Baby killer" is reportedly the most denigrated identity in prison, and it is the most difficult label to counter. With a child murder sentence, as *Veronica* asserts, "you wear it." It cloaks all interactions; it's a constant. "Even your best friend, in a moment of anger, could try to bring up your case and use it against you." In any argument "it's always, 'you're a baby killer.'" Nothing women can do erases the characterization. "I tried to fit in to escape my label [baby killer]. But nothing really made it disappear." Every new bunkie would hear her story from someone in the housing unit. But the harassment can dissipate. Although their treatment from others is harsh, it's not irrefutable. *Veronica* maintains that the stigma can be reduced, if not eliminated, through time and deliberate behavior.

"It's like, if you have good character, and you carry yourself well and you've been doing time, it's not that bad. I think that if you act right, you'll be fine after a while." The longer she's incarcerated, a woman informally identified as a "baby killer" can, by "carry[ing] herself well," reduce the immutability of the characterization. The more time she's down, the more time other women have to evaluate the consistency of her behavior and its contrast to the "baby killer" image. Status within the prison hierarchy can change with time served.

"I KEEP TO MY SCHEDULE TOO": LIVING "AS IF"

Prison is an environment that simultaneously incites and constrains. The extent to which women can express emotions and moral decision making, as well as the forms through which they can manage their feelings, is grounded in the situational and cultural context of prison life.[67] A sentence of natural life offers no emotional rest; life-imprisoned women must always act "as if." "As if" represents agency, that is, a reciprocal relation between the women and their environment, and it reflects a personal reading of and an internal response to the conditions of imprisonment. *Doll's* "as if" is constructed around what her "free world" life would be as she notes, "mostly though, I just try to treat life in here the same way I would treat life on the outside." In a profound reconstruction of reality, she purports to live her daily life inside "as if" she was on the other side of the barbed-wire fence.

"As if" also calls on women to consistently exhibit themselves as deferential, conforming, and positively responsive to all authority while simultaneously masking resistant attitudes and self-affirming identities. *Merrilee* exemplifies this penal expectation in contacts with "black and grays" (correctional officers). Although unspoken, she nonetheless says, with resignation, that "respect doesn't even matter anymore [*pause*], just leave me alone. . . . You don't even like me, so let's not even play."

"As if" is also a fictional, agentic choice in circumstances where reality is too overwhelming to accept. Life-serving women maintain these fictionalized versions of themselves for others' consumption and for their own protection from sanctions, as they wrestle with the truth of their realities. They develop order, scheduling their lives in the already highly scheduled environment. They agentically create informal routines to resist the erosions of time, place, and carceral bleakness. *Monaye*, like many others, maintains a schedule in which she writes short stories and poetry, goes to church, exercises, does craft work, and works her prison job. "I keep to my schedule too." This is the "as if" fiction of decision making in which the women choose how to fill and use unscheduled time. In so doing, they impose order on themselves and on their environment. "As if" creates a measure of control and, therefore, of power over their environment. It creates an impression of forward movement toward normalized goals. "As if" is both a resistance to and a defiance of erosion. "As if" scheduling promotes the image of a woman using time wisely in a challenge to the warehousing, useless waste that is life without parole. It is the public presentation of a worthy self.

Additionally, "as if" behavior is supported by prison personnel, who caution against reversion to reality. *Pooh Bear* narrates her experience with the numbing loss from her mother's death and the concerned advice she received from correctional officers, when she "couldn't move." She tearfully recounts those days: "To know they were having her funeral [*chokes back tears*] and I couldn't go, it tore me up." Correctional officers warned her "not to get into trouble," that is, to act "as if." Their cautions are reminders that visible action, "trouble," as a consequence of *Pooh Bear's* grief, could result in negative sanctions or segregation. Her private crisis is occluded by the institutional imperative to act "as if." It is a warning elaborated by *Martha* and *Kari* in another focus group where *Martha* argued that, "over time, the system turns you into a puppet. It's like you can't have emotions anymore." *Kari* responded, "Exactly! You can't be a human being anymore." Both women claim, like *Pooh Bear*, that they can't express what they feel in context because overt expressions of "negative" emotions result in sanctions from officers. Having a bad day, being emotionally upset, or responding to grief, women can "end up in seg" (segregation) where they're really isolated and "end up feeling worse."

Louise notes that all the women inside must have a "certain level of control" to not attract or involve the attention of the officers, that is, the dramaturgical discipline identified by Goffman (e.g., avoiding slips, keeping the self central, managing facial expressions and tone of voice, in short, behaving "as if"). *Passion* speaks to the emotional and psychological costs of the pretense when she says, "I'm a good actress, but at the end of the day, I need somebody [to end the loneliness and inter-rupt the despair]." *Passion* can manage the "as if" charade for lengthy periods, but "at the end of the day" she also needs support and a "reality check" from a trusted other who embodies an ethic of care. "As if" is movement that contrasts with imprisonment as perpetually standing in place, but it is not without consequence. Imprisoned women are alone in a crowded place, without privacy, so they must enact a protective shield emblazoned "as if."

"HELLOS AND HOW ARE YOUS": ENACTING COURTESY

Another aspect of agency, a central component of an internal compass, a deliberate use of time, and an extension of the "ethic of care" is enacting courteous behavior. Every encounter in a crowded environment where all space is public space is an opportunity for courtesy. Considerate behavior reflects determined actions to take care of each other and to live decently. Politeness requires a minimal level of social interaction, so courtesy inside can be as simple as "the basic stuff" identified by *Shem-etta* as "hellos and how are yous" and acknowledging someone if they're speaking "just out of general respect." The same courtesies expected in the free world are operable in the social world of prison (e.g. social greetings, acknowledging a speaker, queuing in lines, turn taking, and so on). These actions demonstrate a moral code that includes sustained, small courtesies that women extend to one another. But, in a deprivation environment without privacy where all of life occurs in the company of others, courteous behavior necessarily becomes more dimensional. It signals the shared expectation of conduct and a latent capacity for action. In prison "it matters what I think others think," so courteous behavior becomes a kind of "moral code."[68]

To alleviate prison erosions and to avert despair, women must be re-sponsive to one another's needs. Sometimes the needs are immediate. *Sheri*, for example, discusses her response to another woman's pressing desire for someone to talk to. *Sheri* puts aside her own activities as she reports, "I turn my music off and just listen." She also acknowledges the imposition on her time: "for the most part, I'd rather be by myself."

As in other contexts, courteous behavior promotes norms of civility.[69] It engenders and reflects consideration for others in daily interactions and it confers value and humanity on the recipients. Inside prison walls, it also reduces the collateral damage of the mix and establishes informal practices of social control that are so vital to shared space.

And prison is at all times shared space. Women share space with staff and officers, but unrelentingly they share their living environments with other convicted women. They share cells, bathrooms, showers, and even a microwave oven. When chow-hall food is perceived as inedible or unappealing, a microwave oven is a necessity. As an ancillary benefit, the oven supplies the women with a measure of autonomy in preparing their own food and in being able to share it. On the other hand, the microwave also becomes an informal location for enactments of dominance and submission that are ongoing. *Ciara Blue*, for example, contends that "you can have an argument about who's next in line for the microwave that will last the rest of your life."

Use of communal space consequently requires informal rules of courtesy. When they are violated, public-boundary maintenance may occur. Verbal altercations over microwave use (or telephone, or irons, or the TV, etc.) serve important processes inside. In "becoming an inmate" women noted frequent use of language that they had rarely used on the street; however, in developing an internal compass these code-switching, profane language techniques are marshaled in the service of an ethic of care that aims to improve interactions in collective space. For example, in a dispute over microwave use, *Lois* notes, "I'm'a teach you. Don't fuck wit' me." Cussing someone out sets boundaries for interactional behavior as it also enforces the informal norms of shared living in overcrowded conditions. Among its many uses, profanity establishes the parameters of relationships. Loud cursing aims to humiliate and identifies for public notice those women who violate the courtesies necessary in this crowded space. It's a one-on-one exchange with ripple effects. The audience is more than the interactants and includes anyone in the hearing vicinity (officers, staff, and other imprisoned women), as well as anyone to whom the exchange is reported. It serves notice on the violator. It "teaches" that violation of the social norms has public consequences in an environment with very few private spaces.

Everything women inside experience is experienced in the company of others, so they survive "the prison thing" by learning to check other women's discourteous behavior before it becomes routine. While appearing rude or obnoxious, the verbal violence of profanity can be understood as a means of informal social control. It prevents situations from escalating into chaos and positions the women as active agents in controlling their environment.[70]

Courtesy, as a feature of an internal compass, is necessary because in the prison environment there are no opportunities for the unobtrusive discharge of activities of daily life—intimate, personal, and private.[71] Toileting, for example, can become an especially degrading interaction. *Lynn*, who is bunked with another woman in a 6-by-10-foot space originally designed for one and that, therefore, includes a toilet, talks about the "bowel movement battles" that have ensued. She describes the problems of defecation when women cannot leave their cells (during count, nighttime lockdown, mobilizations, sanctions) or when a woman chooses not to observe the courtesy of asking a bunkie to leave while "she takes a shit." In a cost/benefit analysis, *Lynn* describes the options available to her in the "bowel movement battles" with her roommate. She wants to change bunkies, but, with no control over or input into her living assignment, *Lynn* knows that she has to weigh her options: "You have to watch the situation you're in" because "what if I was placed with [named woman]?" With general agreement from other focus-group members, *Lynn* capitulates, "Guess I'll just have to smell her shit because it could be worse."

With personal resources down to the bone, courteous behavior is both available and generous. Deliberate courtesy is meaningful; it directs being and becoming for life-serving women.

"SOME PEOPLE JUST LET THAT SENTENCE KILL YOU": OVERCOMING DESPAIR

Cumulative exposure to stressors, to the attritions of time, to the emotional and psychological consequences of structural conditions, erodes body and soul. One potential consequence of continuous erosion is depression, which may be an appropriate response to losses and the unending repetition of days, weeks, months, and years. Some women report physical and emotional exhaustion and a surrender to circumstances. *Esther* observes, for example, that "some people just let that sentence kill you." In her study of women's identity processes in U.K. prisons, Bosworth noted that "despite the inevitable erosion of their self-images in response to the institutional restrictions, women expend a considerable amount of energy inside attempting to maintain a self-identity as active, reasoning agents."[72]

The life-serving women in this study were also active agents in constructing meaningful lives inside. Their processes were often fraught with obstacles. *Azianna* succumbed to the erosion process and "tried to commit suicide." As a former Michigan women's correctional facility warden, Tekla Miller, noted, many life-sentenced women feel there is little chance for change in their situations and they despair.[73] For some, facing the rest of their lives in a "bleak cell" is not a conceivable option. Suicide ideation and suicide attempts are a means of establishing some measure of control over circumstances. They may also be responses to what *Dennis the Menace* labels a "lifer moment," which she describes as when "you feel helpless and hopeless" as a result of being stuck in an unresponsive, no-exit environment. These ideations are not uncommon among life-serving women as this spontaneous exchange indicates:

> *Merrilee*: Do you make dates? Like, if something doesn't happen by this date, I'm out [suicide].
> *Lynn*: Yes, 2015. If they [parole board] keep sending me "no further interest" then I'm out.

For *Azianna* and others, the foiled suicide attempts force them to go "to the root" and to engage in hard, personal, biographical excavations on their own to understand their journeys to incarceration. Like other women who reported having, at some earlier point in their prison lives, developed advanced suicide ideations, *Azianna* felt that she had nowhere else to go. She could either deal with her life sentence or she could end her life. With suicide thwarted, the only agency she identified was attitudinal. She reported beginning the process toward developing an internal compass. "I came in thinking I have nothing to live for and now I fight every day."

Women's personalities, analytical abilities, personal material and nonmaterial resources, and prison opportunities all advance or mitigate erosion and contribute to the development of a moral compass. As *Anna Bell* observes, "You've got to stay focused on what's important to you. It's so easy to slip off into the madness."

And the madness is not far away. Identity survival in prison is a struggle to maintain agency and a sense of self—self-worth, self-definition, self-confidence—in a system designed to deny individuality, to treat inmates collectively as though they are homogenous objects. Women struggle resolutely to maintain their identities and to develop their own internal compasses. The sometimes valiant emotion-management techniques[74] employed by life-serving women to counter erosion's abrasions are like sandbags in a flood—they minimize the damage and they serve as containment strategies but they rarely stop the flow. For many of the study participants, their efforts are exhausting, frustrating, and disheartening. *Destiny* claims, "I'm currently angry and have been for two years. . . . I'm tired and I don't care anymore." She is worn down, defeated, and losing her "fight." The consequence of not maintaining her resistance efforts is that she was "in seg" (segregation) the week prior to the focus group for four days after 15 years of clear conduct (i.e., time without major misconduct sanctions).

Vulnerable to sanction at every moment from any staff person, correctional officer, or administrator under any personal conditions, prison is a detrimental experience, however many social, political, or personal resources women carry inside (most enter with few). Prison is emotionally and psychologically damaging in its ability to undermine even resourceful women. In each of the identified stages of establishing socially meaningful, self-actualized lives, but particularly so in developing an internal compass, imprisoned women must wrestle with complex social processes. They must manage structured prison time and unstructured "inmate" time. They must control "as if" contemporary impressions. They must monitor the consequences of past experiences and they must contend with the rituals of everydayness, as well as the demands of the institution and society.[75]

Rebuilding Social Bonds

Although life-serving women may say "I pretty much keep to myself," doing time is a communal act.[76] The act of doing time can appear singular and individual, as enshrined in the rhetoric of the inmate code "do your own time." Yet it is quite complex. Doing time is a social activity experienced individually. Imprisoned women traverse their solo prison journeys together. They do their "own time" together. They are constantly in public space while simultaneously removed from public view. In these paradoxical conditions, they engage in efforts to cultivate rich lives and meaningful relationships.[77]

Those women, who traverse the earlier stages of the self-actualization processes inside, ultimately engage in collective efficacy, defined by interdisciplinary scholars Kirk R. Williams and Nancy G. Guerra, and Robert J. Sampson, a Harvard professor of social sciences, as the link between mutual trust and social cohesion among members of a collectivity and their willingness to work together for the common good.[78] The shift in life-serving women's loci of control is reflected in the opportunities they generate to challenge the order imposed by rules and regulations.[79] These women establish, or actively participate in, social networks (collectives) with action orientations (efficacy).

They also contribute to informal social control in the environment by protecting and promoting the common good through their willingness to intervene.[80] *Louise*, for example, asserts the conditions for her interventions: "I've stepped in between fights. They listened and no one's ever touched me. . . . I don't do that for everybody, just those who I really care about." Mediating a physical altercation can be a dangerous enterprise; *Louise* consequently limits her risk taking to those whom she "really care[s] about."

Speaking out and acting out within the constraining circumstances of the prison environment demonstrate active and inventive agency and resiliency. Life-serving women engage in life-affirming practices that constitute basic connections to self and community.[81] *Destiny's* words serve as an illustration, "I'm filling my life up and living," instead of just existing inside. "I continue to strive toward self-actualization."

Research and anecdotal stories establish lifers, like these study participants, as stabilizing forces within the prison complex.[82] Sentencing Project analyst Ashley Nellis argues that individuals serving life are some of the most well-adjusted women in prison for, as *Alexandria* attests, "we have to be."[83] Their institutional safety depends as much on their behavior as on managing prison practices.[84] Prison is their social universe for the long term and, as a consequence, maintaining order in that universe is a priority. *Baby* speaks to this stability: "I'm doing life. I don't need that chaos. I've got to make the best out of what I have."

Tekla Miller supports these understandings and states that penal staff hoped to be assigned to units with "old-timers" who knew how to do time and who therefore fostered calm among the other women.[85] Some life-serving women, like *Linda* and *Jane*, would also prefer bunking with other life-serving women. "I want them to put me in a unit with nothing but lifers" because, as *Jane* argues, "we know how to do our time!"

For these women, maintaining order in their environmental context is essential for emotional, psychological, and even physical survival. Dealing with "drama" and "chaos" long term is exhausting. To combat the corrosive effects of prison time, they scour the setting for support, for training, for emotional and psychological programming, and for opportunities to develop the social skills necessary to create tolerable living space. But, as *Esther* noted previously, life-serving women are not offered the same program opportunities that are available to "short termers." Prison policies ration the spaces with the consequence that, as *Alexandria notes*, "we can't stabilize if we don't get opportunities to better ourselves."

Nonetheless, as those women motivated to do so move through the deliberate, personal processes of constructing their accounts in response to the master narratives of "criminal" and "prisoner," as they simultaneously develop moral compasses embedded in an ethic of care, they also work to (re)establish social bonds based in mutual assistance, empathy, and collective efficacy.[86] They forge bonds of community and friendship to help one another survive. As feminist criminologist Joanne Belknap notes:

> just about everything that is bad in men's prisons is worse in women's prisons (e.g., the increase in incarceration rates; HIV rates; proximity to friends and family; access to educational, vocational, medical, and recreational programs and professionals; and possibly the disproportionate number of prisoners of color). However, one significant gender distinction that is arguably in favor of women is the prison subculture, particularly how the prisoners treat each other.[87]

These self-actualizing women demonstrate guerrilla ingenuity in creating their own informal mechanisms of support and stability.

"THEY TAUGHT ME HOW TO JAIL": MENTORING OTHERS

Perhaps the most obvious form of assistance is the mentoring that life-serving women provide to juvenile lifers. In a world managed at every level by correctional officers, life-serving women need to train each other and the newly sentenced women to adapt in order to survive.[88] To the newly sentenced, everything is personal. To the women with "time in," nothing is personal.[89] Life-serving women have achieved "inmate" relevancy, through experience and status, and so are accorded some measure of social power and authority by their peers.[90] Knowledge inside is power and women with "time in" have it: knowledge of the system, knowledge of survival strategies, knowledge of prison culture, knowledge of the personalities and quirks of the officers, and knowledge of both formal and informal rules of engagement.

Many life-serving women take pride in sharing their hard-won expertise. *Scarlet* claims that "kids" who come in scared are drawn to women who can help them "constructively," specifically "lifers with time under their belts." Because *Pamela* worries about these juveniles, "minors . . . babies," she seeks to connect them to "people like us, to help them" as a direct effort to protect them from predators who want "to get in their panties."

Yasmeen was a beneficiary of this ethic of care. "They taught me how to jail": they taught her how to keep up with personal hygiene; how to keep her room clean; how to not get involved in other people's "messes"; how to choose friends wisely; how to tell a good officer from a bad one; how to forgive others and herself; how to behave during mobilization ("take it as a resting period" and "lay down on your bed without looking out the door"); how to handle "depressing and oppressing" times; how to use the law library to work on her case; how to call a spot for a bunkie in the shower line; and so on.

Lifers who mentor provide strategies instead of answers. *Scarlet* notes that they are "not about control or domination." Their advice reflects the lessons of their unique and diverse efforts to exercise agency in restrictive circumstances.[91] As women like *Yasmeen* gain in knowledge of the system and its various populations, they gain in confidence and experience and many report moving from mentee to mentor.

Mentoring is an emotional seedbed. Life-serving women do the work of the facility by providing a "sense of security" for other women in the system. They teach newly arrived adolescents—terrified and without allies—how to cope with their new realities. Most of these study respondents also reported viewing the younger, more recently sentenced women as difficult to understand and get along with.[92] *Merrilee* metaphorically characterizes these freshly sentenced juveniles as "children of the corn," drawing on the early 1980s Stephen King horror movie about the demonic children in a small Nebraska town who ritualistically murdered all the adults in order to have a successful corn harvest. Forgivingly, she also provides an analytical explanation for their behavior. "There's a pattern. Now you're young, angry, and you've been through Level V [closed custody], before they come to us. The bad behavior is already ingrained." Closed custody, the adolescent's first experience with imprisonment, intensifies the damage of their pre-incarceration lives.

Mentoring lifers seek to work with the young women to undo both the harms of the structural conditions imposed by prison policies as well as their pre-imprisonment injuries and troubles. But they do so very carefully. *Ciara* notes that it's hard getting to know "these children." She relates the mentoring difficulties she encountered with a 17-year-old who has a "25–50 bit" (a minimum sentence of 25 years; a maximum of 50 years). *Ciara* describes the young woman's "mental and maturity level as more like 14" and defines her responsibility this way: "I have to be a constant for her and just let her lead me to what's comfortable for her to talk about in her own time." There's "always something going on" because the girl is new, young, "in the mix," and because her victim is known to an officer, an additional complicating factor. *Ciara* notes that not prying is not easy but is necessary to establish trust.

Many newly arrived juveniles reject the wisdom and experience offered to them, fearful of a "con" or an exchange that will have negative consequences later. *Royal Tee* notes that "it's the small things that make all the difference in the world." She styles young girls' hair without charge: if they "look good, they feel good. When they see I don't want anything from them, they learn not everybody's out to get you. There are some who are genuine." Reflecting her context-based cynicism, *Floyd* immediately responds with "a handful" (of trustworthy women).

The rejection by newly sentenced lifers can be frustrating to the would-be mentors, as *Ciara Blue* acknowledges: "It's like, I'm giving you everything it took me 10 years to get. You hand somebody a beautiful gift that will enhance their life and they like slap you in the face with it." *Ruth* was grown, a mature woman, a mother who had never been in the system before her life sentence. In prison, she had "kids" telling her what to do, kids "who have grown up in the system," "kids from juvie who really know the system," and they'd be telling her what to do. These rebuffs and role reversals result in a double frustration for the mentors who are devalued as "property" in the system and whose devaluation is amplified by the newly sentenced juveniles who discard the experience, expertise, and dignity of the criminalized women inside.

Mentoring is interpretational and embedded in listening for a subtext of fear and distrust, and it requires that mentoring women remember their own prison journeys. *Linda*, a juvenile offender and now a middle-aged woman, draws on her earlier experiences to illustrate how a mentee becomes a mentor and pays forward the lessons she learned from her role models. *Linda's* mentoring path is political. Her mentors were "always on me" about school, talking, cajoling, and nagging *Linda* to take advantage of educational opportunities. She did, and those lessons taught her that "you gotta start something bigger than yourself." One of her role models was released from prison and continued her advocacy work on behalf of imprisoned men and women. *Linda's* mentor "made it [prison advocacy] her life. That's the person I want to be."

Training for her role, *Linda* initiated the Female Youth Deterrence Project and encouraged other juvenile lifers to participate in "the struggle" (to engage young women in empowerment activities so they wouldn't get caught up in "street life"). She tried to involve the juvenile lifers in action beyond themselves, in social movement activities to change the lives of other young women, but also simultaneously to accept the responsibility for the choices that resulted in their incarcerations. Forgetting her own passage through the various agentic processes, *Linda* is often frustrated by those young women still struggling with the first stages of their incarcerations. "I'm, like, are you serious? They just don't put in any effort."

Not all life-serving women are interested in mentoring. Some actively choose not to mentor, preferring to keep others at a distance, as *Belladonna Momma* typifies: "The point is, though, it's my choice. It's my choice who I help and who I decide to stay away from." For her, empowerment rests in agency and choice, not in action. For others, mentoring is an amends-making process. *Scarlet* claims that making a difference in someone else's life, helping someone "jail" effectively, "gives you meaning in the midst of negativity." There are few ways for life-serving women to demonstrate their relevancy, remorse, and reformation. Some attempt to do so through mentoring, thereby demonstrating to self and others that their lives do have meaning.

"I HAVE OUTLIVED MY FAMILY": DEVELOPING SOCIAL BONDS ON THE INSIDE

For women with years of "time down," reference groups on the outside, who respect the authenticity of their remorse and who honor their reform activities, begin to lose their relevance. As the years inside accumulate, former meaningful pre-incarceration identities and nurturing connections to family and friends diminish, crumble, and fade away. People die. *Jesus Lady* laments, "I have outlived my family." Others like *Scarlet* mourn the loss of joy and the interruption of routine from visits with family and friends. She maintains that her "hard time comes from visits." *Scarlet's* incarceration has lasted more than a quarter of a century. During that time, those initially close to her have been getting older and increasingly limited by health concerns. While *Scarlet* previously felt "really down and depressed if I didn't get visits," with time she has had to redefine her expectations and turn inward. It therefore becomes essential that life-serving women, like *Scarlet* and *Jesus Lady*, develop social bonds on the inside.

As feminist criminologist Joycelyn Pollock notes, after years of incarceration the prison world may, by default, become a woman's only world.[93] As *Doll* claims, the importance of "a few close friends" inside magnifies "because I don't have that many people on the outside anymore, only about three or four. People have died." Many of the friends and family members whom she was close to, who were supportive of her, have passed away. Under those circumstances, relationships inside can become more real than any on the outside.

Even with only a few years down, *Caren Sue* reflects on this evolution. "I have best friends at home" but they "don't understand a lot of the things in here, so I don't call home as much anymore." When she calls, "I talk about the same thing every day." She recognizes that, for her friends, "life goes on every day" and "their lives don't stop "just because I'm in here." Her life issues, relevancies, events, and daily gossip are no longer compatible with the interests of friends or family on the outside. Some women inside begin to experience the relevancies in the two environments as mutually exclusive.

Referents for imprisoned women then necessarily become other women in the same circumstances. So they risk outreach and become creative makers of meaningful space.[94] They learn to trust in an environment that renders them constantly vulnerable. As Sister Helen Prejean, author of *Dead Man Walking*, has sagely noted: "The universal riddle of intimacy is magnified in prison: *Letting down one's guard to trust is risking betrayal, grief, rage, more madness.*"[95] Kimberly Greer, a sociologist and a member of the Minnesota Commissioner of Corrections' advisory task force on female offenders, also reports "pervasive interpersonal mistrust inside."[96] Reflecting the ways that women take on the distrust of the system, *DJ* claims, "This is prison and you just can't trust people."

The respondents in this study exposed another prison paradox. *All* the women talked about not trusting "anyone" and simultaneously *all* also talked about other women whom they trusted. Respondents were guarded and protective, selective of friends, wary about who was trustworthy and who should be avoided, but *all* reported trusting specified others. Trust is a commodity that women inside desire, as *Sandy* notes: "I wanted to be trusted . . . and I still want that." But the prison context is not conducive to establishing trust. Trust and trustworthiness rest on consistency, on acceptance (even when behavior is not exemplary), on understanding, on nonjudgmental conversations, on authenticity, and, perhaps most important, on confidentiality. *Ilene Roberts* reflects the oscillation in the paradox: "When you think you can open yourself up to trust, you get hurt. It's never really safe to trust, but we are human, we want to trust."

Critical prison theorist Meg Sweeney notes that "supporting one another is not easy in prison; penal environments breed tension and a lack of trust, and women sometimes betray one another's confidences. Some women nonetheless manage to develop a sense of solidarity in recognizing their shared experiences."[97] *Elizabeth Ashley* is someone who acknowledges these human frailties as well as the contextual features limiting trust: "There are people in here with integrity. A lot of people. But we all fall short." Women develop internal compasses to guide them. They try to remain true to those moral guideposts, but they may end up in situations that undermine their integrity. Unless a women does "some dirty rotten stuff," *Elizabeth Ashley* claims that her errors are probably honest mistakes and bad judgment that "should not wipe out" everything she's done to establish herself as trustworthy. Hers is a generous position in an environment that renders all women vulnerable at all points of interaction.

The constant state of vulnerability reduces some women's desire to be empathetic and substitutes a self-centeredness that protects them from "getting played." Yet developing empathy provides life-sentenced women with opportunities to develop prosocial selves and affirming self-concepts. *Alexandria* notes that being in prison is not the kind of experience one can ever "really leave behind" because prison leaves a "deep impression," but it also opens women up to thinking about, and feeling empathy for, other people in "bad situations, like homeless people who get food on Thanksgiving and stuff at some places. And I was thinking, these are people without homes and food? Why are you only giving them food once a year? It doesn't make sense." Empathy is foundational to developing the means to preserve integrity across discontinuities.

Conclusion

Every prison has a core of activists at any given time who assume leadership and become organizational and informational resources for other women.[98] The life-sentenced women in this study, who traverse the various stages of self-actualization, are those activists. They are committed to building an understanding of the value of community and collective consciousness as resistance to the oppressiveness of the prison environment. They actively engage other women in these processes through directed conversation, through social support, through daily acts of courtesy and recognition, through role-modeling moral behavior and an ethic of care, through their own developing empathy and tolerance, and through their mentoring of juveniles and one another. They use the prison environment as scaffolding for in situ constructions of life changes. They use opportunities and fissures in the system. They discard old habits. They engage others in the processes of crafting different ways of living as imprisoned women.[99] They seek forgiveness, of self and others, through their behaviors as *Joyce* explains: "I wanted to prove to everyone that they were wrong" (for labeling her as a "criminal" and dismissing her for a single act). She cannot convince them verbally, so she attempts to demonstrate her integrity through the ways she behaves and lives her life inside the walls. Life-serving women actively work to self-actualize within the limits of their carceral locations.

6

Desiree

A Journey toward Self-Actualization

I'm not a junk yard. I can't take everyone else's stuff dumped on me. I am a caregiver by nature. I could go years in others' pain.

Desiree's life-course interview opened unexpectedly with her troubled reactions to the most recent suicide at the facility. She was distraught. Her slender fingers folded and unfolded fitfully as she wrestled with the emotional aftermath of the sudden death. The young woman who had taken her own life, a "short timer," had only been out of closed custody and in her unit for three days. *Desiree* said, "[I had] already connected with her . . . knew she was scared. . . . I'm the only one who knew her name. Everyone's just calling her 'that lady' but, it's like, her name is *Sharon!*"

Pushing back against the coldness of institutionalized homogeneity, *Desiree* demanded recognition of "that lady" as an individual, a person of value, who should be accorded the respect of her name. Although newly imprisoned, *Sharon* was apparently friendly with another woman in her residence unit from the same Michigan community. Speaking slowly, but precisely, evoking the helplessness of the moment, *Desiree* said, "I've given her some grief material."

Lost in the blue and orange uniform designed for men, *Desiree* shook as we sat at the stained Formica table in the deputy warden's conference room. A tiny woman restlessly plucking impertinent strands of gray from her tightly curled hair, she lamented *Sharon's* decision to end her life as well as the consequences of her suicide for the other "forgotten women" in the prison.[1] The prison "lockdown" policy, requiring that the women stay in place while officers confirmed the death and then loaded *Sharon's* body onto a gurney and pushed it down the hall, amplified *Desiree's* personal grief. "I had to watch them process a dead body in prison and bring it past my door. I've never seen a dead body before." Acknowledging that *Sharon* "wasn't my friend," *Desiree* was, nonetheless, crying. "I was deeply affected."

Prison is a closed society. Imprisoned women have only one another to rely on for support in circumstances such as this. Questions and guilt inevitably follow a suicide. What if . . . ? Should I have . . . ? Could I have done more? *Desiree* appeared to be overwhelmed by such questions. Reassured that she could reschedule or stop the interview at any time, she chose to continue. "I think I'm OK," she said as she resumed our conversation about *Sharon's* suicide, reflecting about how thoughts of suicide are never far away for life-serving women. "I thought about killing myself last year." She consciously chose not to act on her desperation, considering the suffering that her death would cause her adolescent daughter, "who has already suffered enough from my imprisonment."

Having spent the better part of her 17-year incarceration doggedly resisting "letting time do me," *Desiree* responded empathetically to help other women heal from the suffering that their peer's suicide produced. These efforts—simultaneously selfless acts and strategies for survival— helped her to preserve her estimation of her own value under prison's challenging conditions. Her first ameliorative initiative was presenting an idea for an "encouragement board" to the housing deputy warden. She asked that the deputy approve affixing a corkboard to an empty concrete-block wall in the housing unit. The board would be a place for any woman in the unit to post an inspirational message—a quotation, a picture, a prayer, a story, or some artwork. Intended to be "inviting and colorful," the board would foster connections and responsibilities that might alleviate sadness in the unit's residents. It would serve as a small, but visible, reminder that "we are in this together." "I am hoping to inspire an encouragement board in every unit."

Her other initiative, less precisely formulated, aimed to reduce bullying in the unit. Absentmindedly massaging her earlobe as she spoke, *Desiree* related the rumors that "[*Sharon's*] bunkie was terrorizing her . . . telling her 'don't unpack' . . . you are in with a bunch of lifers . . . they will set you up." *Desiree* deeply desired "to do something as a group to end this [bunkie bullying]." But, in keeping with prison cultural norms, she did not want to involve officers or the prison administration in her initiatives. She is sensitive to the bunkie's circumstances and cognizant of the potential consequences when officers are involved in problem solving. "I don't want her to do more time for being a bully. She has kids." Instead, *Desiree* ruminated about ways to involve her peers. "Maybe we can just set up a panel with lifers who won't take an ignorant approach. . . . Lifers get set in routines, but we try. We do care. We have to stop this. We have to do something." By taking a proactive, collectively oriented approach to the ancillary victimization resulting from the suicide, *Desiree* responded to an internal imperative that sets her apart from women who have given in and given up. When faced with the institution's prohibition against funerals and memorial services, or other opportunities for collective grief or shared sorrow, many women simply shrug their shoulders, pray, and accept that suicide is sometimes a consequence of imprisonment. *Desiree,* in contrast, takes action.

Committed to long-term goals that will make her imprisonment, and the imprisonment of others, meaningful, she struggles against giving in to despair and its stalking companion, depression. "I am trying to make every young woman, every young black woman that comes in, a positive. . . . I want to change the way young black women feel about themselves growing up in a situation close to mine . . . [that] may make [my imprisonment] worth it. . . . I live my life as an example to the best of my ability."

The forms of empathy that *Desiree* displays, an ability to understand the emotional responses of others, to relate to them, and to treat them with care and concern, are central to what it means to be fully human.[2] Empathy is a key factor in the development of social understanding and prosocial behavior and is central to moral development and justice.[3] Empathy is foundational to the social cohesion that is a necessary precursor to the rebuilding social bonds stage of self-actualization.[4]

"I Don't Pray for My Freedom Every Day"

Desiree's empathic work, in the context of institutional power and definitions, is limited in its outreach and its effects. With her life-serving peers, she toils against the generalized despair that permeates the facility. "There's a spirit of hopelessness surrounding this environment. It's like a cancer that's not being treated." The hopelessness of a sentence without exit, the hopelessness of repeated denials of parole or appeal, the hopelessness of feeling invisible to the outside world, and the hope-lessness of being unable to significantly alter the circumstances of their imprisonment—these are the formidable forces against which *Desiree* and others labor to sustain hope. Optimism in prison is fragile. Without some motivation for hopefulness and positivity, life-serving women can easily succumb to despair.

For *Desiree*, as for many of her life-serving peers, hearings for parole often offer the most powerful inducements to both optimism and de-spair. Hope can swiftly be extinguished, for example, by a "no interest" decision from the parole board. In Michigan the parole board is required to complete a "paper review" of the files of second-degree life-serving people every five years, that is, those wo(men) whose life sentences are ostensibly "parolable."

> The factors considered by the Parole Board in making parole decisions include the nature of the current offense, the prisoner's criminal history, prison behavior, program performance, age, parole guidelines score, risk as determined by various validated assessment instruments and informa-tion obtained during the prisoner's interview, if one is conducted. The Parole Board also considers information from crime victims and other relevant sources.[5]

Board members may choose to grant parole, to schedule a public hear-ing on the viability of parole for a particular applicant, or to recommend commutation or pardon to the governor on the basis of a majority vote of the 10 members. They may also choose, on the basis of one parole board member's paper review, for whatever reasons, to show "no inter-est" in the applicant and so no interview is scheduled. Parole board members are not required to provide explanations to applicants for their "no interest" decisions.

Desiree, like her life-serving peers, ultimately hopes for freedom through parole, re-sentencing, commutation, or a successful appeal. "At the end of the day, what you see of me, how I've grown, doesn't matter. . . . I have to sell myself [to the parole board] on paper." Her letter requesting parole consideration becomes one of the board's measures of who she is as a person. After two rejections, however, the crime itself ("the nature of the current offense") still appears to determine the parole board's decision making, overshadowing the depth of her self-rehabilitation. *Desiree*'s remorse, maturity, intelligence, empathy, and desire to contribute to the world seem not to matter. Parole board members, she contends, "only look at the black and white paper" and evaluate her capacity for reentry into the free world through the lens of the crime she committed 17 years earlier. Despite her attempts at self-improvement, the repeated decision of the parole board is "no interest" or, in prison parlance, a "flop."[6] And so she remains a life-sentenced criminal.

A "flop" will often leave life-serving women emotionally unmoored. The possibility of parole, an anchor for their hopes, can be swept away by a single "no interest" decision. When they have done everything available to them to rehabilitate themselves, what, they wonder, is left for them to do? What evidence of remorse and rehabilitation is sufficient? For *Desiree,* clear conduct was not enough. Participation in programs was not enough. External support from family and friends was not enough. Lengthy time served was not enough. Genuine remorse was not enough. What then could be enough? How can she, or any other life-serving woman, ever be "good enough" to exit without some direction, without goals or benchmarks that signal pathways to a different future? What can a life-serving woman look toward to generate a sense of hope? "It [a paper review without guidance] is not humane at all. It's not how you treat people."

Agitatedly twisting strands of her hair as she bit her lip, *Desiree* said the board's "no interest" decision in her case was delivered in a letter slipped, like an advertisement flyer, under her door. "You slide the piece of paper under my door and that's it?? You don't even want to talk to me about it!?" *Desiree*'s deep brown eyes studied the table as she questioned whether or not parole board members considered that five more years of imprisonment without hope might be too much for her to handle.

Idealistically *Desiree* had anticipated understanding and empathy from the parole board members. She thought—with documentation of her successful program completions, letters of support from friends and family, and her own comprehensive statement of purpose—that they would see her as she sees herself. She reasoned that she, like many of her incarcerated peers, had developed understandings of her crime, empathy for her victim and for her own family and community, remorse for the harms she caused, and forgiveness of self for her tragic choices. She accomplished this self-rehabilitative work while she was imprisoned. As a result, thinking within an if X, then Y framework, where she is X and the parole board is Y, she inferred that parole board members, with all their resources, would empathize with the humanity of her self-rehabilitation. Even after two previous denials, she did not expect "this level of insensitivity."

Defeats, like flops, grind away at the personal fortitude that sustains hope inside. Loss of hope erodes the grit and resilience that help women shield themselves against prison erosions. Although everything about prison is impersonal, *Desiree* experiences herself as a woman with value, a woman with contributions to make who determinedly finds hope in the positive changes she can help enact for others. Nonetheless, hope inside is tenuous. *Desiree's* good works and resourcefulness enable her to generate small, localized sources of hope, reflecting the Holocaust survivor and Nobel Peace Prize winner Elie Wiesel's claim that "just as despair can come to one only from other human beings, hope, too, can be given to one only by other human beings."[7]

Hopefulness is not a constant state for *Desiree*. After a "no interest" parole decision or after a denied court appeal, her ability to remain hopeful wanes. *Desiree's* mouth drew downward as she declared, "I don't pray for my freedom every day. I'm sick of it." Demoralized by repeated flops from the parole board and confused by God's lack of response to her prayers for freedom, *Desiree* has come to accept that "maybe my physical freedom isn't in the cards. . . . The weight of my life sentence had to come off my shoulders. . . . It was a cross I had to put down."

After time and with submission of the next appeal or next commutation petition, her hope renews. *Desiree's* faith enables her to resurrect hope after profound disappointments. She believes in the Christian religious tradition that crucifixion is a redemptive process that is followed by transformation. Like many of her peers, *Desiree's* faith is strong. "If God will let me stay in my right mind until the end, I can keep hope." Although she does not have the power to change her sentence, she does have the power to remain hopeful. So she continues to believe in a divine intervention that will transform her circumstances and offer her the forgiveness that comes with redemption. "I learned that if I trust the Jesus in me, he will seek out the Jesus in others. I let the rest be."

"It Is Better to Live Than Just to Exist"

Keeping hope alive in prison is a communal process. *Desiree* collaborates with other life-serving women as they battle against despair. Many women with years down "don't even want to open the door of hope . . . for some reason; the *idea* that the answer may be no is significantly worse than knowing the answer *is* no. People just don't wanna hope" (emphasis is *Desiree*'s). Hope can be cruel. For some life-serving women, the impact of institutional control is total. They stop hoping, succumb to tedium and inertia, and reluctantly accept a lowering of aspirations and the futility of anticipating freedom. For *Desiree*, however, hope is bound tightly to the question of how to live.[8] "Being free on the inside is more important than being physically free. It is better to live than just to exist."

Idle hope is not useful to imprisoned women. Life-serving women must "stay busy" to stay positive. *Desiree* rallies her peers by fostering discussions and activities that encourage them to fashion meaningful lives in spite of their circumstances. "We live in seasons and these past two years have been like winter, dark and gloomy. Now it's like spring." The steady routines of prison life can erode motivations for productive actions and frustrate the possibility of personal change. Yet *Desiree*'s attitudes shift in place. She retains her altruistic other-orientation, but she also becomes more self-determining in her decision *making*. "I'm choosing how I want to be, how I want to live." She invites others to do the same by reframing, or establishing a counternarrative about, their past lives. "The secret to happiness in life is thinking positively about the past. Life is about perceptions. My bad experiences are still bad experiences, but the lessons I learned have allowed me to be someone I like." Being "someone I like" is a hopeful emergence from a "dark and gloomy" metaphorical winter. Her confidence in the reliability of her internal compass makes her sensitive to her own state as well as to the struggles of her peers. *Desiree* willingly shares her insights with them. In so doing, she creates opportunities for them to develop their own internal compasses and to learn to "like" themselves and to be "secure with who you are within yourself" as an antidote to prison ennui.

But she cautions others: "Don't determine who you are by who I am." Acknowledging that life-sentenced women share the same conditions of imprisonment, she insists that other women's responses to those conditions must reflect their own choices and talents. *Desiree* provides one behavioral model, but if other women imitate her choices too directly, they may well lose the potential wisdom that their own creative processes could provide.

Being "Raised Up" by Other Incarcerated Women

Because, after 17 years inside, she knows the system well ("we grew up in here"), *Desiree* voluntarily "schools" recently imprisoned women in the informal norms of prison culture. In a world managed at every level by institutional rules and protocols, life-sentenced women, who tutor each other and their newly sentenced peers in meaningful adaptations, can help those peers live constructive, contributory lives inside. Sentenced at 19 years old as an accessory on a felony murder charge, *Desiree* was the first-time mother of a four-month-old daughter, now 18, when she entered the prison gates. *Desiree's* friend *Simone* characterizes her pre-imprisonment life as a "life that I couldn't even imagine. It amazes me that *Desiree* made it out alive and with brains."

Desiree's plastic, clear-framed glasses reflected the glare of the fluorescent lighting as she discussed coming to adulthood inside prison walls. She was socialized by prison policies and practices and "raised up" by other incarcerated women. With an indomitable will, she learned how to live productively inside the walls. In her self-actualization processes, she was assisted by life-serving women with time down and experiences to share. Those generous women cared for, embraced, and looked after *Desiree* until she was self-aware enough to handle her own "business" in the prison culture. They would tell her "you can do this and not that" and "helped steer [her] in the right direction." Indeed, those life-serving women constituted the village that "raised" *Desiree* after her incarceration. She spoke fondly of them. "*Linda* [*thoughtful pause*], my entire incarceration she has been my grand protector. . . . *Simone* taught me what integrity means. *Ms. Cameron* has always been the exact same person since the day I met her. . . . You pick things up from people that you want to be like when you're in here for a long time. . . . *Annette* helped with everything. She taught me how to do my own hair. I had always went to the hair salon. Taught me what was going on with my body during my menstrual cycle. And how to cook in a microwave. I lived with her for five years. She cooked for me. I bought it, she cooked it. That's how I learned."[9]

Desiree, herself now a "village elder," is in a position to "pay it forward" by using her wisdom and talents to serve others in innovative ways. She empathizes with young women who are learning how to negotiate the mix and who come to her for informal advice, companionship, and an understanding ear. Acknowledging that there are not enough "older" people to go around for all the "young kids" and that the demands on her time and resources are "constant, all day, every day," she nonetheless embraces her role as mentor. "[I keep] about $40 worth of goodies in my room in a bag" and she "rewards" her young mentees for good behavior. "It works for my little ones [*she laughs*], but not all little ones. We have to do something meaningful every day, but it's not easy because there's nothing to do in here at all. . . . They [prison administration] don't offer them anything." Experienced, resourceful women like *Desiree* step into the institutional void and teach newly arrived women the skills that should more correctly be the province of the facility itself: how to cope, how to maintain hygiene, how to choose friends and companions wisely. To those lessons *Desiree* adds listening, caring, and validating, all of which aim to lighten the days of her coterie of "little ones."

Desiree views these mentoring activities as more than simply a means to assist others. Her "little ones" also give her life inside meaning; they help her to survive. Her existential significance is validated by their engagement with her. Her plans, her treats, and her activities all make her relevant and important to these young women. And she is energized by the challenge that her "little ones" pose: "They have boundless energy! We have to find stuff to do . . . and finance it." In the vacuum of institutional inactivity, *Desiree* has "sponsored" creative writing contests where "I'll give out prizes . . . [microwave] cook for them or something." She has also organized book readings, game nights, puzzle competitions, and other entertainment activities in her residential unit so the women can work on "doing something together" instead of giving in to "the drama." Her collective activities are aimed at alleviating monotony and boredom and the predictable slide into drug use. In spite of her best efforts, she notes that "it's very difficult now." When she was mentored, "it was different. . . . We had things to do."

During her life-course interview, *Desiree* excitedly shared the bitter-sweet news that "my niece just got here." The "niece," fictive kin (she is the daughter of *Desiree*'s best friend on the outside), was recently released from closed custody. *Desiree* immediately sought to "school" her in the informal norms of this prison's culture. Recognizing that juveniles inside "need structure and guidance," which she claims the system does not provide, *Desiree* laid out the fundamentals: "Don't get lesbian for the stay." "Don't talk with someone who has been with one of your friends [sexually]." "Don't be a mistress." "Don't invite unnecessary drama upon yourself." "Remember you're not gay. You weren't before you got here and you aren't now." "Do not accept gifts from someone older than you." "Don't borrow, especially from someone you don't know." "Don't talk. You will see lots of stuff in here, but don't talk. . . . When it comes back around it will not be like what you said. If you never say anything, it can't come back to you." In offering these sage bits of advice, *Desiree* aims to inoculate her niece against the often harsh realities of "the drama" in the general population of women. She warns her niece: "You can discuss your feelings with me, but I won't listen to you talk about others." Although she wants to shield her niece from becoming a character in "the drama" of prison culture, *Desiree* also knows that she must step back and respect her niece's life's lessons, simply stating: "She's an adult."

Desiree also appreciates her deep involvement in education, critical thinking, and the fostering of intellectual curiosity among her peers as important dimensions of both paying it forward and developing her own agency. Teaching reading skills, explaining long division, locating capital cities on a map, and developing writing literacy are all activities that she engages in with the GED students that she tutors in her prison job, where she has been present every workday for the past five years. Her tutoring job has been a rare, yet constant, source of profound satisfaction. "I don't work for money. I love to help other people . . . to see the smiles on their faces. . . . I love watching women evolve and mature, becoming more educated. I love my job." The huge smile and the edge-of-her-seat energy that arise as she describes her tutoring experiences reflect a pleasure that is palpable. The delight appears to emanate from multiple sources: her job allows her to infuse her joy of intellectual engagement into her work with students, to contribute something meaningful both to them and to her sense of herself, and it helps to empower them by teaching them necessary literacy skills. Through tutoring, she also shares in their processes of self-actualization.

If, as social work theorist Edward Pecukonis argues, "character is defined not by what a person does, but by the reasons for doing it,"[10] then *Desiree's* character is also consistently, if unconsciously, reflected in her processes of self-actualization, her intellectual complexity, her well-developed internal compass, her empathetic thinking, and her realization of the need for reciprocity and interdependence in relationships.

"Emptying Out and Not Refilling"

Empathy inside is not without consequence. Illustrating the ironic adage "no good deed goes unpunished," empathetic women often pay an emotional price for their caring, generous outreach. Liberal with their time and talents, they sometimes undergo the experience of what *Desiree* describes as "emptying out and not refilling." Other women may not reciprocate *Desiree's* generosity. The women in her friendship network expect her to always be strong, to always be available, and to always be self-sufficient. "No one likes to see me upset because it makes them more tired. . . . [It's] hard to carry everyone's burden. . . . In my culture, [the] strong, black woman is a myth. She's supposed to be the provider; she's not supposed to need help." But sometimes she does. Viewing herself through this mythological framework, *Desiree* recognizes both her limitations and her assets. "I don't wanna say I'm strong. . . . I'm just a woman with strength."

"Most [confidants] just want to dump things on me, but seem to not have time to hear what's going on with me. . . . *Linda* [*Desiree's* 'grand protector'] will not let me cry in front of her. After *Sharon* committed suicide, *Linda* never once asked how I was doing. And I didn't offer it, because the truth is, she didn't wanna hear it." Not one of her friends or "little ones," it seems, noticed *her* suffering. Nevertheless, *Desiree* is an emotional pragmatist. She doesn't expect her friends to offer what they don't have. She's heard their tales of private suffering. She understands without judgment that other women may not have the personal resources to be ready, willing, or able to meet her emotional needs. They have not yet been able to "wrap their arms around the child in them and make it better."

George Herbert Mead, an early interactionist theorist, proposed that empathy is learned through role-taking behaviors.[11] During growth and maturation, individuals acquire abilities to adapt to alternative perspectives by "taking the role of other," that is, by figuratively placing themselves in the situations of people who are in some ways unlike "me." By shifting her focus away from her own reactions, *Desiree* develops empathic reprieves for the emotional limitations of her wounded peers. To a large extent, *Desiree* makes this possible by characterizing herself as "a woman with strength," one who can take care of her own emotional needs. And by keeping her personal demands to a minimum—"I know how to shut *Desiree* off and just do what needs to be done"—she helps to ensure the success of her relationships inside.

Nonetheless, *Desiree* laments the lack of compassionate reciprocity and the toll it takes on her. "Empathy runs deep for me . . . [but] I'm not a junk yard. I can't take everyone else's stuff dumped on me. I am a caregiver by nature. I could go years in others' pain." With too much empathy, *Desiree* risks losing sight of what she needs to take care of herself; with too little empathy, she loses her primary source of hope and relevance inside. Hers is a complex balancing act. She manages the tensions of compassion, in part, because her empathy for others had the unintended consequence of opening a path to self-empathy.[12] As a result, *Desiree* determined "I don't want to die here focused on someone else. I need to learn to work things out for me."

"My Most Intimate Relationship Is with God"

To *Desiree*, an essential source of her empathy and actions in the interests of others is her spirituality. "My most intimate relationship is with God. I pay close attention to my spirit." Maintaining this relationship, she explains, helps "limit the pain" of incarceration, of disappointment, of her own failed dreams and expectations. Listening respectfully to her "spirit" helps her recharge depleted empathy by enabling her to embrace her role as "a child of the greatest God." *Desiree* takes seriously the messages that arise internally and directs them in intentional behavior.[13]

Although profoundly spiritual, *Desiree* accesses God's promises outside the strictures of organized religion. "I don't have a religion. I have a spiritual connection. I pray about his word, not my wishes. . . . Some people pray to God like he's a genie and they are rubbing the lamp. . . . If you do this, I will do this . . . or this will happen." Instead she believes that "his words are promises." In *Desiree*'s view, God understands that his imperfect creations are going to fail. "He knows you will." But he also "tells you to get back up." It is this belief in second chances, in forgiveness and redemption, that *Desiree* also shares with her peers. "None of us are born with a 'how to' guide." People make mistakes. By attending to God instead of people, she avoids the pitfalls of hopelessness, despair, and failed relationships inside, "some sexual, some not." In proof of her faith, *Desiree* is "relinquishing power to the spirit that lives inside of me," believing that, as a human being, "I am powerless."

Conclusion

By presenting *Desiree*'s empathic dilemmas, interpretations, and actions as she discussed experiencing them, I illustrate how the confinement resulting from a life sentence can engender both hope and empathy, as well as the ways that the two are intrinsically related. It is other people who kindle (or deny) hope for life-serving women, and it is other women, living as they do in shared circumstances not of their choosing, who can prompt the development of empathy and forgiveness inside.

Hope and empathy are vital in self-actualization processes behind prison walls. Yet hope in prison is fragile, tenuous, and unstable. Sustaining hope requires continuous, conscious, individual and collective battles fought against the inertia of carceral monotony and boredom and against the crushing losses of "no interest" parole decisions. Ironically perhaps, it is also the case that hope is active, although often shallowly rooted, inside. It is routinely generated in communal activity and foundational to generative relationships.

Life-serving women who develop empathy recognize both human frailties and the adverse effects of the institutional environment on themselves and on others. They try "to do right" but sometimes make errors of judgment, some of which are hurtful. Despite these human imperfections, women like *Desiree* often also realize that the empathy that grounds them in prison is, in part, rooted in their ability to forgive both themselves and others. "To forgive and forget is not possible. You don't forget. But forgiveness is a choice." In making the choice to forgive,

Desiree acknowledges that "forgiveness is not about the other person, it's about you. Most of the time, people have forgotten that they have hurt you. They move on. You are the only one who is still getting hurt." Forgiveness thus becomes a crucial activity in making life imprisonment meaningful.

While empathy is positively associated with forgiveness of others, it is not necessarily so for forgiveness of self.[14] Without it, life-serving women can live in isolation and intense loneliness, where they lose hope and succumb to despair.[15] Perhaps it is forgiveness itself that most directly allows life-serving women to develop and sustain hope; to learn empathy; to create narratives that redefine "criminal," "prisoner," and "felon" identities; and ultimately to communicate in a way that creates cohesive social bonds.

> LL: Do you forgive yourself?
> DESIREE: Yes, but I do have to choose to do that sometimes. I have to make a conscious decision to do that.

7

Correctional Officers or "Us" vs. "Them"

Preserving and Challenging the Binary

Their uniforms make them like Superman. They only have
the power when they put them on. *Ilene Roberts*

We don't want you to be nice. We want you not to be nasty.
Harmony

I actually love some. Some actually care for us. *Sister*

From the perspectives of the life-serving women in this study, correctional
officers are the criminal-processing puppeteers who pull their strings in
the day-to-day, minute-to-minute surveillance and control that is imprisonment. Ironically correctional officers are simultaneously puppets of
the same system of imprisonment. Like the women whose sentences they
enforce, officer "time" is also constrained by physical context, by department and facility policies and protocols, as well as by the additional rigid
proscriptions of in-group institutional behavior expected in their correctional roles. For better or worse, officers and imprisoned women share
conditions of confinement in a mutually interdependent relationship of
domination and subordination through which each group receives legiti-
mation from the other. "Correctional officer" has no meaning without the
incarcerated persons who define them, and "incarcerated women" has no
meaning without the keepers who enforce their imprisonment.

The paths to self-actualization taken by women serving life sentences
occur in constant interaction with the officers who "do time" with them.[1]
The consequences for both keepers and the kept are at best unpredictable and at worst dangerous. This chapter examines the degrees to which
daily compulsory interactions with officers shape the lives of life-serving
women, as well as the ways that the women resist, negotiate, and often

resignedly acquiesce to the conditions that influence these complex relationships. In the focus groups, life-course interviews, and solicited diaries that form the data of this study, women reported positive, negative, and ambivalent exchanges in their interactions with officers. These ongoing and unavoidable interactions are charged with complexities and complications that reflect and challenge, affirmatively and adversely, the institutionally defined positions of "prisoner" and "officer."

"Us" vs. "Them": Context

The interdependency resulting from the legal positioning of officers and life-serving women drives construction of mutually exclusive categories of "other," where "other" is perceived as fundamentally and essentially not like "us." There is a robust literature on the "less than human" or "scum of the earth" correctional officer views of female offenders that is supported by former Michigan warden Tekla Miller's claim that female prisoners "were considered the 'dreaded beasts' of corrections with whom no one wanted to work."[2] Although officers in women's facilities are rarely seriously hurt by the women under their supervision, the conviction that women can and will make officers' lives difficult continues to thrive. Officer perceptions of imprisoned women as demanding and tiresome and as needing more emotional guidance and support than their male counterparts are widespread in the literature.[3] Criminologist Joycelyn Pollock reports, for example, that "officers complain that female inmates argue and refuse orders and that they are verbally abusive and expressive in their frustration and anger."[4] In short, officers characterize incarcerated women as childlike and immature. Like their male colleagues, female correctional officers share the general dislike and disdain for female offenders and are fully capable of using their positions to unnecessarily taunt and humiliate the women under their control.[5] U.K. criminologist Mary Bosworth also contends that female officers may treat women in prison more punitively than their male colleagues do.[6] Female officers are often judgmental about the women's lifestyles, especially as they have affected children, and these issues may serve to separate rather than draw the two groups together.[7]

In a system designed as oppositional and antagonistic, the women report rigid boundaries between "black and grays" (a name for officers based on their uniform colors) and themselves. In carceral interactions, "us" and 'them" categories abound and characterize the perspectives of the two groups. "Us" sometimes refers to officers and sometimes to incarcerated women—the categories shift with the social locations of the interacting parties. When life-serving women talk about "us," they are referencing a loose collective of other time-serving women. When they use "them," the pronoun consistently refers to the officers who control their world. Study participants recognize, however, that their "us" is a limited, particularistic perspective. The power to define the categories in the binary belongs to officers as state-sanctioned authorities. The women acknowledge the officers' characterizations of incarcerated women as "them," identified as such by the officers' sobriquet "trifling bitches" (*Alexandria*). The women also recognize the attributions of themselves as blameworthy "others" in the community of respectable citizenry who are represented in the prison world by the officers.

The "us" and "them" binary may appear static and "natural," but it is not. Using differential resources, officers and imprisoned women actively engage in constructing these mutually exclusive categories. The officers, for example, learn to "other" their charges in numerous ways. Recruit instruction is the beginning of the process of constructing the imprisoned female as "not like us." The one-size-fits-all generic training of officers for dangerous male prisoners may also include informal gender stereotyping of incarcerated women as "selfish, exhausting, needing immediate gratification, having no social conscience, lacking social skills, and being constant complainers."[8] In Michigan, officer recruit training is required by statute (Public Act 415) and department policy and, according to the Michigan Department of Corrections (MDOC) website, is delivered in two phases. "Phase 1 is 320 hours of training delivered by the Office of New Employee Training and Professional Development Officer Recruit Training Unit. Phase 2 immediately follows Phase 1 and is a 2 month period of On-The-Job-Training" colloquially known as a "red tag" apprenticeship because the apprentice officer wears a red name tag.[9] Although the department claims to offer "specific training" for "facilities with female offenders," the training curriculum makes no mention of women, gender, females, or facilities with female offenders. It does however allocate 8 hours to graduation activities and 12 hours to misconduct reporting.

The physical environment is an additional obvious mechanism in constructing "us" and "them" boundaries. The 12-foot chain-link fence, topped by razor ribbon and concertina wire, that surrounds the perimeter of the facility confines officers and offenders and is a reminder to both about who remains and who leaves after an eight-hour shift. Another aspect of the "us" and "them" physical environment is the overt distinction represented by the uniforms that segregate the two populations. Officers don formal black and gray uniforms with their names printed over the right breast pockets; imprisoned "others" wear blue and orange uniforms designed for men. Incarcerated women are not accorded the individual status reflected by a name, or the fit required by female bodies; instead their prison numbers are stenciled across the broad shoulders of the shirts and down the sides of pant legs sized for men. The uniform distinctions vividly illustrate the taxonomy that marks the two groups as conspicuously different populations, confer or withhold authority, and epitomize the embodied gap between "us" and "them."

Uniforms also paradoxically confer immediate solidarity in both groups, erasing any ambiguity of purpose. *Ilene Roberts's* comments on officer apparel in the introduction to this chapter demonstrate the demarcations: "Their uniforms make them like Superman. They only have the power when they put them on." She speaks, of course, to the assumption of institutional roles and attendant power represented by the uniforms, a power vested in otherwise working-class men and women, hourly workers who may themselves be disempowered in broader societal contexts.[10]

Officers may be the enforcers, but, as puppets of the same institutional system, they are not the correctional personnel with authority to determine the specific nature of the intense surveillance that imposes "us" and "them" boundaries.[11] It is wardens and their administrations who are the active creators of correctional environments. They determine the rules on-site for both officers and their incarcerated charges. According to Tekla Miller, prisoner rules are unique to each prison. They concern everything from the number of women allowed to use the restroom at any given time to when a cell door window could be covered.[12] The rules are particularized to individual prisons for issues that cannot be effectively addressed in statewide policies.[13]

"I Came Undone": The Chair

In this prison, for several years and at the time of this study, women were subjected to what many might term institutional sexual abuse under the correctional rubric "security concerns." It is routine practice in prisons for incarcerated men and women returning from visits with family or friends to be searched for contraband. The search is inclusive of body orifices and generally involves bending and spreading of the buttocks. It is not a gender-specific practice, but it is humiliating. At this facility the generic search practice was altered in an unmistakably gendered manner. Women returning from visits were reportedly required to sit naked in "the chair," pull their knees up to their chests, and spread their genitalia for officer inspection. Women claim that the search area was unsanitary and that other women were sometimes present during the procedure. A woman's menstrual bleeding was not sufficient justification for avoiding the chair. *Ilene Roberts* comments that "even on your menstrual period, there's plastic you can put down and bleach in case you cough and something comes out."

This institutional violation of bodily integrity was both site and gender specific. The chair was not used in any other facility in the state. Its use in the women's facility implicates the state in the routinization of specific, sexualized, gender strategies for "us" and "them" boundary enforcement by creating the conditions that make women vulnerable to trauma or to retraumatization. The idiosyncratic practice, specific to incarcerated females—if enacted outside prison walls—would be labeled a crime of sexual assault because it occurred against the inclinations of the women, was uninvited, made the women vulnerable to potential officer misconduct, and was reported as a source of degradation and retraumatization in every focus group where it was discussed. *Yasmeen* captures the essence of many like-minded responses when she says that women are searched "not as a woman, but as an object."

The first time *Destiny* was subjected to the chair search protocol, "I came undone." The officer directed her to "hold my lips [labia]." She refused: "No. You do it. This is not self-service." Other women, like *Louise*, refused visits. "I told my family not to come anymore. I have been raped too many times that [the chair] was horrific for me." Another imprisoned woman, quoted in the *Detroit Free Press*, stated: "I feel as though I am being raped every time I have a visit [from family] and this is done to me."[14]

Resistance to the chair made *Lauryn* a heroine to other women, but it resulted in sanctions that included 12 days in segregation and loss of her prison job. *Lauryn* took a principled position. Her resistance was simple. She was willing to go through the embarrassing "spread your cheeks" search, but she refused the direct order to "spread your labia." Other women seeking removal of the chair "kited" (sent notes of complaint to deputy wardens), attempting to utilize the prison grievance procedure for relief, or they wrote to state legislators, all to no avail. *Jane* tried explaining to prison authorities, who appeared to her insensitive, the potential damaging consequences of the procedure: "I feel like you're prostituting me for the officers' sexual satisfaction." The "us" and "them" boundaries established in this distinctly gendered protocol are clearly drawn.[15]

"We're Just Property to Them": Structurally Induced Inequality

It would be naive to assume that women do not attempt to subvert the system. Of course, they do. So it is an organizational standard for officers to be suspicious of the women they monitor. Treating imprisoned women as "other" protects the officers from games, cons, setups, and manipulations.[16] Self-protection thus becomes normative and systemically entrenched. It justifies the officer "us" who treats the imprisoned "them" in segregating, exclusionary, and demeaning ways.[17] According to Christine Rasche, a founding member of the American Society of Criminology's Division on Women and Crime, this structurally induced inequality in the prison world breeds "periodic contempt for some inmates and a desire to harm others in even the best staff."[18] Opinions of officers coalesce and rigidify and the women they surveil perceive them as indifferent and insensitive. *Martha* summarizes the ordinariness of the experiences of being part of the subordinate, out group: "They don't care about us. Our quality of life doesn't matter to them. We're just property to them."

In her autobiographical memoir of her career in corrections, Miller notes that staff empathy with prisoners is potentially dangerous to employees and threatens control of the prison.[19] She cautions against officer violations of the institutional in-group solidarity that develops from "us" and "them" categorization. She reiterates an institutional prohibition, by law and policy, which forbids relationships between correctional officers and the women they guard. Reduced social distance and emotional attachments blur the lines of authority between the keepers and the kept,[20] a consideration theorized by sociologist Erving Goffman[21] and recognized by *Merrilee,* who asks rhetorically, "Where do you think we come from? We're your sisters and your neighbors." Officers who empathize with their charges are characterized by their peers as "security risks," an interaction noted by *Alexandria,* who asserts that when some officers side with women inside they "catch grief" from their colleagues.

While in-group and out-group dynamics generate solidarity among "us," they simultaneously engender animosity and contempt for members of the out group. Because the need for in-group solidarity is particularly strong under conditions perceived as dangerous, out-group hostility becomes increasingly intense.[22] *Jane* recounted an oft-reported act of emotional violence directed toward her as a member of the imprisoned out group: "I've had an officer call me 'bitch,' 'whore,' and ask if I have Alzheimer's because I don't listen [to her]." Even the most obedient and seemingly genial women reported emotional and verbal assaults by officers, a finding supported by sociologist Juanita Diaz-Cotto's work with Latina prisoners.[23]

Officers' use of profane language and denigrating labels to address the women under their supervision erodes institutional opportunities for successful "correctional" processes while simultaneously catalyzing women's antipathy. Women, like *Jane,* are revictimized by the demeaning and sexually abusive language used by some correctional officers, language that is in clear violation of the women's human rights to dignity and worth as well as a breach of correctional standards for behavior.

These language ruptures foster an institutional climate in which life-serving women and correctional officers become actively invested in interacting with one another in hostile caricatures rather than as complex human beings. *Pamela* relates the environmental consequences of this linguistic erosion of civility when she says, "She [an officer] talked to me like I was some goose shit on the bottom of her shoe." When the "offending" officer's young son subsequently died in a tragic boating accident, *Pamela* could not summon either sympathy or empathy for the mother's loss: "You're so fucking evil that I don't care." Dehumanization is one of the few equal opportunity responses in prison, that is, as long as imprisoned women do not act on it. *Pamela* could not voice her antipathy without anticipating severe sanctions. She could only think it and verbalize it to her peers away from the ears of the officers.

Animosities like these are complicated by the interdependency that is also foundational to the "us" vs. "them" dichotomy. Mutual dependency forms the context and constraints in interactions that are situationally and organizationally circumscribed. As "*the employees* who are front and center in the correctional system," correctional officers serve as "the keepers of the disappeared."[24] They are the day-to-day adjudicators of the environment as disciplinarians, administrators, managers, facilitators, or mentors. They have direct responsibility for the core features of imprisoned women's daily lives (e.g., what to wear, when to eat, how to work, where to work, who can visit, how often visitors can visit, when to write, when to talk and often what to say), as well as the surveillance and regulation of sexual intimacy. They are also the women's first link to outside communications like phone privileges, visits, and contacts. Consequently, as *Alexandria* suggests, the attitudes of the correctional officers are a major determinant of the prison experience and they "set the tone for the [residential] unit."

In the particularities of this correctional facility, the "us" and "them" constructions of "other" are amplified by the prison's history. In 2009 the Department of Corrections spent four days moving 800 women in belly chains and leg irons to their current location, the only remaining facility for women in the state. The newly repurposed facility, which went from being an institution for mentally challenged and dangerous men to a comprehensive facility for women, employed three cohorts of officers: those who remained in the facility through its repurposing, those reassigned from former women's facilities, and new officers. The latent adversarial relationships reportedly became outright hostile during this process of administrative integration. *Elizabeth Ashley* and *Alexandria*, for example, both argued that officers "come in with attitudes" and "take it out on us" in forms that *Ilene Roberts* enumerated: "They'll do a shakedown [toss the cell looking for contraband], send you to seg [solitary confinement], write you up for the contraband *they brought you*" (Ilene's emphasis) and she claims no gender privilege, that is, "female and male guards both do it."

Writing a woman up, or issuing a ticket for a major rule violation, has long-term consequences for women in that it restricts their good conduct opportunities for parole or resentencing. One of the factors considered by the parole board in making release decisions includes prison behavior as assessed by the frequency and nature of misconduct tickets.[25] Contraband tickets, especially for drugs, may be interpreted as demonstrating a willful violation of prison policies and a risk for re-offending behavior. The power to "hand out bogus tickets," as *Tootsie Roll* notes, belongs to the officers, but the consequences belong to the women. Life-serving women, who have no opportunities for freedom, are sometimes sanguine about the reported lack of professionalism among some officers. *Wink,* for example, says, "I have a mandatory life sentence. So give me the ticket to add to my tail, what does it matter at this point?" Without the hope of changed circumstances, sanctioning tickets lose their effectiveness in enforcing compliance.

Writing a woman up for having "contraband" that the officer provided, however, is more than just unprofessional behavior. It is a reflection of asymmetrical power in the interdependency that acts as both a looping mechanism for control as well as a source of deep resentment. Officer hypocrisy is central to the antipathy that *Kari*, and others, fume about: "They have the nerve to act superior when they're bringing in drugs and cigarettes!" It is the life-serving women who have been defined as the lawbreakers, but it is the officers who reflect a lack of respect for the law and who, consequently, undermine the legitimacy of the system that they serve. Blatant officer abuse of discretionary power intensifies the women's anger and bitterness as they are constantly vulnerable to its looping effects. Officers know who has contraband because they allegedly provided it. Therefore, they can control the women through threats of searches. If the woman reports the officer, she is reporting her own contraband use to the same in group that is supplying her and subjecting her to threats. By reporting she makes herself vulnerable to retaliation.[26] As described earlier, retaliation can take many forms but collectively *Sasha Lavan* says retaliation would be "anything that hinders you." *Dennis the Menace* shares an explicit retaliatory story: "Last night, an officer got mad at an inmate and shook everyone's room down and took some stuff, hobby crafts, and something special someone made." The officer applied group punishment for individual behavior and in the process "took" what little pleasures the women had created. It was, in the women's estimation, a routine "petty power trip." The women's allegations of officer misconduct become the word of convicted felons against officers with substantial authority, and the oft-reported outcome is institutional support for the "us" vs. "them" characterizations that benefit the officers.

Although safety and protection are their due as human beings under the care of the Department of Corrections, all of the women in this study told stories, sometimes very detailed, of correctional officer "others" whose behavior ranged from neglect to unprofessional at best and gratuitously cruel at worst. Most women spoke of harsh interactions with officers. Their commentaries about "them" are summarized in these succinct synopses:

"You can't trust officers, no matter how nice." (*Liberty Flynn*)
"They all lie. I don't think I've met an officer here that don't lie." (*Lois*)
"We never know what we're gonna face [in interactions with officers]." (*Jane*)
"Officers here are uneducated and ignorant." (*Destiny*)
"I do not trust officers. I fear them." (*Yasmeen*)

Lynn provides the summative word on mutual "othering" as she presents both her peers' assessments and their understandings of the evaluations of the officers about them: "You've got these officers, they talk to you any kind of way. They think we're all crackheads and hoes." The absolute authority of correctional personnel keeps the women constantly vulnerable to the threat of danger. They must be ready to meet it.

The "us" and "them" dichotomy is so strong for these women that they do not discuss officers with reference to either their genders or their races, two primary categories of oppression and privilege in the free world, or to other identifying personal characteristics. Rather "POlice" or "gray and black" or "guards" are presented as homogenous and monolithic in the women's focus-group conversations and interview narratives. Correctional officer master status trumps race, gender, and physical attributes. In the rare cases where the women identify officers by gender, ill will seems more directed toward the female officers, but it is also ironically the case that some female officers are beloved by the women. Gender emerges only when the women in the study use pronouns to tell a particular story and, therefore, signal gender as "she" indicates female. Race emerges only in my targeted questioning about the potential influence of race on interactions inside. The women's narrative positioning may be an artifact of the data collection methodologies in that the women know which officers they're talking about, so race and gender are obvious to them and not in need of identifying comments. It may also be the case that, at the time of the study, 342 of the 439 officers at the facility were female, so the women assumed that female correctional officer was an unmarked status, that is, it was their default category.[27]

The relations of "other" between officers and life-serving women may be adversarial in nature but they are not entirely fixed.[28] "Us" and "them" does not constitute the only set of perspectives and interactions between the officers and the life-serving women they control. The dichotomy creates a false binary that results in pervasive constructions of officers as law-abiding and incarcerated women as lawless. The institution thus presents itself and its officers as having total power and control over the women in their charge, and the appearance of institutional power is reified.[29] Yet it would be imprudent and shortsighted to assume that the "us" category of officers wields total power with impunity. The binary draws attention away from the small-scale negotiations that characterize daily prison life and that disguise women's roles in configuring power inside the walls.[30] The women are not entirely powerless in their interactions with officers. Cooperation and negotiation also characterize those relations.[31]

Women with years down, for example, will informally and subtly guide newly assigned officers, by providing information and assistance on the policies and procedures they know well and by evoking particular skills and/or interactional behaviors that can make life easier for the women. *Love Evans*, for example, believes it is in the best interest of the women to keep officers informed. "We train them [the officers]" by providing information and assistance. Such training can be positive in that training in particular skills and interactional behaviors may lessen the effect of assumed protocols. *Anna Bell* notes, "We know the rules;

we don't need you comin' in tellin' us what to do and when to do it. The unit will run itself. We know the rules. We know when it's lockup time." But informal training can also morph into snitching and informing. Telling on others offers access to camaraderie with officers but violates the women's informal in-group expectations of behavior. "Training" officers, like all other activity in prison, depends on who is interpreting the behavior.[32]

Relations between life-serving women and officers are obviously more complex than simple antipathy and hatred. Some women paradoxically declare that they "love" a particular officer "with all my heart." These women provided information and judgments of kindnesses and compassion from officers that directly counter the binary, as reflected in these statements:

"She's like a second mother to me." (*Tootsie Roll*)
"You do have officers that actually do their job and protect us." (*Harmony*)
"The officer I thought who would be the worst helped the most." (*Alison*)

The life-serving women in this study challenged dichotomous representations of power and control as resting entirely with officers. *Pamela*, for example, developed two strategic interactions to "let me breathe," that is, to interrupt the oppression of institutional power wielded by corrections officers. The first was to establish her expertise on MDOC policies, which she then quotes to the "offending" officer. She says, "I act like I'm powerful and strong. I'm right and you're wrong." Knowing the formal policies and procedures is a survival tactic, a protective mechanism, used to confront unprofessional behavior. Implicit in the strategy is an insistence on order and consistency. It is a direct challenge to an officer's authority, but it is embedded within the protocols and policies of the department responsible for the women's conditions of incarceration. She simultaneously challenges the legitimacy of their authority as she expresses hostility in unimpeachable legalist terms.[33]

Women can, and do, use policies to challenge correctional officers about the ways that they are doing their jobs. However, whenever they succeed in curbing officer abuse of power and creating breathing space, they frequently also incur resentment and retaliation. Breathing space does not equate with safe space. So *Pamela's* second tactic is to threaten to tell the deputy warden about the officer's offenses. Because "no one wants the deputy in their business," she wields this threat effectively. *Pamela's* strategizing reflects the ability of some of the women to take advantage of the hierarchical divisions between administration and officers. Correctional officers themselves are under administrative surveillance, and women use that knowledge to push back against unprofessional officer behavior. *Pamela* is not alone in her resistance strategies. *Shequetta Tasha Lynn's* resistance, for example, is bureaucratic. Claiming "We both have pens. You write it, I'll fight it," she creates a stream of paper challenges and appeals that demand repeated attention from the ticketing officer and her supervisors. *Lauryn* engages in "psychological warfare" with officers in ways that allow her to feel some small measure of agency in a hyper-controlled environment. In her pre-incarceration life, physical fighting was her "defense mechanism"; now she "takes power" by rebelling against the system, "like with the chair." *Lauryn* refused to comply with a direct order to "spread her lips" so she was punished by being sent to segregation. Rebellions, "like with the chair," are how *Lauryn* maintains "control of my life in some small way. I take whatever [control] I can get" even through the refusal to comply with a direct order. The ability to make choices, even choices that offer only the illusion of control, counters institutional dependency and fosters autonomy.[34]

No one in the study reported an assault on officers as a form of resistance, nor was there any disposition to physically harm officers. This does not represent a denunciation of violence, for women also discuss "settling disputes in the shower" and away from officer surveillance; rather, it represents antipathy toward the oppression, but ambivalence toward the oppressors. Within the boundaries that are dictated by the practicalities of daily life (e.g., counts, chow, work, callouts, visits, med lines, and so on), the relations of power are constantly negotiated.[35] This to-ing and fro-ing is what criminologist Jim Thomas identifies as a "dance of power and control."[36]

Most women in this study report trying, like *Alexandria*, to "not even mess" with officers in attempts to reduce the chances of conflict and sanctions, noting that, "at the end of the day, they're still wearing black and gray." The women report with certainty that the bifurcation between "us" and "them" means "they [officers] will turn on you." Most of the women support the contention that even responsive officers maintain allegiance to the system and to one another, not to the women or justice or fairness.

In the remainder of this chapter, I discuss the subjective assessments of correctional officers offered by the life-serving women in this study. I present the women's stories and accounts of interactions, positive and negative, with officers, as they were related in focus groups, interviews, and journal entries. I do not know if all officers behave unprofessionally, or if some do, or if all the narratives refer to a single officer. However, when the repeated messaging in the focus groups supported the women's narratives, I present and analyze their claims. Several women reported affirmative interactions with officers, as well as a genuine constructive regard for others. The women spoke highly of some very professional correctional officers who conducted themselves knowledgeably and efficiently and who thereby gained the respect and cooperation of the women in their charge. Women spoke disparagingly about those who failed miserably.[37] Some also acknowledged the women's complicity in the creation of a hostile prison environment. As *Kari* notes, some people "dog out the nice officers and turn them into bitches" by playing them and making their jobs difficult and aggravating.

"I Fear Them": "Bad" Officers

Within institutional constraints, there are few ways to be recognized by life-serving women as "good" officers and seemingly unlimited ways to be acknowledged as "bad" officers. Research provides what criminologist Joycelyn Pollock calls a "steady stream" of allegations, investigations, indictments, and convictions of multiple forms of exploitation of women by correctional officers.[38] This study is no exception, as *Monaye* acknowledges: "There are so many ways that the officers [here] are unethical." The women's narratives about their adversarial treatment by officers also demonstrate their own impressive resistance strategies in dealing with patterns of incivility often characterized by petty power displays, inconsistent behavior, and participation in the mix. Similar to the strategies detailed in historian Eugene Genovese's collection of slave narratives, these life-serving women's tactics are defensive and individual, utilized as protection from aggression and abuse, but not as weapons of social change.[39]

Life-serving women reported any number of incivilities perpetrated by officers, ranging from ignoring them, not making eye contact when speaking to them, publicly vilifying and humiliating them, calling them names, refusing to make or accept explanations, creating false wait times, refusing permissions for routine requests, mocking them, enforcing rules in an idiosyncratic manner, to compelling deference from the women, which all reinforce the asymmetrical power relations that define their mutually exclusive positions.[40] Incarcerated women are vulnerable to disrespect from officers at all times due to their stigmatized positions.[41] The incivilities perpetrated by officers are rituals that remind women of their "them" status as criminals and the officers' "us" status as upright citizens deserving of respect and attention. An anecdote from *Alexandria* illustrates the women's vulnerability. "The officer said to me, 'Girl, go to your room.' I said, 'Girl?' She said, 'Bitch, go to your room.'" She "hit me with the door" and "wrote me up for threatening behavior. I fought it and got the ticket dropped. Another officer backed me up on everything, except the door. I told them to check the tapes, but, of course, 'the camera wasn't working.'" Uncharacteristically, *Alexandria* was successful in her challenge to the threatening behavior charge because she had the support of another officer in her claim of innocence. The camera coverage designed to provide both protection and clarity in disputed accounts between officers and the women inside "wasn't working" during this exchange. Women reported nonfunctional camera operations as an oft-repeated condition when they made claims of officer misconduct. *Love Evans*, for example, asked for a camera tape "to be pulled" to document the veracity of a claim she made about an officer's behavior. She reported being told "it depreciates the value of the camera to help inmates."

The petty level of incivilities that beset incarcerated women is best illustrated through issues regarding toilet paper, the commonplace central hygiene product in all developed societies. In the carceral environment, toilet paper is a multipurpose product in the arsenal of women's ingenuity. T.P. is used in its conventional function, as well as a substitute for Kleenex-type tissues, and as additional absorption for menstrual flow. More creatively, it is used wetted, dried, and reformed as hair rollers, dildoes, game pieces, and dice.

Access to most basic needs, like toilet paper and sanitary napkins, is allotted to women on a weekly basis regardless of frequency of cycle or rate of bleeding.[42] If the women run out of toilet paper, they must request, individually, additional rolls from the officer who is their resident unit manager. The request infantilizes women and, with permission affirmed or denied, is an exercise in forced deference. *Glenda Gale*, a woman in her late 50s with 15 years down, asked an officer for toilet paper and the officer responded with "what for?" *Glenda Gale's* "really?" response demonstrated the absurdity of asking a grown woman for a rationale to use toilet paper. Toilet paper is not a right in prison. Its materiality becomes a privilege bestowed, or not, by an officer doing her job. *Lynn* notes that there are some officers who "I won't even ask for toilet tissue." The verbal exchanges are so onerous and hostile that, rather than entertain the incivility, she will go without a basic necessity of good hygiene.

Courtesy in the request for toilet paper is reportedly another occasion for officer discourtesy and ridicule. Wearing a mask of compliancy in the necessary deferential pretenses required of imprisoned women seeking assistance from officers, *Merrilee* uses formal courtesy as a weapon of defense. She politely asks "May I please have a roll of tissue?" when what she says she really wants to say is "Bitch. Gimme the tissue." She cannot show disrespect, but she can maintain antipathy. She reports that the officers make fun of her and "call me a little girl" for her use of correct grammar and her respectful manner. *Destiny* relates an almost identical exchange. She also uses the modal verb "may" when asking for additional toilet paper. The officer asked *Destiny* to "simplify" her speech and use "can" rather than "may." *Destiny* responded: "I have the ability to have a roll of toilet paper, but I'm asking permission to do so." The officer refused to respond, blatantly ignoring *Destiny's* request. In a passive, but powerfully emotive, battle of wills, *Destiny* remained standing in front of the officer's desk. "I've got nothing but time." She refused to ask another officer for toilet paper. "You created this, not me." The deference that the officer assumed as a right was also effectively refused when it challenged *Destiny's* rhetorical competency. *Destiny's* resistance contested the detachment that elevated the officer to a position of power. These small victories are not so small psychologically. They give women some measure of agency in oppressive conditions.[43] *Destiny's* self-confidence and agency destabilized the status quo. Hers was a subtle way of rebelling against perceived violations of authority. Resistance, like power in prison, is everywhere, albeit on a small scale and often subtle.[44]

"Petty power" displays, described as opportunities to "squeeze" or humiliate women unnecessarily, can also occur around toileting issues. "Urine drops," requiring imprisoned women to provide a fresh urine sample for drug analysis, are commonplace institutional security practices. Intended to prevent women from using or smuggling drugs inside their body cavities, officer demands for "drops" are randomized. *Chelsie Marie* registers her outrage over one such drop: "This lady [correctional officer] made me get butt naked and straddle the toilet! Made me get butt naked!" then said "so I can see it." Repetition of "made me get butt naked" was *Chelsie Marie's* explosive exposition of outrage over the humiliation inherent in the demand. A fellow focus-group participant, *Lucy Spencer*, asked the obvious question: "Why do you have to take your bra off to urinate?"

Compulsory nakedness is unnecessary for a "urine drop." Other methods conventionally utilized could accomplish the same goal (e.g., inspecting the stall prior to the drop, conducting a body patdown prior to the drop, or remaining outside the stall door during the drop). Forced nakedness in the performance of what is conventionally accepted as a private, physical waste-elimination process is experienced by the women as a "petty power" exercise in humiliation, exposure, and vulnerability. It is a visceral reminder that the women are "them" and they are powerless, even over their own body integrity, and that officers are omnipotent and institutionally supported in these circumscriptions of their daily lives.[45] As imprisoned women, they have no protection from the security whims of their legally mandated protectors. Women infer malice in these exchanges and characterize them as "us" vs. "them" "petty power" displays.

Participants in this study agreed that consistency in behavior and stability in the enforcement of rules and policies were, after respect for basic human dignity, the most important qualities in a "good" officer. Women do not complain about sanctions consistently delivered. They do complain stridently about arbitrary and inconsistent sanctions. Life imprisonment is difficult enough without the added daily insecurity of unpredictability.

For life-serving women, officer inconsistencies are akin to being trapped in a hall of mirrors. They distort people, relationships, and definitions. No one is immune. Distrust permeates interactions between officers and imprisoned women. Prison's coercive potential is "always coiled in the background" and, with inconsistent behavior and capricious rule enforcement, life-serving women cannot predict when it will be activated.[46] Consequently every officer's behavior is loaded with meaning and is often perceived as a threat or test because, as *Anna Bell* claims, "They change the rules in the middle of talking to you." When behavior that is required of the women is unclear and the requirements for them appear ambiguous and unattainable, life-serving women report anxiety resulting from a state of constant vulnerability and the fear of getting something wrong and, therefore, of being sanctioned.[47] Because the power to initiate and define interactions belongs to the correctional officers, life-serving women always run the risk of violating a rule or protocol that is unfamiliar to them, for, as *Ilene Roberts* notes, "just as soon as you think you know something, it changes."

Sandy details the tension inherent in this vulnerability with regard to the only relatively fixed, stable material items of her life inside. Her bed, her locker, and her footlocker are the "tool kit" of her prison identity.[48] Yet any officer at any time can enter her room and rifle through, touch, search, handle, discard, and break her possessions for the stated reasons of looking for contraband or simply enforcing a general claim of "security." About this helplessness, she says, "Your space is always vulnerable. Everything you are is in that space. Everything you own is in that space. You are defined by that space." But in prison, no space is private and none is inviolate.

As criminologists Mike Vuolo and Candace Kruttschnitt note, "Prison staff have the ability to improve the lives of their charges or to further damage them."[49] Officer consistency in attitude and job performance enables time to pass more foreseeably for the women. Inconsistency, on the other hand, destabilizes the women's daily routines and leaves them feeling vulnerable to officer caprice as almost anything can be a violation if the officer frames it that way.[50] *Ilene Roberts* claims that "all it takes is an officer to be in a bad mood." If women are lost in their own worlds daydreaming, or maybe thinking deeply about a loved one who died, officers can and do give "tickets" for "walking slow" or "loitering." As previously noted, these infraction "tickets" have adverse effects on opportunities for probation or parole and reflect the pervasive reach of institutional power. Any response from the women that is agentic and autonomous, rather than deferential and quiescent, is likely to result in punishment. *Martha* cautions, "You really have to choose your battles."

Rather than being random occurrences, such inconsistency characterizes the routine monotony in the lives of life-serving women. A fiction of prison is its representation as a uniformly consistent, one-size-fits-all, rational institution. For the life-incarcerated women in this study, prison living is more often reported as erratic, even chaotic. *Ilene Roberts* argues, for example, that "policies are just a preconceived notion of structure. Every day is a different day, different rules, different officers." Administrative policies are written, reported, and available. They stipulate exactly what an imprisoned woman can and cannot do in her daily routines, as well as the consequences for violations.[51] However, all the women in the study report idiosyncratic enforcement of the rules such that a rule is sometimes a rule and sometimes not, sometimes enforced and sometimes not. *Dennis the Menace*, who was at one point "$600 in the hole" for drug debts incurred inside the prison, makes the case for inconsistent enforcement. She claims, "The officers knew I was high, oh yeah, they ignored it. I was bad." She rises in the focus group and demonstrates how she would stumble around while she was high. "Oh yeah, I was bad." Her "bad" behavior was ignored. She was not cited for drug violations, or referred for substance abuse treatment. The care, custody, and control of women is an assumed responsibility of the staff.[52] Yet officers, legally mandated to protect her, reportedly ignored her behavior while citing others for "not having your shirt tucked in" (*Elizabeth Ashley*).

Criminologists Shanhe Jiang and Marianne Fisher-Giorlando argue that the ambiguity in institutional rules implies that no correctional officer enforces all the rules all the time or even enforces all the rules equally.[53] Which rules are applied and to whom depends on officer discretion. *Martha* supports this research conclusion, noting that officers "do what they like, or don't like." One officer reportedly told her, " 'They pay me to run inmates. They don't pay inmates to run me!' " Differences in age, education, and race between officers and life-serving women can, and reportedly do, exert influence on officers' judgments.[54] The women's only protection against officer caprice is *Martha's* strategy. "You've gotta have it in writing."

In the institutional surety of the system, incarcerated women are not trustworthy, having established themselves as rule breakers through their crimes. The external definitions of them, reified in their life sentences, trump all potential other definitions and are the context for all interactions inside. Officers define them by their crimes. *Sheri* narrates a very real consequence of this "us" and "them" positioning: "They [officers] don't pay attention. [Named woman] woke up having an episode [mental health breakdown] and they see it, but they waited for her to do something to herself" before calling for mental health assistance. The us vs. them bifurcation is so strong and the normative "in-group" belief that imprisoned women are always trying to con the system is so robust that officers do not trust the women, even in life-threatening situations. The event must be clearly unambiguous, as when a woman does visible, physical harm to herself during a mental health episode, before the officers will act on her behalf. At such an extreme, criminologist Hans Toch noted that "malevolent neglect by staff or peers can place an inmate's physical existence at risk."[55]

The routines of inconsistency result in physical and emotional vulnerability, a constant, enervating state for life-serving women. *Doll* notes, for example, that "an officer switching up on me makes time hard." Unable to resist head-on, they must accept what can't be avoided. After more than a decade of imprisonment, *Glenda Gale* has reconciled herself to the inevitability of the stress of helplessness. It's unavoidable. Inconsistency is routine prison protocol: "The house rules change day to day. So we're never sure of what's what." *Scarlet* attributes the inconsistency to officer intentionality: "They keep you in constant limbo all the time." Vulnerability, like other susceptibilities of imprisoned women, is used as a social control mechanism to keep them destabilized and conforming. There is no period of relaxation for imprisoned women. They must maintain constant vigilance or fall prey to any officer's "bad attitude."

As a consequence, the contacts between officers and life-serving women are so dichotomized that the only two interactions reportedly experienced by many study respondents are named by *Monaye*, that is, "some officers just ignore us. But that's still better than them harassing us."

According to organizational theorist Sarah Tracy, officers engage in the mix as a means of interrupting the routine boredom of their jobs.[56] They often do so as voyeurs characterizing the women's behavior as entertainment, relishing and encouraging the bizarre, and creating opportunities to reify the women as "other" and themselves as "normal." Real and apocryphal stories about incarcerated women that are strange or deviant relieve the tedium of the job and reassure the officers of their own normality and status.[57] *Glenda Gale* agrees; she maintains that officers create the volatility because "it's like entertainment to them." Yet the boundaries between "us" and "them" are not altogether distinct when officers participate in the mix. Officers often come from the same communities, know people in common, and frequently have the same behavior patterns as the women they are guarding.[58] Consequently, as *Baby* notes, "They make a point of being in everybody's business, knowing who's with who and spreading it around."

Gossip is ubiquitous in the mix. With the lack of privacy, there are few opportunities to hide or disguise behavior or personally discrediting information that might, under other circumstances, only be shared with close friends if at all. When officers engage in, or participate in, generating the gossip that is pervasive, they create a general environment in which officers, staff, and other women are perceived, as *David* claims, as "trying to make a mess of my day." Intentionally or unintentionally, in a closed environment, officer behavior has ripples and *David* experiences these ripples as individual, eroding assaults. She cannot remove herself from the "confusion." She can only try to develop a protective layer because any reaction from her could result in negative sanctions. So she tries to keep herself away from and out of interaction with officers, but that is not always possible. For, as *Shequetta Tasha Lynn* declares, "Some officers gossip more than the inmates do." Sometimes if a woman tells an officer something, the officer will go to the woman complained about and tell her what was said. "Then they get mad" and the situation can become both explosive and dangerous.

Officers also have access to information not readily available to the population of women that they control. *Sheila T.* offers an example of an officer using such information in the public arena of the mix: "The other day an officer came in and yelled to another [officer] about a new prisoner and what she did." As unprofessional as the officer's public claims may have been, they are worse when they're erroneous. As in most circumstances where gossip is the currency of information, the officers don't always get it right. Due to an error in the departmental records of her crime, officers privy to those records were openly characterizing *Bella* as "an assassin, a mass murderer. Officers ran with the story that I was a hit woman, an assassin." *Bella* was not charged as the do-er in her crime. Nonetheless, current officers would publicly pass her "presumed" criminal record on to new officers. Tired of denying their rumors, *Bella* now just says, "Look it up on the Internet." She has little faith that they will, believing that they prefer salacious gossip to the truth.

Over and over, study participants spoke about the damage caused to them by officer gossip. As the following focus-group exchange demonstrates, life-serving women's vulnerability increases with officer participation in rumormongering.

> *Liberty Flynn*: You can't trust officers, no matter how nice.
> LL: Why not?
> *Liberty Flynn*: They talk to other people, other officers.
> LL: So officers pass gossip?
> FOCUS-GROUP MEMBERS (emphatically): "Oh yeah." "Big time." "Officers talk a lot."

Baby's assertion of the consequences is typical: "I have so much hurt because of her."

Women, under the best of circumstances, are at the mercy of the officers who guard them. When the controllers are engaging in the behavior of the controlled, the potential for personal and environmental damage increases. The situation becomes frightening when correctional officers, who are supposed to be a source of institutional stability, intentionally destabilize the environment. One consequence, as *Sasha Lavan* illustrates in her claim that "the officer will tell others," is that the gossip then starts the domino cascade with other incarcerated women that "you don't want to start." Gossip and violence feed on one another, sometimes with devastating consequences.

* * *

It is ironic that equal opportunity employment for female correctional officers has had the unintended consequence of opening doors for men at every level of women's prisons.[59] Historically, offending women were separated from men in male prisons because they were routinely, sometimes savagely, assaulted by male prison guards or incarcerated men. The assaults served as an impetus for separate prisons for women with female matrons to oversee their care and correction.[60] When female corrections officers realized that their promotion opportunities ended at being wardens of female facilities, far fewer in number than men's facilities, and that men could be wardens of female facilities, while women were not similarly appointed at men's facilities, they sued for parity.[61] Their success literally and figuratively opened doors for male officers in women's facilities. The consequence for incarcerated women was an intensification of the patriarchal standard that the control of women by men is acceptable, a standard that is further amplified when men's heightened surveillance of women is legally sanctioned, institutionally legitimated, and backed by state-endorsed use of physical force.[62]

Cross-gender supervision results in a unique set of institutional concerns regarding privacy, sexual harassment, and sexual misconduct.[63] Legal proscriptions regarding the potential for such behavior became encoded in the Prisoner Rape Elimination Act (PREA) of 2003. PREA sustains zero tolerance for officer/inmate relationships, prohibits cross-gender strip or unusual body cavity searches and patdowns, and further bans nonmedical staff from viewing opposite-gender incarcerated persons who are in the nude or performing bodily functions.[64] Additionally, PREA recognizes that no incarcerated woman's relationship with an officer is consensual. There is always a power differential. Nonetheless, a number of women in the study reported sexual relationships with officers and defined those liaisons as "consensual."

Characterizing their liaisons as consensual is empowering to women who have little power otherwise. By labeling their asymmetrical sexual engagements with officers "consensual," the women lay claim to some measure of control over their own bodies. Ignoring the obvious differentials in power, status, and authority, they construct themselves as agentic decision makers who choose to engage in illicit sexual relationships with officers. Three examples will serve to illustrate the nature of these relationships and the challenge to their "consensual" definitions.

Linda is a juvenile lifer; she was imprisoned at age 16. Now a mature woman, she discussed a "consensual relationship" that she had with an officer when she was a newly imprisoned adolescent. She "fell in love" with him but notes in retrospect "I had no reason feelin' that way. He was 38 years old. I only knew how to feel, not to think." Their relationship ended when she heard that he was having sex with another incarcerated woman rumored to have a sexually transmitted disease. *Linda* did not report the relationship. The officer was never sanctioned.

Miriam "became a drug addict in prison" as a consequence of her "consensual" relationship with a male staff member. When she sought to end the relationship, he savagely beat her and left her "strapped to the bed" and in a "comatose state" where she was discovered by other officers, resuscitated, and rushed to a hospital. She was diagnosed with a closed head injury and still struggles with its aftereffects. "For something like that to happen to you, when you're supposed to be protected, you're gonna be different." The officer was prosecuted, pled guilty, was sentenced, and "just got out." *Miriam* remains incarcerated and continues to deal with the reverberations of the relationship and the assault.

Bella reports enacting what social work theorists Avery Calhoun and Heather Coleman refer to as "sexual trading," purportedly the most common form of contact between correctional personnel and incarcerated women.[65] *Bella* has had "a few" officer-initiated liaisons but claims her own agency in the encounters. "I was mostly in it for gifts and favors." For *Bella*, the sexual encounters were "worth it": "It came to me having everything I could possibly want, except my freedom." As a captive, she views using her body in assignations with correctional personnel as agentic. She traded sex for the material goods and privileges that would ease her confinement, even if they could not end it, an exchange also found by Diaz-Cotto in her study of incarcerated Latinas.[66] To the extent possible, *Bella* deliberately hid her relationships with officers from prison administration and other women.

The women's claims of consent mask the predatory nature of the sexual liaisons. As criminal justice theorists Mark Pogrebin and Mary Dodge note, and as is enshrined in PREA, no incarcerated woman's relationship with an officer is consensual.[67] The asymmetrical power relationship and institutional context obliterate any claim to consent. Why then would any incarcerated woman become sexually involved with an officer? In response to the question in a number of focus groups, participant answers came quickly: loneliness, boredom, power, special privileges, money in their personal accounts, and the fairy-tale fiction of falling in love.

For those other women who are not in "consensual" liaisons and who were reportedly coerced, bribed, or fearful of retaliation for non-compliance with sexual demands from correctional personnel (i.e., "are you refusing a direct order?"), the *Neal v. Michigan Department of Corrections* class-action lawsuit validated their accusations of patterns of sexual abuse spanning more than 20 years and several facility administrations.[68] The astonishing success of the suit clearly illustrated that sexual abuse is a particular dimension of the privatized punishment of women.

The plaintiff women in *Neal* alleged that the MDOC director and facility wardens were aware of the widespread and systemic sexual abuse by male officers of women consigned to their care and that they failed to take action to halt abuse that was "pervasive, routine, and horrific."[69] The women's allegations included rapes, sexual harassment, forced abortions, privacy violations (e.g., observations of gynecological exams or showering by male officers), cross-gender patdowns, forced public nudity, threats, and retaliation against women who reported the extensive sexual abuse.[70] So effective was lead attorney Deborah Labelle in establishing that the State of Michigan "invited men into the women's prison unit areas without training, without restriction and without precautions for these women's safety" that at the end of the first of a series of trials, in an unprecedented, history-making move, one jury foreman read aloud the following prepared statement: "We, the members of the jury, as representatives of the citizens of Michigan, would like to express our extreme regret and apologies for what you have been through."[71] As Rachel Culley wrote, "It was one of the most extraordinary courtroom moments the attorneys had ever seen."[72]

A year later, the plaintiffs agreed to the MDOC settlement offer of $100 million. After 13 years of class-action litigation, ongoing sexual harassment and abuse of over 900 women, as well as "swift" and "harsh" correctional personnel retaliation,[73] the plaintiffs received financial compensation: $37 million was earmarked to resolve sexual intercourse, oral sex, or digital penetration claims; $18 million for claims of officers' groping, exposing their genitals or masturbating, forcing women to touch their genitals, or inappropriate cross-gender patdowns; and $5 million to resolve claims of sexual harassment or inappropriate viewing of nude inmates.[74] The remaining money covered two sets of plaintiffs who won verdicts at separate trials in 2008.[75] The settlement also included extensive injunctive relief:

> Prompt and streamlined sexual harassment investigations and follow-up, advisement of the legal right to report sexual abuses upon release from prison, the formation of a Retaliation Review Committee to promptly evaluate allegations of retaliation, and ongoing counseling and psychological services for victims paid for by MDOC. MDOC also committed to conducting semiannual review of sexual abuse allegations by MDOC's Internal Affairs and investigating additional means of conforming to the recommendations of the Prison Rape Elimination Act.[76]

By the time of the settlement, male officers had already been removed from the residential units. No officers were sanctioned as a consequence of the suit.

Life-serving women have to cope with sexual harassment and officer misconduct, sometimes on a daily basis. They have no exit. *Ever.* Unlike women on the outside, who can move, change jobs, or simply shop in different neighborhoods, there is no place that imprisoned women can go to escape predatory, unprofessional officers.[77] They are literally and figuratively locked in to interactions with officers who can and sometimes do assault them—physically, verbally, and emotionally. Professional boundary violations by even a few officers reduce the legitimacy of all officers' orders and the enforcement of policies determined by prison administration.[78]

"Someone Who Doesn't Treat You Like Shit": "Good" Officers

Officers who were described as behaving badly were ubiquitous in the women's narratives, but many study respondents also described morally responsible officers who were professional in performing their jobs. Good correctional officers won the affection of life-serving women who praised them as "attentive and caring, not picky or petty" (*Caren Sue*), as someone who "encourages you, cares for you" and "is a Christian lady" (*Sister*), takes their jobs seriously "instead of making it personal" (*Kari*), "someone who does their job" (*Martha*), someone who is "not hollerin' all the time and not dealing with petty stuff" (*Chelsie Marie*), and someone who will give "heads-up warning" about minor infractions that can be fixed before they are sanctioned (*Shemetta*). Descriptions of "good" officers in this study only developed in contrast to "bad" officers, that is, the women's articulation of "good" was only raised in contrast to "bad." In the us vs. them Manichean worldview, the women's default construction of a generic correctional officer was "bad." A good officer then was described by her opposition as "someone who doesn't treat you like shit," which was the frequently repeated, expected interaction. Most women agreed that a "good" officer "treats you like a human being" because s/he has respect for unconditional human dignity.

A "good" officer is akin to a respected employer, that is, someone to whom the women accede control, but who does not micro-manage and is consistent, approachable, empathetic without being intrusive, courteous, supportive, kind, understanding, and "real" and authentic, "not fake." Good officers are acknowledged, sometimes in indirect ways. Women report reciprocity, for example, in not aiming to take advantage of "good" officers because, as *Sister* notes, "that's disrespectful." Life-serving women don't want to get good officers in trouble so "they do what's right."

Grace tells the story of women in a housing unit who, using their meager resources, artistically designed and created a going-away card and secured signatures for an officer who was leaving. The homemade card was a gesture of recognition and acknowledgment for an officer who did her job with respect and integrity.

The good officer exceptions conveyed by the focus-group participants permitted the women to cling to their unrecognized stereotypes of "them," while carving out exemptions for officers who make them comfortable by being different from what women view as the norm.[79] Pollock notes, and these data support, that women do not adopt the social distance from officers that characterizes imprisoned men and their minders.[80] Some of the women in this study reported looking to staff to provide nurturance and support and wishing for officers who were a combination of professional service providers and informal sounding boards. Others, like *Harmony*, set the bar much lower. "We don't want you to be nice. We want you not to be nasty."

All focus-group members who discussed interactions with officers adamantly stated that, after recognition and respect for their humanity, consistency was the primary quality desired in a "good" officer. *Lynn* and *Merrilee* both report appreciating "Ms. [name] because she's always a bitch." They like her consistency; they know what to expect; they have no illusions about her, "not like these officers who be changin' all the time." They value her predictability, the reliability of her bitchiness, and the order and stability it provides. To get that constancy, they are willing to excuse her unprofessional manner. "This accommodation represented a commitment, shared by most peoples, however oppressed, to the belief that a harsh and unjust social order is preferable to the insecurities of no order at all."[81] *Lynn* and *Merrilee* make realistic adjustments to their prison world. They acquiesce to the circumstances. As do *Pooh Bear* and *Lois*, who claim that the same officer called one of them "a damn crackhead" and told the other "You just ugly today." They report a perception of care in these unprofessional remarks. *Pooh Bear* declares that "it's like getting cussed out by your mama."

Under the U.S. Constitution, imprisonment imposes responsibilities on the government, the least of which is the duty to protect prisoners.[82] Correctional officers have the legally imposed duty to protect inmates from themselves, from other inmates, and from mistreatment by staff.[83] Imprisoned women are entitled to the stability and consistency of professionalism, of protective control over the environment, and of protection against informal bargains.[84] Sometimes they get it. *Faith* argues that "they actually do try to protect you in here," talking about a time she "got help" to exit an abusive relationship with another woman. An officer, upon learning about the physical abuse *Faith* experienced from her inside lover, took action to protect her. The officer "filled out a form" and "put it in writing" that she would have "no contact with that person" and the abusive partner was moved to another residence unit on the grounds. "So I was safe." In a confined, oppressive environment, physical safety is a paramount concern.

Harmony's experiences support this assessment of the protective function of correctional officers. "You do have officers that actually do their job and protect us. They see that you don't feed the madness, don't do the girlfriend thing, do your work, and go about your business." She claims that officers "saw my good behavior" and "looked out for me" and warned her of threats against her. In those circumstances, where officers recognize positive behavior and mature choices, they will protect. *Har-*

mony attributes the official protection she experienced to *her* choices and to the ways *she* comports herself and not to the professionalism of the surveilling officers.

Meme relates a similar experience, claiming that when she arrived in prison, she was "plumb dumb." She had never used drugs, never drank alcohol, and never smoked. She was unprepared for the mix.[85] Some officers "took [her] under their wings" because she so obviously did not know how to present herself in this new environment. Other women would "borrow" her stuff, use it, share it and then "bring it back almost used up." An officer noticed these exchanges and tried to "coach . . . and teach [her]" to not allow people to take advantage. Under this tutelage, *Meme* learned to be "penitentiary smart" and to "keep busy." The need for protection that these women identify is a consequence of forced dependency. Officer control over every aspect of their lives instills dependency, and then women are held in disdain for their lack of sophistication in the environment. *Meme* continues to spend leisure time with staff because "it helps." When she needs a pressure-cooker release or time to vent, she talks to staff, claiming that their conversations relieve her stress and tension. She has developed a treasured camaraderie with some institutional officers. She is validated in the exchange, as they reportedly call on *Meme* when "something needs doing in the unit." Their influential attention validates her in this harsh environment.

Officer behaviors and attitudes can facilitate successful adaptation to the complex prison environment or thwart positive adjustments because, as *Alexandria* noted earlier, the resident unit manager "sets the tone for the unit." On the line in daily interactions, officers determine the climate of the facility. This influence is particularly salient for juvenile women incarcerated for life. *Linda*, incarcerated at 16, has spent more of her life in prison than she had lived as a child in the free world. She reports being grateful to the officers at her former facility because they "raised" her. Skirting the rigid boundaries of us vs. them within the institutional structure, some officers nurtured and cared for her as an adolescent and a young woman. These good officers knew who she was and influenced who she came to be. They recognized her adolescent foibles and the limits of the context in helping her develop social skills and maturity. Those officers would give her the benefit of the doubt in discretionary judgment calls. Most of the good officers at the previous facility—the only prison she knew, the prison where she grew up, the prison where she matured from a child into a middle-aged woman, the prison where officers recognized her personal changes and growth, and where she earned enough trust to be given the benefit of the doubt—were transferred to other facilities when that prison closed. *Linda*, whose life experience in the free world was truncated as an adolescent, struggled in the new facility where the officers didn't know her and judged her harshly. "I've resigned myself to not getting respect." She has had to start over as a woman with a stigmatized identity. Unlike her previous experiences, "We [correctional officers and incarcerated women] just coexist and that's no way to live."

That good officers can have a profound influence on the young women in their charge is underscored by *Caren Sue*, another adolescent who has been incarcerated for life. *Caren Sue* came to prison when a group of "red tag" or apprentice officers were being trained. "They have seen me grow." In the carceral environment, with few positive opportunities for recognition, the attention and affirming comments of these officers provide her with external validation of her maturation. As prison's authoritative sources, they make her "feel good" when they acknowledge the changes in her behavior. This tacit approval from officers is a challenge to the stigma and sense of worthlessness that a life sentence imposes.

Other women recounted forming close familial bonds with officers. *Jesus Lady* warmly declares that some officers "were more like family members to me" and they "ended up giving me protection and support." While these relationships sometimes took years to develop, Christian bonds reportedly enhanced the emotive, nonmaterial connections. Prayer is ubiquitous inside. A life sentence can annihilate the human spirit, but religion, or even simple faith, offers life-serving women transformative possibilities denied by a retributive society. Some of these women experience opportunities for mercy and forgiveness through the religious interest of correctional officers who represent the outside world to them. *Tootsie Roll* identified an officer who is "like a second mother to me," as she highlighted the officer's Christian outreach through the provision of "motivational papers" and directions regarding "which scriptures to read." These faith connections are perceived by

Jesus Lady, Tootsie Roll, and others as gestures of good will and validation. *Jesus Lady,* who reports being without family in the free world, "didn't get anything out of them [officers] except a replacement family, since I never had anyone close to me like that." These officers become surrogates for the family, the nurturance, and guidance that life-serving women lose during their years behind bars.

Other women, like *Alison,* discuss the empathy extended by good officers when life-serving women experience trauma through the death of a loved one. The loss of a family member is a particularly soul-crushing experience inside, in part because the woman is isolated from conventional supports for grieving. She has no other family members with whom to share her memories and emotional suffering. She cannot attend the funeral or memorial service. She cannot grieve in private. She cannot withdraw, even temporarily, from the daily schedule of the prison. She has no access to people or places to remediate the intensity of her grief. And she has little support for the emotional instability that often accompanies intense sadness. She is required, at all times, to maintain prison routines.

Alison lost her mother after her incarceration for a particularly high-profile case that alienated her from the other women imprisoned with her. "The officer I thought who would be the worst helped the most." When an imprisoned woman loses a family member, she is allowed to call someone to help her through her initial grief. Estranged from the population of life-serving women, *Alison* said, "I was the only person ever to request an officer as my call, but I did." The officer hugged her "even though it's against the rules." *Alison* was moved by the extent of humanity that the officer displayed through the physicality of touch across the us and them boundary. She claims that "everything" in news reports about her was "a lie," although believed by other women and correctional staff. "But here an MDOC could see the real me." The officer's care validated *Alison's* humanity and reestablished her worth. *Alison* continues to see the officer every once in a while and "she always asks about my family." The inquiry is a token gesture of courtesy with great meaning for *Alison* because "that's human." The gratitude of women for small gestures of civility from correctional officers is amplified in this rarified environment of us vs. them. *Alison's* narrative demonstrates the possibility that genuine sympathy, even empathy, might exist across the bifurcated boundaries. These border crossings were few in reported numbers, but important to the women when they occurred.

Good officers also emerge from bad situations. *Jannel* notes, for example, that most people deal with "maybe one suicide" in their lives. "We've dealt with six." Suicides test the mettle of correctional officers as they are closely watched by the women under their supervision. *Harmony* speaks of an officer who tried to resuscitate "the last suicide victim." She learned that the correctional officer "took time off work and had to get counseling." This fracture in the Superman aura of control and detachment allowed the women to transcend the us vs. them dichotomy and to recognize the officer's humanity. The uniform and responsibilities of her role did not erase the effects of the loss. There was a caring person wearing the uniform. The officer's personal challenges demonstrated her boundary crossing, her empathy, and her caring, in the unnecessary death of a woman in her charge. The care is illustrative of the genuine intimacy of lives inextricably bound together.

For most women, it's the small courtesies extended by good officers that are most significant. They remind women of their worth and value. *Yasmeen* related an incident in which she was reading late into the night and an officer came into her room and said, 'You're not usually up at this time of night, are you OK?' *Yasmeen* experienced the inquiry as one of care and concern. Alternatively, however, her skepticism about officers surfaced when she noted that the officer might simply have been doing a "suicide check," reflecting institutional requirements.

These narratives of exceptionalism in the discourse of "good" correctional officers challenge the women's us vs. them binary. *Merrilee*, who chooses to maintain strictly instrumental exchanges necessary for functional discourse with officers, and whose stated opinion of most correctional officers is "respect doesn't even matter anymore. . . . You don't even like me, so let's not even play," nonetheless says that she loves "Officer Z with all my heart." Officer Z works on holidays, "is not fake," and for days she "helped me like a baby," consoling *Merrilee* when her mother had passed. *Merrilee* "loves" Z and simultaneously feels antipathy for Z's colleagues. Within this paradox, *Merrilee* embodies the inconsistencies of life-serving women and their keeper counterparts. She doesn't trust or even like anyone in a black and gray uniform, *except* the officer that she loves "with all my heart." Nonetheless, *Merrilee* asserts that it would be "hard for me" to come to Z's defense if someone was "to get on Z," that is, to physically assault her. The us vs. them boundary is so strong that she feels ambivalence about violating it to assist an officer in need, even one whom she "loves."

Conclusion

Women perceive rigid boundaries between black and grays and themselves, an us and them dichotomy that appears impermeable but that is under constant negotiation. Locked into mutual interdependency by institutionalized penal structures, antipathy and hostility between the two groups are tempered by cooperation and collaboration, if not by respect and appreciation. Life-serving women and their criminal-processing puppeteers reciprocally create, negotiate, and modify prison protocols and policies. They exist, as anthropologist Lorna Rhodes notes, in a calculus of risk and opportunity that is foundational to their mutual interdependency.[86]

8

Eating the Life-Sentence Elephant

"One Day at a Time"

I stay as busy as possible. I work, and I do my job the same way I would on the outside. *Doll*

You can't stop. When you stop, it's hopeless and you want to die. *Destiny*

It's not just me in my room. It's me, my bunkie, and a toilet. *Grace*

How do you eat an elephant? One bite at a time. How do you manage a life sentence? One day at a time. Life-serving women claim that engaging the whole elephant—the burden of existence in an oppressive present and an unchanging future—is annihilating. "It can kill you." As an antidote to "letting time do you," the women in this study intentionally engaged in self-actualizing behaviors. They adapted and learned to exploit opportunities that allowed them to fashion portions of their lives on their own terms and to thereby resist erosions of body and soul. These efforts required daily, sometimes minute-by-minute persistence, fortitude, attention, planning, and commitment to self-imposed agendas, as well as some measure of self-defined spirituality and patience. These life-serving women anchored themselves in the present and coped with their situations "one day at a time" by being both deliberate and reflective.

To appreciate their agency and strategies for coping with and developing autonomy within the confines of their incarceration, it is necessary to understand imprisonment as both formal structure and informal negotiation. The constant interplay between the prison structure and the women's negotiations with officers and administration over rules and procedures incorporates active elements of process and performance.[1] Ceaselessly regulated and controlled by the institution, life-serving women nonetheless act and possess some autonomy. They focus. They plan. They obstruct. They create time-management schedules that shape their lives and infuse them with meaning. They interact with others in consequential ways. They develop devotional practices.

Their coping strategies illustrate relationships between agency and structure. They make choices within the limited ranges available to them. Their agency is visible through their strategies, but it is not always visible in conventionally expected ways. Their sometimes small, sometimes routine actions are not always public, organized, formal, or unambiguous, yet the participants in this study report being unremittingly resistant to the control and erosions of imprisonment. Sometimes life-serving women simply engage in what sociologist Catherine Kohler Riessman calls "resistance thinking" or "transformative thoughts and actions in everyday life" that substitute for speaking out when the costs of confrontation are high.[2] Given the forms of institutional power with which life-serving women contend, their strategies of resistance and self-actualization are often covert. My study of their resistance practices then is contextual and accounts for the conditions and possibilities for action within the constraints of 24/7 surveillance and control.

The agentic strategies of the life-serving women in this study, I found, converged around four axes of decision making: (1) normalizing chosen activities inside using "as if" outside world analogues; (2) maintaining individualized action orientations generally described as "staying busy"; (3) forming affective and instrumental relationships with peers inside; and (4) developing and sustaining a self-defined spiritual center, often expressed as having "a personal relationship with God." Although the strategies are enacted idiosyncratically, they are ubiquitous in both sustaining and enabling female lifers to create their paths through the carceral stages of self-actualization from becoming a prisoner through rebuilding social bonds (see chapters 3 and 5). Some strategies served some women well; others did not.

All the women reported enacting behaviors in *all* four convergence areas, although not equivalently. Women "doing life" may have similar opportunities for self-actualizing behavior, but their interpersonal skills, interests, life experiences, and personal orientations vary widely.

Therefore, strategic choices within this study population were neither uniform nor singular. They were at all times complex and nuanced. Still achieving in these adverse circumstances by speaking out or choosing silence, acting out or choosing compliance, and using guerrilla ingenuity to survive demonstrates that their individualized strategies are active and ongoing and that the women are resilient.[3]

"Just Living Like I Would in Society": "As If" Normalizing Strategies

Imprisonment forces women into consent to the overarching authority of the institution and to the loss of conventional adult choices and decisions. Incarceration is not an anticipated condition for adult women, but it is one to which the women in this study must adapt. They report becoming active in preserving their identities and in garnering some measure of control over their unpredictable environment. As social work theorist Sheryl Pimlott Kubiac and her colleagues note, prison offers a "compromised range of options for coping."[4] Using subversive ingenuity, life-serving women locate the interstices in the system and reframe their options to create thin replicas of the lives they would be living in "the real world." Determined to reshape their circumstances, they draw on the normalizing activities experienced, or expected, on the outside as their models. *Lucy Spencer,* for example, prepares for a return to hoped-for civic life by engrossing herself in the programming on the Home and Garden TV (HGTV) network. After 20-plus years of incarceration, the homemaker role that she left behind when she killed her abusive husband is no longer familiar, so she seeks contemporary lessons on how to create a new "happily after prison" life. Home and Garden "keeps you knowing what's out there, especially the latest colors and gadgets." These commonplace activities are at the core of her poignant fantasy about a dinner salad. "I laid back in bed last night thinking about ripping up salad in a bowl. . . . It's been so long since I've been part of society." Her food-preparation fantasy ends. Reality intrudes. She has gone too long without a kitchen, pots and pans, or food with which to cook a meal. Nonetheless, HGTV provides her with the fodder for imagining a reconstructed life. She intends to be ready if and when opportunity knocks. As does *Esther,* who says, "Right now, I'm designing a farm. I'm gonna have a farm." She loves to grow things, trees, food, animals. She came in to the focus-group meeting carrying a book about planting small fruit trees. If a battered woman and her child are in need, *Esther* is "gonna hide 'em" on her farm, because "if a battered woman had time to think clearly, maybe she wouldn't do what we did." *Esther's* "what we did" speaks to the collective of life-serving women who were imprisoned "behind a man," that is, their incarcerations were the consequence of having aided and abetted violent men or having murdered their brutal male partners. *Esther's* desired future, her projected rebuilding of social bonds, anticipates providing care to other women caught in circumstances similar to her own as it simultaneously addresses her need to redeem herself and "to grow things."

To prepare themselves for hoped-for future freedoms and to normalize present circumstances, life-serving women like *Lucy Spencer* and *Esther* set goals, work diligently, navigate obstacles and setbacks, stay focused, and resist the desire to "use dope to cope" and other temptations always available in the mix. In a solicited diary entry, *Kari,* who is 38 and has been incarcerated for more than 20 years, demonstrates how this "as if" normalizing is linked to the passage of time. "My mind isn't in here. Everything I do is focused around my friends on the outside and preparing myself for the demands of life on the outside. I never have looked at my being in prison as permanent. I just get through my days as simply 'going through the motions,' something I must do, surviving, and before you know it, it's 5, 10, 15, 20 years later."

Imitating life practices is a strategy that life-serving women utilize to cope with prison erosions in individually particular ways. *Caren Sue,* for example, embraces the gendered practice of "looking good" in public space in order to normalize her prison experience: "I do my hair and makeup every day. I do it for myself. If I look good, I feel good. It's fun for me. I look forward to doing it every day." Although she is challenged by the very limited cosmetic options in the prison commissary, the "same four colors of eye shadow forever," she is undaunted in her desire to continue to represent herself as feminine and attractive in this female-dominated environment. When women leave their rooms, they are immediately in the public arena of shared institutional space. Using the steel-case mirror affixed to the wall in her cell, *Caren Sue* prepares herself for this public display as she would if she were in "the real world."

Other life-serving women describe planning and maintaining schedules for unscripted time, often anchored by prison jobs, as another "as if" strategy to normalize their lives and to make them feel useful.[5] Women report designing self-imposed schedules, on top of the already highly ordered prison protocols, to enforce their own order on themselves and on their environments. Most, like *Cameron*, claim that they "have a daily and a weekly schedule." Determining how to use their unscheduled time offers women a measure of control and, therefore, power over their circumstances. Self-scheduling promotes the experience of using time wisely versus the prison warehousing that is a commonplace experience for life-serving women. Their schedules are also used as analogues to their imagined lives on the outside. *Martha*, for example, embraces normality in her chosen prison routine: "I try not to think about it [life sentence]. I distract myself by just living like I would in society. . . . I make a schedule, what I would be doing if I was at home. . . . [I live] like I would on the outside. I'd probably be studying and working, so that's what I do in here."

Journey provides the most extensive example of using her routine to normalize her circumstances and to sustain a sense of autonomy and agency. "I do my time by having an agenda." She compares her imprisonment to her earlier process of graduating from high school after which she had a go-to-college agenda. *Journey* was living her plan as she was an undergraduate before her imprisonment for life at 19 years of age. She has now been incarcerated for more years than she had been a child or adolescent in her pre-incarceration life. Offending and imprisonment were huge missteps in life for which she needed a new plan. "Coming here wasn't on my agenda" but she adapted to her circumstances, developed a new agenda appropriate to her location, and "I've stuck to it." She wanted to continue her education, so she has completed all the programming available to lifers inside, including college classes coordinated by the author. Another item on her agenda was earning a paralegal degree; she is "learning everything" she can "about that field." "I'm still working on that." One reason that she "sticks to it so hard" is that she's "always planned" on going home. "If your plan is to go home, you need to act like it." For *Journey*, acting "as if" means taking her agenda seriously, envisioning her freedom, educating herself, and creating a viable means of economic support when and if she is released or paroled.

For most Americans participating in the labor force, work is a normative state. Their work requirements schedule their lives, that is, when they work, where they work, how long they work, what their work responsibilities entail, the payment structures for the work they do, and so on, determining the parameters of their life choices. Labor-force participation is a key feature of the identities of most adults. As sociologist Erving Goffman noted more than 50 years ago, the role dispossession that accompanies imprisonment ends work as a component of the incarcerated woman's "identity tool kit."[6] Consequently, upon release from closed custody to the general population, most women actively attempt to gain some prison employment, preferring menial work to the tedium of leisure inside. Prison jobs allow women to demonstrate commitment to conventional behavior, to the ordinariness of having a job. In a study of incarcerated women in California, criminologist Barbara Owen found, for example, that "the majority of women shape the day around a job, vocational training, or a school assignment."[7] Those findings are also replicated in the importance of work assignments for the women in this study.

Like life on the outside, work inside structures daily living for those women lucky enough to secure prison employment. Jobs reportedly give them "a reason to get up in the morning," a place to go, and people to interact with as well as helping them to "keep [their] sanity." Ironically, work also allows some to withdraw from social engagement with their peers. *Merrilee* claims, for example, that she's become "real reclusive." She goes to work where she voluntarily "picks up 16-hour shifts. I've been real isolated." Alternatively, if their work involves assumptions of responsibility, jobs also lend purposefulness to life inside. *Sandy*, for example, had a job as a clerk. She had "daily conversations" with her civilian supervisor who reportedly treated her like a person, not an incarcerated subordinate. "That helped [in her personal transformation]." Those unscripted, ordinary conversations enabled her to feel normal. *Sandy* engaged in talking to people who were part of the "real world." Such jobs and such experiences "give you meaning" in an environment where voicelessness and namelessness are facts of life.

The jobs available to women inside are jobs that run the facility— cleaning buildings and grounds, doing laundry, cooking in the kitchen, transporting people in wheelchairs, tutoring in GED and vocational programs, serving as administrative clerks, cutting and styling hair, painting the facility, maintaining electrical services, providing institutional maintenance—and, like those jobs on the outside, the work shifts varied often due to the protocols of the facility for counts, chow, and other security needs.[8] The pay scale inside is not equivalent to market-based salaries, nor is there a career ladder.

While paid employment has more financial value on the outside, it may have more anchoring value on the inside. *Doll*, a legal writer, says she makes "$3.34 per *day* [emphasis added]," which is "good money" for a job inside. "Obviously, I'm not in it for the money." At the other end of the wage spectrum, *Shequetta Tasha Lynn* says that she "earned $0.17 an hour in the factory." From those limited funds, unlike her counterparts on the outside who have access to credit cards or layaway programs for expensive purchases, *Shequetta* had to put herself on a lengthy budget regimen so that she could purchase the black and white TV that was administration approved. "I earned $0.17 an hour in the factory, but I would put away $5 from my work money or $20 from what my family sent me. . . . Everything in here takes time. Nothing is instant gratification."

For some, as for their peers on the outside, their work was "just a prison job" necessary to structure time and to generate income indispensable for purchasing commissary supplies like soap, deodorant, "noodles" (ramen noodles are sold in the commissary and are reportedly the gold standard of exchange inside), and shampoo. Not thrilled with her present job, *Journey* notes in her diary how she came to terms with continuing: "At the end of the day . . . I needed a job. I needed a meaningful job that kept me busy and [where] I could make a decent living."

Despite the limited financial remuneration, life-serving women reported finding meaning in their jobs. Some women "treat [the job] as a skill" that they can utilize if they are released or paroled. Through long-term employment inside, *Antanashia,* for example, has developed confidence in herself as a creditable employee. She is "15 years down. Kept a job my whole bit." This remarkably long, single employment history inside reflects trust in her competency by her civilian supervisors. Trustworthy, competent in position, and reliable are all descriptors denied "prisoners" in public discourse. *Antanashia*'s 15-year history of employment is an implicit challenge to the cultural stereotypes of life-sentenced women.

Some women's work assignments provide them with more than money and scheduled time; some gain access to wares that they can sell or barter.[9] *Wink*, for example, worked in the kitchen and started stealing chickens and peppers to sell as a means of making "$30 in a few days." She was caught and lost her job. Sanguine about the outcome, she said, "I hustled at home. I had to hustle in here."

Unlike incarcerated men, whose resistance tends toward violence, imprisoned women work to undermine the system of control.[10] Their activities contribute to the thriving underground economy that provides the goods and services that create the prison luxuries that, at the end of the day, modify their environments and allow them to act "as if."

Paid little in their jobs and provided with only basics of daily living, women find ways to soften the material deprivations of incarceration and normalize their lives inside. As Karlene Faith, a Canadian feminist, scholar, and human rights activist, notes, people who are desperate are often creative.[11] These life-serving women are creative, inventive, and resilient in their guerrilla ingenuity. Like *Wink*, they develop economic "hustles." Sometimes the hustles involve legitimate activities, like washing dishes, washing and/or ironing clothes for others, selling paper towels or bleach, running errands for people, making greeting cards, doing hair; sometimes the activities are illicit, like bringing in contraband, "tricking" (selling sex) for commissary goods, or slinging drugs. Drug hustles inside reportedly function in two ways. The first and most obvious is selling. If a drug seller can get a woman hooked on heroin, then she can make a steady income off the woman's drug habit. The second hustle is to hustle the seller by hiding her drugs during a "shakedown" (cell search). Alternatively, some women are coerced into hiding drugs for someone else. *Shequetta Tasha Lynn* cautions that "if you don't [hide the drugs], [the seller] might talk about you like a dog or beat you up in the bathroom, or both."

Reflecting the social circumstances of her pre-incarceration life, *Ilene Roberts* claims that "everyone finds some way to scam the system. This is just a world in a world. There ain't nothin' you can't get away with." At a focus-group meeting, *Ramona* dubbed herself "the contraband queen." Her claim to fame was not contested by the other participants. Her assertion reflected pride that was contradicted by her following declaration that she's "not proud" of her hustle. Nonetheless, she bragged: "Give me 24 hours, I got you." . . . She then listed items that she ostensibly had smuggled in—alcohol, underwire bras, 300 tubes of lipstick, diet pills. All, but one, were feminine products necessary to promote the semblance of "as if" normality in this abnormal circumstance. Unlike many others, *Ramona* engages in premeditated hustling. When the author inquired about how she managed to import all this contraband into a presumably secure facility, her response was twofold: "hustling skills learned on the outside" plus "I had friends in low places." She claimed correctional officer assistance with her entrepreneurial activities.

Hustles, contraband, clothing sales, ironing for others, tricking for commissary, and selling prescription medications are all responses to deprivation. They reflect limited options to enhance the comfort level, especially with regard to food and personal items. "I sold my meds for probably about six months. I didn't want to, but I did it only for my basic needs, toothbrush, etc." (Women would secure pills under their tongues or in their gums until they could extract and sell them later.) Contraband scores and hustles are responses to market economics, where supply is driven by demand. But they are also status involved: *Ramona's* claimed title as the "contraband queen" situates her as an acknowledged underminer of the system. Hers is a high-risk endeavor that assuages the desires of her peers to act "as if." It is a status occupation inside.

Hustles occur both inside and outside legitimate employment venues. Some jobs provide opportunities to bring in, move, and/or distribute contraband items (e.g., drugs, weed, cigarettes, cosmetics, food). While the luxuries that women gain may seem minuscule by outside standards—noodles or a tube of lipstick—the extras provide more value than simple materiality. They sustain illusions of normality. They soften women's lives as well as reinstate them as active resistors of the erosions of imprisonment.

"Getting over" on the institution, even in small ways, is also motivational. Women working in the kitchen, like *Wink*, steal food to share or sell, although both sanctions and surveillance to prevent theft are significant. Women also creatively use job locations in order to gain access—through eavesdropping on supervisor conversations, paying close attention, and reading upside down—to valuable information affecting their lives but otherwise withheld from them.

In addition to its potential to temper systemic control, employment also provides many women with their niche in the prison culture. For those who avoid the hustles, according to *JoAnna*, "working" and/or "getting a job" is a standard route to status and legitimacy in the prison hierarchy. Jobs help women to stabilize their identities for, as *Destiny* claims, "we become our occupations—the GED lady, the HIV lady, the library lady." *Cameron*, whose job has a service orientation, reports being "approached [by other women] every day because of what I do." The women also identify themselves by reference to their jobs. In her solicited diary, *Journey*, for example, identifies herself this way: "I am the line leader in [X] department," a supervisory position over other women that, with departmental managerial support, provides her with status and authority in the work environment.

In a crowded facility, however, not everyone is awarded a job. Job positions are limited. Without a job, there is nowhere to go and nothing to do. With no work hours, unscheduled time has no structure beyond administrative counts and chow (mealtimes). *Linda* faces this dilemma. "I like to work. . . . I don't have [a job]. They won't give me one. I lay in bed all the time." She is not lazy. She just cannot get a job. The consequence of unemployment is stultifying inactivity. "I take pills to comfort myself. . . . I just peed dirty for using heroin in [the last month]. . . . Unfortunate, but true." The drugs helped, "but not long term . . . I just try to do as best I can." Drugs inside are short-term solutions to long-term problems. As in *Linda's* case, they may blunt the edge of the pain, but they don't change the conditions that cause the pain. If all possible job positions are filled, there are no jobs available for the women who want them. As in life on the outside, unemployment is a structural condition but its deprivations are experienced by jobless individuals.

Ultimately, women employed "as if" analogue strategies—maintaining self-defined schedules, engaging in work assignments and responsibilities, developing economic hustles—to provide the foundational bases to both normalize and resist their circumstances. For most, the strategies were smart, effective ways to handle overwhelming circumstances. These women acted agentically so that they would not succumb to "letting time do you." In describing a formula for coping inside enumerated by others, *Anna Bell* said, "Basically that's what I do. Work. Go to church. Go to bed. And do it all over again." The endless repetition is a reflection of her compromised choices, but of choices nonetheless.

"It's a Matter of Self-Rehabilitation": Staying-Busy Strategies

For the women in this study, the oft-repeated refrain "I stay busy" signaled the importance of attention to activities that provided purpose and created safe space in their lives. "Staying busy" reflected a sense of both achievement and accomplishment that eroded the fixity of being locked in place. By organizing the unscheduled portions of their lives, these life-serving women created a measure of control and, therefore, power over their circumstances. They resisted prison losses by engaging in activities that they chose: reading, writing, craft work, creative work, educational TV programs, learning new skills, televangelist ministries, and so on. Most often their choices focused on self-improvement strategies over collective action. Individuals engaged in prayer, in programs, and in whatever resources they could access to improve their lives and rehabilitate themselves. As *Ilene Roberts* claimed, "It's a matter of self-rehabilitation. They [prison administrations] don't give it to you."

Meme's "I stay busy," although tied to her work life in the facility, like many other women's claims, really goes much further than empty busyness. "Working keeps me focused." Being focused prevents her from dwelling on the deprivations in her life, on the losses she has incurred through imprisonment, and on the endlessness of her incarceration. *Meme* is recognized by both officers and other women in her unit as the "go-to" person to get work done, "anything, walls, doors, waxing floors, anything." By her own account this attention serves multiple purposes. It keeps idleness at bay, for as *Meme* notes, "idle hands are the devil's workshop." It distracts her from "all the mess" going on in her unit, which, at the time of the study, she described as "off the chain" (out of control) due to a "maggot" infestation from one woman's neglect of her food storage. "Staying busy" also keeps *Meme* in top physical condition. "I look good for my age." When she's busy, the repetition and mindlessness of the work she does provides her with quiet time that removes her from "the mess." She uses the time to reflect, think, and motivate herself. As all her work involves facility maintenance, a corollary consequence of *Meme's* busy-ness is a clean collective environment.

In a study population of men sentenced for capital crimes, criminologists and critical prison scholars Robert Johnson and Ania Dobrzanska found that men who organized their unscheduled time avoided trouble, took charge of their lives, engaged in agentic behavior, and provided security "without resort to deception or violence."[12] For the women in this study, "staying busy" has these and other ancillary benefits. For them, it also kept corrosive forces at bay. It temporarily refocused attention away from the pain of their internal states. It acted as an antidote to depression and despair. As *DeDe* noted, "It's not easy in prison." Yet the hard time of a life sentence can be constructive if the pains of imprisonment are met with mature coping strategies that are responsive and responsible and that also seek autonomy, respect the rights of others, and support affirming interactions.[13]

Toward that end, life-serving women expend considerable energy and effort to keep their minds active and engaged. In theorizing total institutions, like prisons, sociologist Erving Goffman noted that they are the "least intellectual of places."[14] *Linda* graphically articulates the intellectual void that women with life sentences face: "In here our minds turn to mush. If you keep around mush, your mind will turn to garbage." Reading is one remedy for the "mush" that develops from the lack of intellectual stimulation and the ennui of monotonous routine.

All the women report "reading" as a popular tranquil strategy in staying busy. As Ronald Aday and Jennifer Krabill, criminologists who study aging, argue, reading provides incarcerated women with links to the outside world, valuable information, and opportunities to learn.[15] It also fills endless time. For example, in the 23-hour lockdown of her initial closed custody, *Cindy* claimed, "I read until I thought my eyes were going to bleed." There was nothing else to do.

The women's reading interests, however, are individual and particularized and vary widely from those like *Belladonna Momma* who says, "I read my Bible," to others who read devotional religious tracts to those who read scholarly tomes and engage others in their discourse. *Linda*, for example, is "reading Plato for my class." *Linda* is enrolled in a college-level class coordinated by the author and offered at the facility on a voluntary basis by professors from a local university. The women's successful completion of the courses is rewarded with Continuing Education Units. Prior to 1994, academic study leading to undergraduate degrees was available to incarcerated men and women. However, under the Clinton administration, Congress voted to deny federal Pell Grants to persons incarcerated in state and federal prisons, although only 0.1% of the Pell support monies went to imprisoned people. College degree programs in prisons fell precipitously from 350 to about 12 in spite of research evidence that indicates that successful completion of even one college course during imprisonment reduces rates of recidivism.[16]

Linda's study of *Plato's Republic* also engages her intellectual friend in discussions about the philosophical arguments. Although her friend is not enrolled in the class, they're "reading it together." *Linda* claims that there are not many "intellectually stimulating" people inside, but once she finds them "it's, like, maaaan! These people have their own ideas and opinions." Reading together provides women with self-help opportunities to maintain vibrant intellectual lives by engaging in collaborative intellectual work. As an ancillary benefit, reading provides reasons to seek others out for intellectual companionship and stimulation.

As a resistance strategy, reading also serves multiple purposes. Some women report being avid readers of the Department of Corrections' policy manuals and directives. Policy knowledge is a protective strategy accessed comprehensively by *Shequetta Tasha Lynn*. In order to understand the implicit and explicit directives and policies, she says, "I read everything closely." *Jesus Lady* is another expert reader of policy manuals. She claims to "never give up. [Others] convince themselves that there's nothing they can do . . . and so they get nothing. I just stick to it." She was acknowledged by other women in the focus group as relentless in requiring correctional officers to adhere to policy, to "going by the book." She provided the reasoning sustaining her choices: "It validates that we are human beings. We have rights, and we will not be walked on and treated like trash." For most women, however, their reading selections are more conventional than department policy manuals.

Reading provides entertainment that offers women respite from their current circumstances. *Cindy* laughingly narrates this distraction: "Right now I'm in the middle of Harry Potter." If someone comes to her door, she responds, "I got a date with Harry! Leave me alone!" Many other women also report immersing themselves so completely in the texts they've chosen that they can temporarily escape their environment.

As a strategic maneuver of avoidance when women encounter problems like the drama of the mix, reading is effective. *Ciara* says, "I don't go in the TV room or the day room. I don't engage with that [drama]. I do my time in my room. . . . I read." Women also use reading to mediate their own experiences.[17] The texts they choose create the necessary distance for them to come to terms with their experiences. *Liberty Flynn,* for example, writes in her diary, "I am a voracious reader. I do want to find out WHY when something breaks or goes wrong. I can't touch the WHY in myself." For women like *Liberty Flynn,* reading provides distraction from situations or emotions—"the WHY in myself"—that are too painful or too overwhelming to manage.[18] Reading thus fills emotional space.

As literature scholar Megan Sweeney notes, imprisoned women draw on available reading materials for more complex reasons than escape, avoidance, or staying busy.[19] They also read to find sources of inspiration and guidance to reinterpret their pasts in ways that allow for growth and healing. The women in this study reported turning to self-help texts for personal change. *Raine* is one reader of "self-help" books. She was motivated by self-improvement. Like many other life-serving women, she accepted the prison narrative that her personal deficits were responsible for the choices that resulted in her imprisonment. She was "told" that she could write up book reports and take them to the parole board as evidence that she was rehabilitating herself. "Told" is part of the prison information mill. Women inside develop their own, informal means of sharing sometimes erroneous information. *Raine's* self-help reading obviously had a pragmatic objective beyond her personal growth.

Reading is not the only calming activity for staying busy. In creating a regimen for effective use of unencumbered time, women develop a sense of ownership of time and autonomy over a range and variety of activities. Like many others, *Jane* engages in craft work. "Now I'm at a place in my life where, if I have a bad day, I go to my room and get my crafts out. . . . If they took my crafts away from me, I'd probably be hanging somewhere [suicide]. I crochet, I knit, that's my release. It helps me refocus." *Jane's* craft work extends beyond staying busy. She describes its soothing effect on the tenuous hold on her emotions inside, where suicide ideation is never far away. The material acts of knitting and crocheting engage both mind and body and serve as a release for *Jane*'s pent-up emotions. Working with her hands keeps her busy and helps her to re-center herself when she is coping with negativity in her environment. The repetition involved in knitting and crocheting can be lulling to a troubled spirit as can the physical properties of holding and touching. Through craft involvement, *Jane* has chosen to make constructive use of her time. She produces material products that she sells or gives as gifts and that are physical manifestations of her triumph over environmental adversity.

Craft work, reading and writing, and journaling share some common properties. All are individualized strategies to relieve potentially dangerous and/or painful emotions. They draw mind and body together and help women to heal. They provide opportunities for temporary evasion, which is evident in *Monaye*'s claim: "I use writing as an escape." They serve as creative outlets. *Linda*, the self-described "writer who doesn't write," is innovative in her approach. To make writing "fun" for herself, amid the hearty laughter of a focus group, *Linda* shares her particular topic choices: "This is why I'm hot" and "This is why I'm not." Like others, *Linda* uses writing to take her own social inventory. In this subtle self-actualization process, she is both amusing and reflective. "I'm writing down all the feelings and thoughts I have, about my past, [as well as] my experiences I have in here now." Her writing helps her to reinterpret and rescript her life. Other women, like *Lucy Spencer*, eschew journaling because, for her, it's "never been safe for me to write a journal." Inside or out, she's "always felt" that someone—her mother, her husband, or a corrections officer—might read it and she would be left exposed and vulnerable.

Beyond journaling, women write to create and, as Erin George, a poet, life-sentenced woman, and prison ethnographer, notes, to establish "reconnection with the world beyond these walls."[20] *Liberty Flynn* exemplifies these processes when, in her solicited diary, she says, "I like to write. I'm currently working on a murder mystery, a series of children's books, and a humorous tale of two women in prison, and the daily exploits and problems they have." She is reaching out through one of the only viable means at her disposal. She creates texts for the enjoyment of others that simultaneously resist the invisibility she experiences as an imprisoned woman.

Ultimately, *everyone*, at least during the early years of incarceration, also reports being engaged in "working on my case." As *Lauryn* laments, "It takes a little bit of time to get caught in the system, but forever to get out of it." Carol Jacobsen, who is the Michigan Clemency Project director, and I have summarized the lengthy appeal process that imprisoned women face.[21] First the appeal moves through state courts and often through federal courts as well. By law, imprisoned people are entitled to one appeal only, for which the state will pay an assigned attorney (either an attorney employed by the State Appellate Defenders' Office or an appointed attorney) to represent him or her in that initial appeal. The State Appellate Court rules on the conduct of the case *only* (e.g., the legal technicalities in the handling of the case). It does *not* rule on guilt or innocence. If the Court of Appeals reverses the trial court, the case is sent back to the State Circuit Court for remediation. If the appeal is denied, which is most often the case, and if the woman cannot afford to hire attorneys to continue, she must do the legal work on her own. That appeal is filed "pro se," or without legal representation, in the State Supreme Court. When state remedies are exhausted, the woman has the right to file a petition for habeas corpus (Latin for "you have the body") in the United States Court of Appeals for the Federal Circuit for relief from unlawful imprisonment. Most habeas petitions are filed as *pro se* cases and it may take the court two years or more to issue an opinion. Because only about 2% of federal appeals by imprisoned people are successful, with the exception of death penalty cases, which had a 40% success rate between 1978 and 1995, the habeas petition is penultimate in the appeal process.[22] In Michigan, when all else fails, a one-time "Hail Mary" option exists in the form of a Motion for Relief from Judgment, which can be filed with the original trial court. A successful Motion for Relief from Judgment is extremely rare unless it contains new, and compelling, evidence and, even then, the woman might only be awarded an evidentiary hearing without relief.

For women with few resources, limited educational backgrounds, and no legal training, the processes and procedures are daunting. Most life-serving women were represented at their trials, or plea bargains, by public defenders. They did not, and do not, have the financial resources necessary to secure paid legal representation. Nonetheless, legal remedies are their only hope for freedom. Left to her own devices and desiring her freedom, *Sister*, with an associate's degree but no legal training, "took a paralegal course" to become informed and proficient in the legalities of an appeal. She reports "fighting issues" for three decades that resulted in repeated denials of her petitions. Undaunted, she "found errors" and would start her legal technicality research all over again. "After it got 30 years, I was like somethin's gotta give." She began to lose hope, as many other women do in the same or similar circumstances. In her solicited diary, *Liberty Flynn* describes coming to terms with the court processes and consequent disappointments: "I spent the first three years of my bit in the law library looking for a miracle. Miracles don't happen anymore. . . . I started doing legal research and helping people get out of prison. I seem to be able to help others, but can't help myself, no matter what I do. . . . I'm still waiting for that miracle that won't ever happen, I guess." Most women sentenced to life imprisonment will never experience the miracle of freedom. Some, like *Doll*, embrace the eventuality. "I know that one day I'll get out of here. Whether it's my body, or only my soul, I've made my peace with that." Nonetheless, they must all learn to live in the environment delivered to them. They do so by "staying busy."

Women cling to staying-busy strategies as a means of managing the unremitting consequences of a life sentence. Busy-ness can be profoundly satisfying. Being physically busy allows for action within confined space, especially in inclement weather when there is little opportunity for movement or choice. Yet staying busy is more often a social, psychological getaway strategy. It removes women from lengthy introspection that may lead to despair and hopelessness. Work assignments and concentration on personally scheduled activities serve as ways to distract from thinking about losses and context, fill time, relieve boredom, discharge tension, promote self-control, stimulate personal improvement and productivity, provide satisfaction through creative outlets, set them up as earnest in contrast to "slacker" peers, gain information, and empower, in that women may modify their environments by broadening their ranges of experience.[23] As *Passion* notes, staying-busy activities help women to "stay mentally healthy." Crafts, reading, sharing ideas, work assignments, and self-improvement all prevent "dwelling in the helplessness" of life imprisonment.

At all times "staying busy" is an individual choice that manifests idiosyncratically and is centered in resisting erosions to self. *Sandy*, for example, reports that she paints, draws, writes, watches TV, and does her time "alone. I've pretty much done my time without one-on-one interactions." She does her time "alone" in the presence of over a thousand other women. The primary function of staying busy is self-actualization and regulating an unpredictable environment. Sometimes being "alone" in the crowd is the best strategy.

Most of the life-serving women's staying-busy activities are rule conforming. While they may individually be active obstructionists or they may innovatively work to undermine institutional protocols, they do not report engaging in collective protest or organized challenges to the system in part due to institutional restrictions on their ability to meet in groups without supervision. Life-serving women learn to internalize the process of prisonization, that is, they come to recognize that they are without institutional power, so they acquiesce and discipline themselves to accept indignities or accede to punishment.[24] Simultaneously, they enact individual strategies that compensate for deprivation and they remain present in the moment. They choose adaptive, action-oriented, problem-solving strategies that allow them to act "as if" and to "stay busy." For the most part, they do so individually, not collectively.

"It's Absolutely the Real Thing": Fictive Kin Relationship Strategies

Since the early work of sociologists Rose Giallombardo, David Ward and Gene Kassebaum, and Esther Heffernan, and the more recent work of criminologist Barbara Owen, historian Regina Kunzel, and sociologist Juanita Diaz-Cotto, researchers of women in prison have found that a long-standing and durable feature of women's institutions is the formation of pseudo-families, formal alliances of fictive kin that provide emotional support, decrease fears and isolation, and socialize newly sentenced women to institutional rules and the informal codes of prison culture.[25]

In their pre-incarceration lives, life-serving women functioned in multiple relational roles as mothers, wives, girlfriends, daughters, and sisters. Once they were imprisoned, they were left with limited support systems and few resources. External social support from family and friends is significantly reduced through stringent prison-visit schedules, transportation costs, body searches, as well as child-care expenses and responsibilities, and eventually death and disability. So life-serving women create and develop new relationships to replace the old.[26] Some participate in pseudo-families that mimic the cultural expectations of nonincarcerated women.[27] In these prison families, women assume the formal, gendered, familial roles of mother, father, sister, cousin, auntie, and so on.

Kunzel established that incarcerated women take their pseudo-family roles and responsibilities very seriously.[28] A few life-serving women in this study, like *Bella*, laid claim to these relationships. "Oh, it's absolutely the real thing. They really become your family to the point where it doesn't even occur to you that it's not by blood." Pseudo-families function not only to protect as media portrayals would have us believe, but also to provide affective, social, and economic support. *Bella*, like other women who had no children of their own on the outside and whose incarcerations have confined them beyond child-bearing years, has assumed pseudo-motherhood as a readily available and socially valued identity.[29] She interacts with a young woman inside who "became my daughter." *Bella* describes her "daughter" as young, in her 20s, "sweet and vibrant," clinging to and hugging *Bella*, but "she's still kind of in a stubborn place [in her behavior]." The young woman is currently confined to closed custody (lockdown for 23 hours per day) as a consequence of institutional sanctions imposed on her behavior. "I can't get her to get her shit together." *Bella* is confident, however, that her "daughter" is getting to "that point where she's getting tired . . . calming down" and so will be more amenable and open to instruction and advice. As tokens signifying their closeness, the daughter sends *Bella* pictures and Mother's Day cards. "I feel like she really is my daughter. . . . Even my mom asks how my daughter is."

These nurturing, compassionate relationships provide women with a safe haven. *Caren Sue*, who is both young and recently sentenced, has adapted to prison by being cared for by her pseudo-family. She states forthrightly that *Daphne* and *Demona* are her "gay parents." "My dad," *Demona,* "looks like a boy." *Caren Sue's* fictive prison family embraces traditional gender roles. When she came out of closed custody and joined the general population, *Caren Sue* said, "I was 18. I had a mouth on me." *Daphne*, the surrogate mother, reportedly observed that "she needs guidance" and *Demona,* her surrogate father, reportedly assumed responsibility for her saying, "I'll be her dad." *Demona* has enacted that role "ever since." She's protectively "kept me under her wing." While this concerned engagement has sustained *Caren Sue,* it has also raised an ethical dilemma. "When I first started calling *Daphne* 'Mom', I would catch myself. I felt disrespectful to my real mom who died when I was [a child]. . . . Now I think she would appreciate me having another mother figure." *Caren Sue,* like lucky children on the outside, reports feeling nurtured, protected, and embraced by her prison parents.

Some women who develop pseudo-families inside do so, in some measure, to create the nurturing ties that were absent in their pre-incarceration lives. *Grace* claims that in these pseudo-familial relationships "women get from each other what they couldn't get from their families at home." *Baby,* whose mother passed when she was young, exemplifies this creative role-filling function. "I loved [my mother], but she wasn't really there for me." "Things" (a generic code word for experiences too painful or too shaming to share in a focus group) were happening to Baby, and her mother "would never believe me." *Baby* self-medicated with drugs and "caught a case" (was arrested and charged with a felony). Now "I got me two moms in prison. One white and one black. It's not about color." *Baby* articulates Kunzel's finding, and the evidence of this study, that pseudo-families are often formed across race lines.[30] In focus-group interactions, *Brenda Olds* assumes her role as *Baby's* prison mother with pride: "I'm her white mom." *Baby* goes to *Brenda Olds* for advice, support, and "just to have someone to talk to." Both women report feeling unconditionally loved by the other. As evidence of their ease together, a focus-group scribe noted that "during the focus group, they were sometimes whispering with one another. It was a very carefree, friendly-seeming occurrence that was a complementary visual aid to the discussion."

While some study respondents reported affective fictive kin relationships, many other women did not. They practiced what sociologist Catherine Kohler Riessman calls purposeful strategic avoidance, a self-imposed exile that gives women some measure of control over their environment.[31] *Alexandria* illustrates this positioning: "I am in pain for a reason." She alleges that no one knows what she went through, not her life, not where she came from, not her childhood; others don't know the reasons for her behavior. She chooses "backing away before I get hurt" and eschews pseudo-family entanglements.

Still others create emotive bonds reflective of their particular circumstances. The close relationship *Cindy* and *Louise* share, for instance, is a kind of hybrid pseudo-family. They exhibit close, non–sexually intimate ties built on the comfort of generational wisdom, that is, *Cindy*'s youthful incarceration and *Louise*'s 20-plus years of imprisonment. Although they describe their relationship in familial terms, the terms are applied loosely, out of respect, rather than as a replication of the structured pseudo-family reported by Giallombardo and others.[32] *Cindy* addresses *Louise* by a domestic term of endearment that captures their close relationship: "Hey, Nana, look at this." She also embraces both her status and role. "I'm the kid." Yet they report that monitoring *Cindy*'s youthful naiveté is a shared responsibility of *Louise*'s friendship network. All the women in the group take care of *Cindy*, lavish attention on her, and tolerate her sometimes childish behavior (e.g., mooning one of them in the hall). It's gang mentoring of a sort, where all the gang members are incarcerated, middle-aged, middle-class women. *Cindy* loves the attention. She reports spending most of her time in the company of "older" women where she is "the kid" and they all fuss over her. *Grace* explains these hybrid relationships through this analogy: "You don't just go look for it, it just happens. You know how you can't pick your family members? There might be that one uncle you don't like or something? We have that in here also. This is our society."

Many of these life-serving women have spent more time with peers inside than with blood relations on the outside. Many, like *DeDe*, have incurred heart-wrenching losses in the compositions of their outside families. "I lost my mother. I lost my father. My one son was killed. I was diagnosed with cancer. I had disfiguring cancer surgery." Staggering personal and physical losses like *DeDe*'s cannot be erased, but they can be soothed by caring, companionate relationships with other women inside.

These fictive familial ties anchor life-serving women and serve as public declarations that they are relevant to others. *Louise* describes their shared circumstances. Prison is "a world of inconsistency. Our families [other life-serving women] are constant." Companionate relationships sustain women as they struggle against the erosions to body and soul inherent in natural life sentences.

Like families everywhere, fictive kin prison families are not without tensions that are magnified by the oppressive context in which they are formed. They are not immune to problems seen in relationships on the outside.[33] Trust, for example, was discussed in several focus groups as a particularly salient feature of commitment to a pseudo-familial relationship. *All* the women in this study reported a distrust of the system and of other women. Some, like *DJ*, claimed, "This is prison and you just can't trust people." *All* of them also went on, like *Dennis the Menace*, to name women whom they trusted. "There are two people I trust. They're my moms. They're doing time like me." Life-serving women are cautious and wary of committing to trust, a necessary condition for fictive kin alliances. Because prison restrictions and the influence of the mix are not conducive to establishing trusting relationships, *Sandy* notes, "It takes a long time [to develop trust]."

Women surveil one another to determine trustworthiness, specifically to attend to "where they are coming from." Surveilling one another is an emotional nucleus. It's interpretational. Watching concentrates attention and ascribes motives in the presumed subtext of interactions. Because prisons have no exclusionary policy, women are in constant contact with others not of their choosing. Everything—movement, eating, recreation, showers—occurs in a group environment. If women are alert to individual interactions, they can predict behavior and assess trustworthiness. In this informal surveillance, *Lynn* says "you have to prove yourself" to be trusted. *Sheila T.* warns that "you just don't meet today and trust tomorrow."

Uniformly these life-serving women identified trust as "practicing confidentiality," as keeping secrets, as not repeating what is told to them, as not gossiping, and as demonstrating this discretion over the long term. Longevity of interactions is important. As evidence of her confidence in her two "moms," *Dennis the Menace* explains: "I've said some pretty horrible things and none of it's come back to me." Nonetheless, these life-serving women claim more breaches of trust than fulfillment of expectations. *Ilene Roberts* summarizes their experiences: "When you think you can open yourself up to trust again, you get hurt. It's never really safe to trust, but we are human, we want to trust." When prison is all they have, some life-serving women seek to establish close, familial-like bonds, but they also acknowledge that they cannot avoid the hurt of disingenuous exchanges.

"Not Everyone Inside Is Bi or Gay": Intimate Relationship Strategies

The world for women incarcerated for life is a small, bounded place. Their survival, emotionally and psychologically, requires that they remain in the moment. In this place at this time, one of the strategies that women use to manage and resist the dead-endedness of their life sentences is engagement in same-sex intimacies. Life-serving women report that these intimate encounters can, and often do, feed both their bodies and their souls. Those women who engage in same-sex sexual activity are unintentionally reconstructing the conventional social meanings of "lesbian" and "homosexuality." In their particular "sexual universe," they are creating definitional frames that are linked to the control present in prisons.[34] Homosexuality infringes on the dominant culture; sexuality that is enacted infringes on prison rules.[35] Prison officials seek to enforce the external meanings of sexuality in this controlled environment and women are sanctioned for behaviors interpreted by officers as sexual activity (e.g., hugging, hand holding, comforting one another).

It is important at the outset to caution that in this study, as in other research, forcible rape in prison by another woman is so uncommon as to be almost nonexistent.[36] The same-sex relationships reported in this study were consensual, chosen, and agentic. Physical rape by another imprisoned woman was neither reported nor discussed in focus groups, solicited diaries, or life-course interviews. That does not also mean, like all other reports of incarcerated women, that this population has avoided rape. Many of these life-serving women have suffered the traumas of rape, incest, and sexual abuse in their pre-imprisonment lives as well as by correctional officers once they were imprisoned. In 2006, women incarcerated in Michigan prisons filed a class-action lawsuit against the Michigan Department of Corrections alleging patterns of sexual abuse spanning more than 20 years and several facility administrations.[37] Their case settled with a $100 million award to the female plaintiffs.

As early as 1965, sociologists David Ward and Gene Kassebaum identified women's intimacy, often manifested in sexual relationships, as the most distinctive type of gender adaptation to prison circumstances. That claim has been repeatedly supported by research on women in prison.[38] As cultural anthropologist Mark Fleisher and criminologist Jessie Krienert found in their more recent study of prison rape, prison is not an asexual environment.[39] Women bring their sexual identities and experiences with them into the prison and they adapt in idiosyncratic ways to the hyper-sexualized culture in which they find themselves. In focus-group discussions, in-depth interviews, and solicited diaries, women in this study spoke to the many ways that same-sex intimacy is structured, visible, and commonplace inside prison walls.

Representatively *Martha* speaks to both the ordinariness and the public nature of these encounters, noting that once women become acclimated to prison culture, they treat the sexual environment "like it's nothing." After years of incarceration, she has accepted "that's just how it works." She provides an analogy: "It's like you see pictures of people in Third World countries who don't even bother swatting the flies away from their faces. They're just tired and they know there's no use in even trying." *Martha*'s remarks reflect carceral pragmatism in the acceptance of the ubiquity of sexual activity inside, of intimate behaviors played out in public space, and of the aftermath of relationships gone bad within the "drama" that drives prison life.

Prison sexuality is a complex sociocultural network of mutable sex roles that is a defining element of women's prison culture. For example, *Doll* argues, "I don't think it's so much gay or not gay. I think it's whether or not you're willing to be in a relationship." For *Doll* external labels bifurcating sexuality into gay or straight are not relevant in the prison context. Intimate contact between women is simply one means by which relational dynamics are manifested inside. There are others. Same-sex engagements reflect the limitations of the institutional environment, not necessarily the sexual preferences of the participants.

Fleisher and Krienert found that, "in prison, the labels 'gay' and 'straight' are not necessarily mutually exclusive categories."[40] The either/or duality of gay/straight is not germane in this artificial world. Perhaps "sexuality" is not even the appropriate term to describe the reported sexual behaviors of these life-serving women. Their intimate behaviors do not mirror conventional sexuality, as defined by desire and preference. In *The History of Sexuality*, Foucault argues that those human acts and sensations that come to be defined as "sexual" are social products borne out of the interactions of history and culture.[41] Desire and sexual excitement are not "naturally driven" human experiences. Foucault argues that both are political constructs. Within particular historical and cultural moments, we learn who the appropriate objects of desire are within our cultural context. Even the manners of expression of desire are embedded in networks of cultural meanings. According to Foucault, sexual desire, behavior, and identity are not necessarily mutually implicating phenomena. They are discrete: sometimes consonant, sometimes not. "Bodies and pleasures" only become subjective through social, cultural, and discursive mediation. Because erotic dimensions of human sexual experience are elements in a changing discourse and sex (and the assumption that sex is the primary force conditioning human relationships) is always a discursive construct, then sexual desire, preference, choice, and activity are all political behaviors. In any social context, the construction of a "sexual universe" is fundamentally linked to the structures of power. Imprisonment is one node in the web of interactions out of which the idea emerges that sexuality "is" something in and of itself. Incarceration for life then results in an anomalous "sexual universe" that structures sexual behaviors and intimate sexual relationships as well as their definitions.

Although the same-sex activities of incarcerated women are a popular cultural stereotype, research on incarcerated women's participation in same-sex intimacy within correctional facilities is sparse.[42] Most research on imprisoned women focuses on the history of female incarceration, explanations of women's criminality, gender issues in sentencing, lack of appropriate programming, treatment during imprisonment (particularly for sexual abuse), and the role of pseudo-families. With a few notable exceptions (e.g., historian Regina Kunzel's *Criminal Intimacy: Prison and the Uneven History of Modern American Sexuality* and historian Estelle Freedman's work on prison lesbians), extensive research rarely focuses on women's same-sex sexual relationships inside.[43] Smaller-scale studies, however, have made significant contributions to understandings of these activities. In their study of 245 incarcerated women in a southern U.S. correctional facility, for example, criminologists Mary Koscheski, Richard Tewksbury, and Christopher Hensley found that 8% of the women identified as lesbians pre-incarceration, while 28% identified as bisexual, and 64% identified as exclusively heterosexual. Postincarceration, 13% identified as lesbian, 31% as bisexual, and 55% remained exclusively heterosexual in their identities.[44] Findings such as these demonstrate that the conventionally polarized border between homosexuality and heterosexuality is both blurred and permeable in women's prisons. In a study of women incarcerated in the United Kingdom, criminologist Mary Bosworth found that "sexuality divides the inmate community because lesbian relations are accorded conflict status."[45] Although some women in her study appreciated opportunities to form intimate ties, others were "extremely critical" of any lesbian activity and reported being made uneasy by same-sex relationships. Nonetheless, Bosworth also found that "lesbian relationships were fairly common among the inmate community."[46] Sociologists Candace Kruttschnitt and Rosemary Gartner studied women in two California prisons and found "sexual relations among prisoners was reportedly 'just a part of life in here.' "[47] They note that affective sexual relationships helped life-serving women manage their sentences but were also a source of conflict, as they remained a central element of the mix in women's prisons.

Women's reported sexual activity notwithstanding, all same-sex intimacies are prohibited in prison and—historically and contemporarily—prison authorities have established long-standing patterns of policing and prohibiting girls' and women's sexuality. In this study, sex, sexual relations, and same-sex intimacies were recounted as ongoing activities,[48] and disapproval was robust for sexual relationships that involved concurrent relationships with multiple partners. Most often, discussion of same-sex intimacy was raised by the women themselves. Two of the study scribes noted this pattern: "drugs, homosexual relationships in prison. They're mentioned every time without it even being brought up and probed by you. Both are an outlet for comfort, for emotional release." Another scribe at a different focus group noted, "I was also slightly surprised by the candid sexual conversation the women had. They talked in a way close friends talk and felt comfortable enough to talk like that in front of us."

The relationships reported and discussed by the women were usually dyadic, consensual, and offered differing degrees of emotional involvement. Nonetheless sexual activity is strictly prohibited, policed, and punished inside prison walls.[49] Officers interpret sexual passion as a threat to prison order,[50] so correctional sanctions are purportedly swift and decisive for any violations of expected institutional celibacy. Incarcerated women are not allowed to hug, hold hands, or comfort one another, even in times of intense grief. *Shequetta Tasha Lynn* reports getting a ticket because another woman had her head on *Shequetta's* shoulder when she was crying over missing her child. "People get more tickets for hugging." Such contact, interpreted by officers as sexual, puts women at risk of a "ticket for sexual abuse" (a prison misconduct citation, often with penalties that can affect parole/commutation considerations). Given the clearly enforced prohibitions, women who engage in same-sex sexual liaisons are unmistakably choosing to engage in resistant and transgressive behaviors.

As a strategy for conformity, empowerment, self-actualization, and resistance, same-sex intimacies serve multiple purposes in the lives of life-serving women. As *Lizzy* notes, "Not everyone inside is bi or gay." Women discussed multiple forms of sexual behaviors that were commonplace. Not all women engage in all these activities. Some women choose celibacy or autoerotic behavior and so have no sexual engagements with another person. Other women arrive and begin "right away" looking for a relationship. "Well, the girls who are looking for girlfriends want to know straight up who they should hit on and who they shouldn't waste their time on." Still others are in committed monogamous relationships. Some women report running the gamut of sexual opportunities. For other women, sexual relationships happen unexpectedly. For some, not at all.

The primary sexual goal, according to poet, prison ethnographer, and incarcerated woman Erin George, is getting sex and hiding it from correctional officers.[51] As a consequence, as *Tootsie Roll* notes, "this relationship stuff gets intense." It seems that it has been so for a long time. In a study of New York's Bedford Hills Prison for Women during the Progressive Era (1890–1920), historian Sarah Potter found that women incarcerated there expressed and embraced passionate desire and a need for love regardless of the sex or race of their partner.[52] So, too, for the women in this study, who reported, sometimes with passion and intensity, multiple means, methods, and motives for hiding from the officers their sexual encounters, their ingenuity, and their distraction ploys.

In a context of 24-hour surveillance, in an institution that has 1,400 security cameras, where the only persons allowed in residential cells are the bunkies assigned to them, women who engage in sexual activity must, of necessity, be creative, innovative, and determined. Sexual logistics inside are complex. To "hook up" and protect themselves from the scrutiny of correctional officers, women employ "chalkers." Chalkers are other women, friends providing assistance or simply employed lookouts, who watch for and warn the lovers about the approach of an officer or a bunkie; who distract the officer with requests, questions, conversation, or complaints; or who involve officers in fruitless errands that temporarily move them out of the area. All the women make note of which officers will actually check rooms as part of their job responsibilities. Life-serving women connect for sex when enforcement is lax. Unanimously, they claim, "you sneak."

For those women who have toilets in their rooms, correctional officers are required to "knock and announce" before entering. Women sexually engaged will respond "I'm using the toilet; I have diarrhea" to cover their erotic activity. Because there are no cameras and no officers in the showers, the shower room is a choice location for carnal pursuits. Additionally women, through trial and error, have located the spots that the surveillance cameras don't monitor. Those unsecured sites provide women with opportunities for fast-service sex. In spite of their utilization of the cracks in omnipresent surveillance, all study participants agreed that, given the potential sanctions, "the less people that know the better." Nonetheless, in one venue or another, they discussed the following eleven categories of sex and sexual activity.

1. *Entry sex.* Recently sentenced women, who want to "fit in" to the perceived prison culture, describe engaging in same-sex sexual relationships, sometimes for the first time. *Sheri* had just turned 20 when she arrived at the prison compound. She had a high-visibility, media-saturated case and "no one wanted to be my friend." Inside she was mentored by "dope addicts," was using drugs herself, and describes her entry by saying, "I was cute and I

got a girlfriend too." Using sex to fit in reflects the normative aspect of sexual relationships in women's prison culture. The context *Sheri* entered was sex-saturated and sexual activity was integral to *Sheri's* initial prison adjustment.[53]

2. *Sex for sex's sake.* Women who engage in sex without commitment, as a heterosexual substitution activity, or simply because it is available, are engaging in intentional, proactive initiatives. They refuse to allow prison policies to constrain their sexual appetites. In their recountings, they express no emotional ties to their assorted sexual partners. Their sexual activities are unencumbered by relational bonds. They are simply instrumental responses to cravings within a deprivation environment. *Shequetta Tasha Lynn* provides one such example: "I wanted sex for the weekend. I didn't have a prom." She had completed a vocational program and it was spring break on the outside. "I didn't have my spring break out there, so I had it in here." Imprisonment prom sex was, for her, a festive activity, an "as if" celebration of her vocational success.

Sex and sex alone is *Ciara Blue's* expressed motivation. "I have lots of sex. But I don't get emotionally attached. I've been here since I was 17 [now 34] and I'm *going to* have sex! Go ahead, move me, I'm going to have sex" (emphasis is *Ciara Blue's*). Her challenge to the authoritative order, her capacity to insist on sexual activity, is evidence of her autonomy. She is willing to endure prison sanctions, that is, being relocated to a more secure residence unit, in order to have her sexual yearnings satisfied. She will not be denied. *Ciara Blue* reports that, "most of the time," she doesn't communicate with her sexual partners to arrange their meetings. Instead someone will pass her a note suggesting a time and location. She responds, "I'm there." Although eschewing selection criteria in her partners, she enacts rigorous rules of engagement. "I don't lay with kids" and "I don't speak on it." Her sexual activity is not predatory; it is consensual. She maintains strict confidentiality. "My private life is private."

3. *Diversionary or distraction sex.* Sometimes described as situational homosexuality, or colloquially as "gay for the stay," diversionary or distraction sex eases the isolation and the aloneness that Erin George describes as "the perpetual punishment of those con-

fined."[54] Some heterosexually identified women respond to the loneliness of imprisonment by engaging in same-sex intimacies. *Ciara* is clear about these processes: "Gay for the stay comes out of loneliness." It is not, as sociologist Rebecca Trammell claims, a "transitional lesbianism."[55] Trammell's error is in assuming that the sexual act reflects both identity and preference. As Foucault argues, they are discrete phenomena. *Doll*, for example, speaks to sexual intimacies and their role in the endlessness and seclusion imposed by a life sentence. "I think if I wasn't a lifer, I would've never ended up in a relationship." When asked why, *Doll* says, "Because it was such a long time to spend alone." Later she ruminates, "It could be why I let the first woman catch me."

The losses, the surveillance, the "drama," and the constant vigilance and loneliness erode women's abilities to cope and manage a lifetime of imprisonment. "It happened more because I was lonely than because I was gay" was an oft-repeated message in the focus groups. Same-sex sexual relationships inside help fill the voids and soothe the pains of imprisonment.

4. *Emotional fulfillment and personal growth.* Women with life sentences sometimes choose to engage in intimate relationships out of a longing to have a deeper connection with another person. Koscheski and Hensley found that women imprisoned in a southern correctional facility adopted same-sex relationships in order to share joys and sorrows and losses and triumphs with someone who cared.[56] In this study, *Ciara* provided support for their findings. "We [lifers] get in these codependent relationships with people that are more draining" than beneficial. "We are emotionally stagnated in so many areas." Suffering both visible and invisible losses due to imprisonment, "all we want [out of these relationships] is love and appreciation."

Not all same-sex intimate relationships inside are loving and caring. Many do not end well. *Doll* describes her experience in such a bittersweet relationship. "It wasn't good, but what I got out of it was really vital to me. She loved me despite everything; no matter what I did, she still loved me. And I needed that." *Doll* "spent my whole life being judged and I . . . never felt worthy" so, when she paired up for a sexual relationship with a woman inside, she felt bathed in unconditional love. *Doll's* agency and self-actualization were facilitated by being soothed and nurtured. Like mulch in a garden, the unconditional love enhanced *Doll's* self-actualizing processes. "In my case, after coming from a lifetime of abuse and judgment, being with someone nonjudgmental is what helped me grow." For *Doll*, as for many other study participants, the same-sex intimacies were not about sex or lesbianism or homosexuality. They were about care, concern, and acceptance.[57]

5. *Bed buddies.* Bed buddies serve the sexual and comfort needs of women whose partners live in other units and so are not easily accessible. *Sasha Lavan* eschews such behavior in her claim that "some people just have bed buddies and still have their woman. I just couldn't see myself doing that." However, she also acknowledges that, without freedom of movement, "sometimes you find yourself being by yourself and you wish you had someone else beside that one person." Bed buddies are instrumental, not affective, sexual interactions. They serve the particular purpose of filling a short-term, loneliness void, but they do not extend further into a relationship.

6. *Transactional sex.* For some women, sexual relationships are simply an economic exchange, a form of institutional barter. In a study of imprisoned women's relationships, criminologist Kimberly Greer noted that unequal access to money and material goods inside was sometimes the driving force for sexual liaisons.[58] Canadian social work scholars Avery Calhoun and Heather Coleman termed these trades of sexual services for material goods "sexual extortion." In this study, women acknowledged such transactional exchanges, but those women with more time down reported intervening in the negotiations of their youthful peers.[59] *Joyce*, for example, gives "noodles" to young girls so they don't have to "kiss ass" for a snack. *Meme* will take these young women under her wing, talk about their options, and make clear that they are "disrespecting themselves for a $0.29 noodle."

7. *Predatory sex.* New, young, or naive women, particularly juveniles, may become targets for older predators. When juveniles are incarcerated for life, they enter the prison world without the social resources to cope effectively. They become prey to the unscrupulous.

Wink disdainfully depicts an environment where "some women prey on babies," noting that some girls are 16 and the older women are "50, 52." *Ilene Roberts* discusses the grooming behavior of these predators, who "play a certain role, mother, etc., then they try to touch you. They'll buy all your personals for you [soap, deodorant, shampoo, lotion, sanitary napkins]" until the young woman is indebted. The informal prison code proscribes that "if you took gifts, you owe [whoever provided them]." The predator can then demand repayment in the form of sexual favors. It is a form of coercive sex in which the prey acquiesces to the encounter in order to reduce or eliminate her indebtedness.

8. *Autonomy.* Imprisonment denies women control over their own bodies. Same-sex intimacy is a means of reinstating, in small measure, some of that control. *Faith* chooses to be sexually active in a consciously intentional, political decision that signals "control of my own life." In prison, engaging in any relational sexual activity is strictly prohibited and severely sanctioned. For *Faith,* "control of my own life" comes from choosing to be in a same-sex intimate relationship in an environment with few choices. Her choice to remain sexually active is transgressive behavior that is voluntary, consensual, and—when undetected—empowering.

9. *Gay on the outside, gay on the inside.* *Tootsie Roll* and *Dennis the Menace* exemplify bringing outside sexual orientations into the facility. They are what criminologist Angela Pardue and her colleagues label "true homosexuals," those women who identified as gay prior to and continuing beyond incarceration.[60] *Tootsie Roll* and *Dennis the Menace* are not "gay for the stay." They both engaged in homosexual and/or bisexual behavior prior to imprisonment. After incarceration, their options were limited to women. *Tootsie Roll* says, "I was bisexual since I was 16. I've been in two real relationships with women here—emotionally, mentally, and physically."

   Dennis the Menace adds more dimension to the transition from outside to inside sexual activity. "It's hard for my mom to accept. My mom knew I slept with women on the streets. When I go home, I don't think I'll be with a man again. Women are a different kind of love. More emotional and sentimental." *Dennis the Men-*

ace has established her preference. The sexual behavior of other women, who were gay or bisexual before their incarcerations, was shaped outside of prison but sustained by the hyper-sexualized climate inside.

10. *Committed couples.* George writes, "To deny the possibility of bona fide sexual relationships is to deny what little autonomy the prisoners feel they have."[61] Many women involved in same-sex relationships report being steadfast and devoted to their partners. Their relationships are dyadic and monogamous. They take pride in their connection and are dedicated to one another. *Lizzy* exemplifies this variation on sex inside as she asserts, "In my relationship, it's more than just sexual; it's a friendship. I mean, yes, it's a relationship and there's a sexual element to it, but really she just keeps me positive." *Lizzy* sets herself apart from the "gay for the stay" women engaged in sexual activity. In contrast, she presents her relationship as more dimensional than just sex; it is relational as well. "It's a friendship" that implies caring, sharing, depth of knowledge of one another, reciprocal obligations, pleasure, and delight. *Lizzy* summarizes her relationship with her partner: "She's there for me as a friend, but [she] also fulfills my sexual needs." These multidimensional, committed relationships reportedly achieve the balance that helps sustain life-serving women.

11. *Celibacy and/or autoeroticism.* For reasons of heterosexual orientation, of choice, of religious proscription, or of cultural or familial sanctions, some women eschew participation in same-sex intimacies. They report choosing self-stimulation over same-sex engagement. Autoeroticism and same-sex intimate relationships are not an either/or choice. Some women engage in both. For those choosing only autoeroticism or celibacy, there are social consequences. *Sasha Lavan* avers that "if you don't participate . . . in here, you find yourself being by yourself."

Most of the dyadic sexual relationships described by these life-serving women appear to have little to do with sexual orientation or sexual preference. They have more to do with the deprivations of the prison context, accessible resources, and choices available to cope with loneliness and the unremitting pressure of time. For those, like *Journey,* who say, "I've had a girlfriend, but I'm not gay," same-sex sexual activity is not synonymous with a homosexual identity. Relationships matter. The reported sexual intimacies most often serve as pathways for emotional gratification. Sex is simply the method enacted to deepen emotional connection. These study participants do not describe, or discuss, sexual relations between women as "homosexual," except for those who previously identified as bisexual or lesbian. For most, it is the relationship that matters; even if the relationship is described as predatory or economic, it is still a relationship. The heterosexual/homosexual binary is not relevant in this context. In meeting their sexual needs and desires, life-serving women present more fluidity and more sexual flexibility than is available in a simple gay/straight dichotomy.[62]

Although using sexual activity to fill time, to conform to perceived culture, to seize some measure of autonomy over their bodies, to self-actualize, and to resist, these women are also actively reconstructing the social meanings of sexual identity. They are actively enacting a range of sexual identities. Although engaged in same-sex sexual intimacies and relationships, they do not define themselves as homosexual, nor do they define themselves as lesbian, bisexual, or gay, unless they did so prior to incarceration. It is a misnomer to describe their sexual intimacies as "homosexual relations" or "lesbian relationships" unless both partners identify as lesbian. The majority of women in this study who engaged in same-sex relationships did not view themselves as homosexual in their identities. Like *Journey*, who had a girlfriend but did not identify as gay, most women presented themselves as maintaining the heterosexual identities that they embraced prior to imprisonment even as they simultaneously reported engaging in same-sex intimacies inside.

Although enacting behavior that conventionally defines people as homosexual, they are not homosexual in their awarenesses of self, in part, because their engagements are not driven by orientation or preference, but by loneliness, economics, availability, or predation. Calling same-sex sexual intimacies "homosexual" creates a mismatch between enacted behavior and self-identity. *Journey* has not "become" gay by engaging in same-sex sexual behaviors. In her identity, she's "not gay." As criminologists Mark Pogrebin and Mary Dodge have argued, same-sex intimacy in prison is consensual and enacted for emotional fulfillment;[63] it has little to do with homosexuality.

"A Personal Relationship with God": Prayerful Strategies

"I start every day with tears. . . . If I didn't have faith, I couldn't have survived in here." *Louise's* testament to the role of faith, of spiritual practice, like the claims of many of her peers, links prayer to the emotional and psychological coping skills that are necessary for surviving life sentences. Meditative prayer is a potent individual strategy enacted by life-serving women to protect themselves from the corrosive processes inherent in the prison experience.

Life-serving women pray, in part, to commune with a nonjudgmental higher power. *Cameron,* for example, describes using "count" (the four-times-a-day institutional requirement to ensure the presence of all the incarcerated women in the facility) for spiritual practice. During count, work ceases. Recreation stops. Phone calls end. Women are required to sit on their beds until "count clears." In her solicited diary, *Candace* (see chapter 9 for *Candace's* spiritual story) says, "This is also my quiet time with God. Count time 11 a.m. I read my devotionals and my Bible and have a chat with him." Daily devotion, a practice noted by many women in the study, is a public symbol of obedience to religious precepts.[64] For these women, God is powerful and all-knowing and consequently knows the purity of heart and genuine remorse of the women who seek his comfort. Life-serving women may not receive societal forgiveness for their crimes, but they do receive God's forgiveness. *Jannel* speaks to this surety: "Forgiveness comes as a result of repentance. If I choose to repent for the wrong I have done, forgiveness is granted [by God]." When social processes do not prove to be forgiving, an alternative is present in God's mercy.

It is an acknowledged cliché that people find God in prison because, as *Royal Tee* notes, "who better to grab onto than God? There's truthfulness to it." She notes that after her incarceration, she thought about God as "Big God" and "if you mess up, he'll zap you. . . . I made God the God-of-get-me-out-of-prison." Eventually, through "reading his word," she let go of her get-out-of-prison demands and developed a "relationship with God" where she "could talk with him." Now her petitions are less specific and less insistent: "I ask Him to keep me healthy and give me peace." The manifestation of God's response to her talking is "a still, strong voice inside your soul" that relieves the feelings of frustration and powerlessness that can become obsessions inside. *Royal Tee*'s personal relationship with God offers her the elements of connection that help to provide her life with meaning.

For most life-serving women, having a relationship with God is not a cliché. "It gives us hope at the end of the day and that's what matters." Without hope, there is despair. In the face of daunting fears, belief in God is a wellspring of hope; it assures women that they are not alone in the world.[65] Communing with God through prayer provides women with faith in an alternative future. They believe that, through prayers, they can exert some measure of control over the unpredictable circumstances of their lives.[66] *Alexandria* speaks of her confidence, and the repeated confidence of others, that "God wasn't going to do this [life imprisonment] to me. I wasn't going to stay. God set me aside for something." Her imprisonment has a moral component. God is a rational planner who makes selections and chooses women as instruments in his plans. God has set *Alexandria* "aside" for reasons as yet unknown to her.

Women, who report believing that God can be influenced by appropriate behavior, by prayers, and by their sacrifices inside, also expect rewards or punishment for compliance or disobedience.[67] Most frame these understandings in the befores and afters of incarceration. *Ciara Blue* claims "I was born and raised in church. I turned my back on it. No sooner had I turned my back, [then] bad things started happening." In a discursive exchange *Meme* disdains the find-God-in-prison cliché. "It's not that I found God in here," she says. She always believed in God, she "just didn't pay attention to God" or "didn't pay attention to what I already knew" until she was imprisoned. She waves her hands to demonstrate how she was running straight through the "yellow caution lights" that God was "flashing" at her and the accidents that ensued. "Zoom! . . . In prison, it's a red light." *Meme* had beliefs without practice. She reports that she chose to ignore the "yellow caution lights" that could have interrupted her momentum and changed the direction of her life. Now she, and her life-serving peers have time for God, for the religious practice that demonstrates their remorse and their new obedient-to-His-word identities. *Meme* says, "God keeps me focused, grounded, and on my course." Everything else in her life is halted by the imprisonment "red light" but God forgives the egregious errors committed by her pre-incarceration self.

Merrilee is skeptical of the faith statements of her prayerful peers. To demonstrate her suspicion, she inquires about the emotional and psychological survival of "women who have been down 20 and 30 years, how do they do it?" Focus-group respondents chorus their uniform answer: "God." Not easily swayed, *Merrilee* continues her questioning: "Do you really think it's about 'being good in God's eyes' to get out? How could it be about God? If it is, me and Him, we've got issues." *Merrilee* has been "good." So have hundreds of other women in the facility, as evidenced by their clear conduct records and genuine remorse, yet they continue to be imprisoned. If it is about being good, *Merrilee* is challenging her peers' deeply held beliefs and she is holding God accountable for a failure to act. *Merrilee* and God have "got issues."

Imprisonment unhinges women from their moorings. Without social anchors, prayer and devotional behavior become significant coping strategies. Prayer is ubiquitous in this women's prison. It is reportedly the most important and most effective tool that women can access without fear of sanction. *Love Evans,* for example, claims, "The best tool I have is prayer. I can't carry all that weight." The weight of time erodes. It bears down on life-serving women and it can crush them, but, for those who believe in the efficacy of prayer, God makes their loads lighter. Through prayer, God shares the burden and relieves the loneliness and isolation of living through a life sentence. *Ciara* claims, "That's the best thing about him, he does what he does because he chooses [to love me]" and "he's the only one who ever has." For some women God becomes the spiritual manifestation of lifetimes lived without temporal love.

Trust in God and his love is implicit in prayer. These life-serving women trust that their imprisonment is part of a broader, spiritual plan for them. Like *Alexandria, Jannel* believes that "God has a plan for my life. Man has given me a life sentence, not God. . . . I was not angry with God." Akin to many of her peers, *Jannel* does not accept that her life sentence is her endpoint. *Jannel* believes prison is God's plan for her, so she is not angry with God over her imprisonment. She trusts that her incarceration is part of a more universal plan for broadening her ministry. "Ministry is in me." She can sit in the prison yard and share his teachings with other women. Being locked away and labeled a criminal "cannot stop God from doing with my life what he wants." Nonetheless, she asks, "OK, God, how can you bring good out of this horrible situation?" She thanks God for the experience of her imprisonment because "He's using me here." Her submission to God's authority reestablishes her dignity and worth as an individual and as a "child of God." She reinterprets her imprisonment from a stigmatizing experience into a highly moral enterprise. She is confined so that she can be an instrument of God for other imprisoned women.

In a study of the religious engagement of incarcerated men, criminal justice scholar Todd Clear and his colleagues identified a number of intrinsic meanings of religion that are also supported by the narratives of women in this study.[68] Like their male counterparts, women found that religious practices were helpful in dealing with the guilt resulting from their crimes, but, unlike the men, in a gendered spin the women also prayed for relief from the guilt of leaving their children and families behind. *Ciara* calls herself a "child of God" but steers away from organized religion, claiming "I'm very spiritual. . . . I believe you live your hell on earth." She has "lived my hell" in retribution "for the life I took." She cries as she talks about how her children have paid as well for her "not being there. . . . I reap what I sow. It all comes back." *Ciara's* life also reflected the pre-incarceration rejection of religious obligations, noted by others, which presumably led to her criminality, collectively defined as an undisciplined desire for worldly pleasures. About her early spiritual life, *Ciara* says, "Before imprisonment I went to church every Sunday, even during my addiction. I stood in church with crack in my purse and sang 'Amazing Grace' and I cried." Then reality bit. She was charged and sentenced for a death that occurred in the commission of another felony. "When I got locked up, I was at my lowest point and that's who you turn to." Now she says, "God is why I wake up every morning."

Another intrinsic meaning of religion in this study that resonates with those identified by Clear and colleagues[69] is what they termed a "packaged alternative to previous ways of living"; that is, through use of the Bible ("God's written word") as a blueprint, women develop new pathways through life. They reinterpret unpleasant present events as challenges from God. Women, like *Jannel*, are "in my Bible" all the time. "There are a ton of women in here that try to tell you how to be"; by "listening to this [she touches her Bible], it keeps you grounded." *Jannel* tries to "use this gift" (of her ministry) as best she can. The Bible is her guide. She says, "You have to be set on something or you can be swooped into anything." Many life-serving women report profound connection with their Bibles as resources, as indexes of advice, as the sources of answers for problems, and as guides to survival. *Journey* says, for example, "When people come to me for advice, or want help, I just give them a biblical message. I don't think there's anything the Bible can't help with." Her response to others carries the weight of the word of God. It provides her and other women with the space to read their own meanings into the text as it simultaneously brings them into a community of other believers.

In the religious prison narrative reflected by these life-serving women, straying from the religious path for false worldly pleasures resulted in their imprisonment. Their incarcerations were divine, and temporal, retributions for choices that took them "away from God." But imprisonment was also "God's plan" for each of them; it was a moral wake-up call to return to religious practice and to become instruments for spiritual work inside through outreach to others. *David* speaks to these understandings when, in her solicited diary, she writes "my journal is a spiritual journal because this is how I do my time in God's word and my focus is becoming a new me inside out. . . . I want God to use me in this prison to help speak good into these women. . . . they [correctional officers] treat us like shit and not everyone is strong enough to face these hard times. That's one reason I try to stay in the presence of the Lord. For peace . . . I'm in prison to become a good role model. . . . I have a good reputation with staff and inmates. I don't get in the way of nobody. . . . when I look back over my life, I know it was God who carried me threw [*sic*] these storms. . . . my time here in prison to me means that I have to redirect my life and find purpose and realize that God makes no mistakes." *David's* remarks reflect a commonly described sense of communion with God as a source of solace and hope in difficult circumstances. That "God makes no mistakes" locates her crime and resulting imprisonment as challenges from God that she addresses by reaching out to other incarcerated women as a role model. Belief in God gives meaning to her existence. She is not invisible. Her imprisonment, and the imprisonment of other life-serving women, is—in these terms—"God's plan" for them.

An additional intrinsic meaning that Clear and colleagues found in their study of religion in the lives of incarcerated men dealt with the loss of freedom, the obvious primary deprivation of imprisonment.[70] In their religious practice, the men found freedom by developing a personal sense of peace more concentrated on spirit and less on material comforts than they had had in their pre-incarceration lives. *Raine's* personal account is consonant with those findings, as it also indicates the gendered nature of freedom. "I've had conversations with God since before I was locked up." She illustrates with a narration of the lowest point in her life. "Homeless, drunk, high, and tired" after a night of heavy drinking and prostitution, she came undone at 4 a.m. in an elementary school yard. She asked God, her refuge of last resort, to help her get sober and "out of this life." She did not imagine prison as the answer to her prayer, but "it turned out that prison was what I needed" to get clean and sober. Having been incarcerated for more than 20 years, *Raine* continues to reflect the confidence of others in God's intention to secure her freedom. "I know that one day God will open that gate for me." God has reasons for her imprisonment: *Raine* is certain that there is "something he's protecting me from out there" by keeping her confined. Through her faith in God, she is both free and safe within prison walls. By submitting to their versions of the will of God, women can escape the reality of their present circumstances and enter a state of grace where they are not judged, threatened, or demeaned and where they are enriched and nurtured. Belief in God provides an embracing response to their yearning for connectedness.

For many women, sentenced "behind a man," who have been manipulated by men, who were abused by men, who had been "gullible" and "stupid" in the service of men, who aided and abetted violent men, or who murdered their brutal male partners, it is only in a spiritual incarnation as God that the male figures in their lives are experienced as nurturing, loving, and dependable. In such iterations God becomes emblematic of the ideal partner or father, the essentialized, idealized version of a physical man who honors, comforts, and protects women. In focus-group discussions, God was often, if unwittingly, presented as a male figure substitute. For example, when *Jannel* was first charged and sentenced, she reported going through a phase of hating men. Yet, she also claimed, "it was God, the man, who has held me . . . and comforts me." "I don't depend on earthly men, I have a heavenly father." Envisioned as a male nurturer, redeemer, and exonerator of past errors in judgment, God has gendered obligations. His responsibilities are representatively iterated by *Royal Tee*: "to make decisions for me . . . to keep me informed . . . to protect me. . . . If I'm doing my part, he's like my overseer, a guardian, a father, protector, provider, a comforter." In these presentations, God begins to sound like the hegemonic male, described by sociologist Michael Kimmel,[71] who follows the four basic rules of traditional masculinity: (1) "No sissy stuff"; (2) "be a big wheel"; (3) "be a sturdy oak"; and (4) "give 'em hell." Not all life-serving women agree with these characterizations of God's gendered responsibilities: *Jannel* disputes God's obligation to anyone. "The way I see it, He has no obligation to me. He sent his son to die. He's already done it all. He doesn't owe me anything."

While having "a personal relationship with God" was the preeminent spiritual description among women who identified as Christian, other women embraced different religious practices or none at all. *Simone*, for example, overturned her previous belief system and now locates her spiritual center "within myself. I don't believe in God. [My belief in God] changed when an occurrence happened to me. I just take [imprisonment] day by day. . . . I don't have anyone to rely on now. Every decision I make is a conscious decision." God abandoned *Simone*, so *Simone* abandoned God. Without God, she's alone and self-guiding. *Simone's* reoriented spiritual center reflects the fatalism shared by many other life-serving women who claim that, with a life sentence, there's "nothing more that can happen to me." *Harmony*, however, reports coming "from a different place." She claims Buddhism as the "closest thing you can come to the spiritual path that I'm on" and she embraces a Buddhist worldview that "God is everything, including the conscience that I am."

In an environment that enforces conformity, even personal religious beliefs can result in shaming experiences. *Wanda* says, "When I first came to prison, I was ashamed to admit that I am Wiccan. I catch a lot of shit for it sometimes." Before her death, *Wanda's* grandmother taught her this loosely structured, duo theistic religion and encouraged her to honor both a goddess associated with the moon, stars, and Earth, and a god associated with the sun, forests, and animals. In spite of difficulties with her bunkie, who called *Wanda* a "Satan worshipper," *Wanda* has continued to celebrate lunar and solar religious rituals in order to honor her connection to her grandmother. In a closed environment, with high rates of religiosity, being Wiccan is a high-profile identity. Negative depictions of *Wanda*'s spiritual beliefs are heightened by characterizations of Wicca as "Satan worshipping," particularly when a significant segment of incarcerated women subscribes to "get thee back, Satan" religious beliefs.

Other life-serving women, who lack a connection to organized religion or a personal relationship with God, reportedly search for one. *Azianna*, for example, says that in "trying to get God" she has explored every religion looking for a "fit" that she can embrace. She reports "even" trying her bunkie's Jehovah's Witness religion, but "it didn't work." Although she reads the Bible "religiously" and she "sticks with God . . . I pray constantly," nothing helps. She can't "get God." Upon hearing her religious struggles, her focus-group peers attempted to help *Azianna* develop additional insight in her quest.

> *Scarlet*: What gives you peace then?
> *Azianna*: Nothing. I've never found a religion that fits.
> *Joyce:* Why continue if it doesn't work? You don't keep taking a medication if it's not working.
> *Azianna*: Because I hope . . .
> *Joyce*: Can't hope. You gotta have faith.
> *Jannel:* Don't look for religion. Look for a relationship with God.

Azianna is seeking an understanding of God through organized religion and religious practice. She reads the Bible and she prays as she searches for an indistinct outcome that confounds her. She can't find the path to "get God." She cannot find a "fit" in the organized religions she has known. The personal relationship with God that other women seem to have realized is elusive for her. *Scarlet* is incredulous. Her own faith is what provides her with "peace." *Joyce* aims for the pragmatic in providing assistance. "Why continue if it doesn't work?" She provides a medical analogy that frames *Azianna*'s desire to "get God" as akin to getting a spiritual inoculation. *Azianna* nonetheless clings to "hope" for an eventual religious epiphany. Hope is central for women who are sentenced to life without parole. It enables them to envision better, different futures than their present circumstances allow and so is central in the struggle against the erosion of generalized despair. A positive outlook, enabled by the confidence in a meaningful relationship with God, helps women to preserve emotional wellness. *Joyce* resolves that *Azianna's* idle hope, however, is not useful. She counsels *Azianna* that she "can't hope. You gotta have faith." Raised in a "Satanic home," faith is difficult for *Azianna* to grasp. *Jannel* offers a way out. She advises *Azianna* to turn away from organized religion and to "look for a [one-on-one] relationship with God." One that is unmediated by formal proscriptions. *Jannel* expresses the oft-repeated imperative "You have to have a source of support that isn't a human being" so that you can maintain "hope in something higher than this mess." Prison is a hostile, unpleasant environment, and "God does not like ugly."

Religion and the hope, forgiveness, and acceptance that it offers is embedded in life-serving women's prison culture. Life-sentenced women don't just have a religion. They actively "do" religion. Their spirituality is performative and deeply definitive of who they are as individuals. *Floyd* provides an example. "He [God] touched me so much in prison. I've seen so many miracles in prison." When asked to give an example of a miracle, *Floyd* responds decisively, "He changed my life." As a source of hope and communion with the sacred, religion becomes the primary tool for rehabilitation and self-actualization.

Religion matters inside. Spiritual practice and belief in a higher power provide women with a sense of direction and purpose.[72] When all other problem-solving avenues are closed, denied, or unavailable, prayer is accessible. It is one of the few activities that prison administration cannot sanction or control. Prayer is an empowerment strategy that women actively employ to connect with a higher power, to diffuse tense situations, to maintain hope, to reinterpret their lives, and to support them as they engage in self-actualizing behaviors. When *Shemetta* gets into "bad situations" with officers or other women, she acknowledges that sometimes "all I can do is pray."

Religious practice orders the prison world of life-serving women and provides them with a vantage point from which they can reinterpret their crimes and punishment from stigmatizing experiences into moral enterprises, believing that "God has a plan for my life." A life sentence annihilates the human spirit; religion provides the balm that allows life-serving women to move through the pain they caused and the pain they experience. Women discipline themselves to follow religious proscriptions, subsume themselves for hoped-for higher goals of redemption and a second chance at life. If a second chance remains beyond reach (as *Ciara* says, "I accept God needs good people in prison"), prayer is the most-reported strategy used to create meaningful lives behind the prison wires.

Conclusion

The agentic strategies identified by the life-serving women in this study converged around four axes of decision making, that is, normalizing chosen activities inside by using "as if" outside world analogues, "staying busy," forming affective and instrumental relationships with peers inside, and developing and sustaining a self-defined spiritual center. Having "a relationship with God" was by far the most-reported strategy. Religion is life-serving women's primary tool for rehabilitation and self-actualization. No matter where they are or what conditions, challenges, or obstacles present themselves, prayerful women can always turn inward. In conversations with God, their sufferings and remorse have greater purpose. "A relationship with God" provides them with wholeness and offers them comfort. It is also the most agentic strategy as it can be enacted idiosyncratically in religion or practice, individually in prayer or meditation, or collectively in Bible study, religious services, or prayerful singing. Prayer and "conversations with God" do not require institutional approval or permission. Nonetheless, the powerful force of prison control remains omnipresent, even in faith gatherings. While outside the confines of prisons, it is conventional practice in many religious groups to hold hands for a moment of prayer. Inside, *Louise* comments on the "no touching" policy. "We were told that we couldn't hold hands because it wasn't a church."

9

Candace

"God Is My Answer"

Every time I am on my bunk, I look out the window. I start
with the sky and work my way down to the trees, buildings,
and finally to the ground watching for any wildlife that is
walking or flying by. The Canadian geese are my favorites!
This is one of the ways that I can cope with having to live
in this environment, twenty-four hours a day, seven days a
week. As of three days ago, I have now been incarcerated for
18 years.

In a gentle, musical voice serenely attuned to her big-boned, square-
jawed body, *Candace,* a life-serving, middle-aged, white woman,
contemplates her loss of personal time, that is, time that she can structure, organize, waste, reflect on, plan, anticipate, shape, or envision. "My
time has just disappeared. I always say, 'My clock doesn't work.'"

Permanently banished from society by a life sentence, *Candace* experiences "time lost" as an ancillary cost of imprisonment. More substantive than a simple quantification of years, her time lost is a significant,
if abstract, void: "It's like I can't remember the timeline of my life." One
consequence of the loss is that the oscillations of cause and effect that
led to her incarceration are absent from this study's data: neither her discussions in the focus groups nor her solicited diary narrative acknowledge this relation between past and present. She, of course, remembers
events that occurred both pre- and postimprisonment, but she can no
longer place those events in a meaningful narrative sequence that yields
a unified life story. Time, as an historical link between her past self and
present circumstance, has been eroded.

Candace has also lost time as a measure of daily living. She has spent
18 years in carceral time that is both shaped and shapeless. Prisons

maintain security through predictably scheduled daily activities at pre-dictably scheduled time intervals (e.g., count at 7 a.m., 11 a.m., 4 p.m., and 9 p.m. every day; chow three times per day; and officer shift changes at 6 a.m., 2 p.m., and 10 p.m.). Every day is shaped by repetitious institutional routines with the consequence that each day becomes individually shapeless and days, months, and even years can pass without notice or remembrance.

Institutional timetables vary in times of crisis only: power outages, water-main breaks, tornado alerts, winter ice storms, escapes. *Candace* notes one such interruption in her solicited diary, written in the early spring: "The whole facility has been on water restriction since 6:00 a.m. this morning. No showers at all and limited water use. Again, no information is given as to why we are on water restriction or for how long.... It is now 4:30 p.m. I am waiting for count to clear so I can make a mad dash to the showers, if the water restriction has been lifted. If it has, I guess I will have to sacrifice going to dinner for taking a shower instead ... [restriction remains in place].... Count time 9:00 p.m. I get ready for bed and pray that we will be able to take a shower tomorrow." The unexplained water restriction lasted for two days.

The many years of *Candace's* incarceration cannot be measured by rites of passage or significant events, only by the monotonous, unceasing present of prison life, occasionally interrupted by system anomalies. For *Candace* prison timetables and routines have become so embedded and embodied, so controlling of her life, that she has released her hold on time as it is conventionally marked outside the walls. Her cognitive timepiece has malfunctioned. She has lost the experiential recognition of her own life narrative.

"I just can't gauge time anymore," she notes dispiritedly. When every day is a replica of the day before and the day following, it is easy to get lost in the larger flow. She forgets little details, like dates and birthdays, that mark time outside the walls. Sociologist Rik Scarce, who spent 159 days in prison for refusing to cooperate with a grand jury request to turn over confidential research communications, noted of that experience that classical clock and calendar time can "haunt and taunt" imprisoned people.[1] Calendar years mark the passage of time in their unspent lives, haunting them with loss and taunting them with what-could-have-beens. *Candace's* life imprisonment, and that of some of her peers, has resulted in this forfeiture of classical time. The importance of conventional notions like "on time," "double time," "overtime," "pastime," "in due time," and "taking time out" cease being relevant. Suspended in time, she surrenders to the overarching carceral measures of "time lost" and "time down."

Additionally her life sentence has had the additional consequence of consigning *Candace's* ovaries to lockdown. Engaged and childless when she was sentenced in her mid-30s, she is now past her reproductive window. Her biological clock "ran out of time," another invisible cost of a life sentence for women. As she laments the lost opportunity for childbirth, her watery blue eyes betray her longing and regret. "I am not a mother, though I have always wanted to be. I was and still am engaged to be married . . . after the crime and my incarceration, my plans for having children began to disappear. Unfortunately, since I have been down for so long, I am no longer at the childbearing age." Then, drawing on her wellspring of religious conviction, she adds, "But with God, nothing is impossible!"

When I ask how she copes with both the obvious and the invisible costs of her life sentence, *Candace* sheds her quiet, self-effacing demeanor and animatedly provides the oft-repeated lifer mantra: "God is my answer." I ask what that means, and *Candace* replies, "It's a connection that's hard to explain. It's spiritual." She struggles to convey how, in the communal environment of prison, women have to know how to keep their own peace, especially when "you're getting it from both sides [other women and officers]." She notes dolefully, "If you want peace and quiet [in prison], you're screwed. There's always someone yelling in the hall." As is the case with many of her life-serving peers, *Candace* uses her personal relationship with God as her primary strategy for securing personal space and "the little joy that I find in this place." Her resolute control of unscheduled prison time and her discipline of daily devotional practice to achieve peacefulness are the central organizing principles of her life inside.

Control of time and "a personal relationship with God" are inextricably linked for many life-serving women and—particularly so—in *Candace's* iterations of her self-actualization strategies. The shaped and simultaneously shapeless quality of prison time creates a crucible within which *Candace* develops her close personal relationship with God. This relationship provides the spiritual tethering that enables her to reduce her emotional range and to dull her affect in response to the challenges of life imprisonment. Withdrawal from active personal engagement with other women and officers through prayer is an advantage in dealing with the vulnerabilities of penal life. Her "personal relationship with God" shields her from the risk of becoming too despairing, too angry, or too disconsolate. It also shields her from confrontation with the consequences of her own life choices. Indeed, the tranquil engagement with others that results from her religious practices enables her to present herself, and to be accepted by her peers, as a good person of religious character.

"God Has Blessed Me with the Availability to Use the Telephone"

Like many of her life-serving contemporaries, *Candace* imposes discipline and meaning on her life through rigorous scheduling. Her self-control is exacting. To avoid dealing with the "chaos" of the communal restroom, for example, *Candace* controls what and when she drinks, consciously regulating her bodily functions so that they accord with the daily scheduling of the institution. With pride, she attributes her institutional stability to being "very regimented. . . . I'm almost like a robot."

Although she experiences erosions of time as a consequence of pervasive institutional scheduling, *Candace* resists other slow attritions to her personhood and identity. She maintains some authority over her life by asserting control of her unscheduled time and by keeping God perpetually present in the progression of her days. Indeed, prayer is the single, most effective strategy that life-serving women report drawing on to maintain hope and to reduce despair. Criminal justice theorist Todd Clear and his colleagues, studying the religious practices of incarcerated men, propose that the deprivations of the prison context influence imprisoned men such that they become more receptive to religion.[2] This contextual framing illuminates the otherwise unnoticed intersections of two social institutions: prison and religion.[3] As a case study, *Candace's* devotional life highlights those intersections as well as the many ways religious practice informs her perceptions of time and provides a vantage point from which she interprets her imprisonment.

Her intentional daily scheduling, for example, reflects the two strategies central to her stability and self-preservation, that is, her control of
accessible time and the solace she finds in prayer.

"God wakes me up just before 6:30 a.m."
6:20 wash face, brush teeth, etc.
6:30 Joyce Meyer Ministry on TV
7:00 count, prayer for 15 minutes
7:15 wash, dress, "down one glass of Tang, 2 multi-vitamins, 1 vitamin E, 1
    Calcium vitamin D, and 2 vitamin C pills . . . read my Bible and devotion-
    als" and go to work
7:50 work
10:30 early detail lunch
11:00 count and "quiet time with God"
12:15 [or when count "clears"] work
3:30 return to unit
4:00 count, if count clears early, either "mad dash to the showers" or if "I am
    blessed to get a telephone that is free, I call my mother"
5:00 dinner
6:00 evening program: Bible study, college class, choir practice, or yard
    [weather permitting use of outside recreational area]
8:40 back to unit for ice in summer or to heat water for coffee/tea in cooler
    weather
9:00 count
TV and prayers "Thank you God for your mercy"

While prison protocols mandate specific times for institutional responsibilities (count, chow, shift change, etc.), women can choose to fill
unspecified times with their own "staying busy" activities. *Candace* fills
her time with an array of devotional practices. Like many others inside
and out, her religious observations are more formalized on Sundays. In
observance of the Sabbath, she says, "I get up and begin to get ready to
go to church. I [sing in the Gospel Choir], so I attend all three Protestant
services each Sunday."

Although *Candace* most often prays alone, she also looks forward to
opportunities to worship with others. Collective participation in religious services, or Bible study led by religious volunteers, is one means of

sharing values and emotions in a context with both formal and informal limits on emotional sharing. *Candace* mines these occasions of religious engagement for the nuggets of wisdom that will brighten and improve her life. From one Sunday sermon, for example, she gleans a life lesson: "I learned that love is thinking higher of others than of yourself. Like Jesus did for all mankind." She takes the lesson to heart. She makes service to others part of her daily interactions. "I set out on the day thinking 'what can I do for other people?'"

Sunday religious service anchors the week of prayers for *Candace* and for the other religiously observant women serving time with her. Shared prayer serves as both an emotional outlet and a place to experience spiritual solidarity.[4] These communal devotional practices embody the moral rules that religiously observant women in this community observe toward one another, simultaneously strengthening the friable social fabric inside and enhancing their fragile solidarity.[5] Sharing the experience of faith and communal prayers is also an "as if" activity that restores a sense of normalcy to their lives by replicating pre-incarceration experiences of spiritual connection.

Knowing that praying together can help their peers to cope with difficult memories, religiously observant women often plan special spiritual events on days that might "trigger" these painful recollections. *Candace* recorded one such Mother's Day service in her solicited diary. "The Mother's Day Program was so emotionally and spiritually charged, it affected everybody in the auditorium. . . . we decided to address deeply repressed issues that women deal with in their lives, especially in prison. Rape, suicide, incest, physical and emotional abuse, etc. We had music and dance and a play about these issues. There were religious volunteers at each show. For the last half of the show, they spoke on these topics. It was very cleansing and encouraging. There wasn't a dry eye in the auditorium."

"God Blessed Me with a Corner of Pizza"

To further understand the ways that *Candace* thinks about God, I asked her to keep a diary for two weeks. In her entries she explicates the methods she utilizes for personal reformation through devotion to God, as well as the moments during which she calls upon him for help and assistance.

Candace begins her daily journaling by announcing that this request is a challenge. "I absolutely detest writing," she says. Rather than refuse my invitation, however, *Candace* redefines the task, presenting it as both determined by God and as positive preparation for her future. "God obviously had other plans for me [than her previously unstated desire for a life-course interview]. Actually it makes a lot of sense. When I get out of prison, I am going to enter a world full of emails and twitter. I need to practice expressing myself more clearly with written or typed words." *Candace's* ability to redefine unpleasant experiences optimistically and to plan for her desired freedom is characteristic of the aphorism "when life gives you lemons, make lemonade."

Candace's diary entries are steeped in the permeating presence of God and in her constructive use of unscheduled time. God travels with *Candace* through the "staying busy" activities of her day; she consistently invokes his presence in the days' pleasant and difficult moments. In health care, for example, "Praise God! I have a health care call out for 10:00 a.m. I have been trying and trying for weeks to see a doctor. I have extreme lower back and sciatica issues." The focus of her delight, attributed to God's intervention, is successfully getting an appointment. She discounts or ignores the weeks of pain she endured while waiting to see a doctor, which included borrowing a coworker's back brace. Or with commissary: "I'm all out of Tang. . . . Everyone in the unit is in what I call the pre-store frenzy. They are out of coffee, sugar, creamer and food that helps us survive the kindergarten portions we are given in the chow hall." Yet the following day she writes, "Store has arrived. Thank you Lord." *Candace* experiences both pleasure and divine intervention in the implementation of a routine prison distribution of the women's commissary orders. By assigning these and similar moments as gifts from God, *Candace* focuses her attention on the small, attainable rewards of prison life, rather than on its grimmer aspects. Even about weather, she enthuses: "I woke up about 4:00 a.m. last night to a wonderful rain, hail, thunderstorm. I really enjoyed watching the lightening, the wind and the rain. God truly blessed me with a good show!" She does not experience the early morning awakening as an interrupted night's sleep or as a feature of climatic weather patterns; instead, God has provided her with the natural entertainment of a lightning storm. Chow hall, too, has its blessings: "Count clears and it is time for the telephone dash [3 phones for 60 women]. I miss getting to an open phone. It's alright because they call our unit first to the chow hall. God blessed me with a corner of pizza."

Because she experiences God's influence everywhere, nothing in *Candace's* prison life is experienced as coincidental. She finds God's supportive influence in every large and small event. Even the gaps, omissions, or limitations of her imprisonment are experienced as lessons of the spirit. "If you wake up in a bad mood, for whatever reason, just being in prison is reason enough, you can make a choice not to be that way. You can allow yourself to stay in that state of mind in this environment, but it can be dangerous to your health and well being. . . . I pray that this day will go well."

Of the choice to have "a relationship with God," *Candace* writes:

Every inmate must make this decision at the dawning of each day, especially lifers. Both women ["short termers" and lifers] are incarcerated, separated from their families and former lives. The core difference is *knowing* you are leaving prison by man [out date] and *not knowing* [life sentence without parole]. The lifer must choose, if they want to be stable and functional during their incarceration. They must choose faith/trust. The faith/trust decision the lifer must make is given either to God or to man's mercy. Common sense (trust) is not faith, and faith is not common sense. They stand in the relation of the natural and the spiritual, of impulse and inspiration. (emphasis in original)

"This Is My Quiet Time with God"

Like many of her life-serving peers, *Candace* attains a modicum of serenity by actively creating an inner landscape. It is a self-constructed, interior space dissociated from, yet embedded within, institutional time frames. This inner landscape is a personal and prayerfully fashioned place for intense reflection and spiritual communion. In this sacred space, *Candace* experiences God as a felt presence. Time mists into irrelevance in her inner landscape. There, she is safe, neither fearful nor vulnerable. Although other women speak of similar prayerful experiences, their inner landscapes are highly subjective; they become each woman's experience of them. The construction, meanings, and devotional conduct and rituals that *Candace* employs are idiosyncratically hers.

In her inner landscape *Candace* engages in dialogic conversations with God. "Count time. This is my quiet time with God. I read my devotionals and my Bible and have a chat with him." Among other benefits, these conversations help to satisfy her yearnings for connectedness. Here she isn't invisible or forgotten; here she has a "personal relationship with God." She savors the moments of connection. *Candace* listens to the voice of God in these "chats" and uses the quiet time and his messages to become more reflective and more introspective. During this time in this space, she can center herself, "hold [her] own experience in empathic attention,"[6] develop self-caring narratives, and experience both mercy and forgiveness. "It gave me an understanding that God can and will guide, teach and shape you, step by step into this wonderful individual that can do anything through Him." The one-on-one correspondence with God that she experiences offers her opportunities to create boundaries that keep depression and despair at bay. Instead of remaining static in place, contemplating the deprivations of her sentence, *Candace* "spend[s] time with God, with my daily readings and prayers."

In her inner landscape, *Candace* is not ostracized for her crime. Prison authorities cannot take away her inner space. She has developed a strategy that has allowed her to create a sense of personal freedom within prison walls. No matter where she is or what her conditions, or challenges, or obstacles, she can always turn inward and access tranquility through prayer. "[I] pray to God for Him to give His guardian angels charge over my Mother, my fiancé and the rest of my family and enemies. To keep them safe from harm and to be at peace. I pray this will be a day of peace for myself and [my bunkie]. Having discord in this tiny room longer than twenty four hours is not acceptable."

Prison losses also find purpose in *Candace's* inner landscape, as they do for many of her religiously oriented peers in their own sacred spaces. Loss is integral to *Candace's* understanding of the meaning of her life sentence. "In a deep reworking of personal life issues"[7] through her dialogues with God and his spiritual agents (religious visitors, ministers, chaplain, other prayerful women, etc.), *Candace* writes in her solicited diary, "I have learned after being in prison all these years, when something or someone has been taken from your life, it is not always a sad loss, it can be a happy loss. When you receive Jesus into your heart you understand that this all had to happen, just as it did, so I can be the person I was truly meant to be." Christ's transcendent authority, as a judge of worthiness and value, offers *Candace* an alternative route to understanding her life imprisonment. It is an understanding that is defined by the person she has come to be, not by the person who committed her crime 18 years ago. Her feelings of guilt and remorse for her crime remain salient but they are no longer of primary import. Her communion with God provides *Candace* with a sense of wholeness and comfort that validates her existence and significance. Their inner landscape conversations offer her hope and a rationale that gives meaning to her life imprisonment. Through redefinition of her crime and punishment as "God's will" and not simply her own flawed choices, and through her personal processes of reformation, *Candace*'s incarceration and removal from the distractions of the world become moral instruments, not criminal punishments. She understands her crime, her sentence, and her imprisonment as acts of the divine that have assisted her in becoming "the person I was truly meant to be."

"God Is So Good!"

Candace begins her days of spiritual connectedness when "God wakes me up in time to watch Joyce Meyer at 6:30 a.m." With spiritual leaders limited to religious visitors and a single chaplain for 2,100 women, tel-evangelists become important messengers of God's word for life-serving women. They are easily accessible to anyone with a TV, are available at predictable times, can substitute for church services, and their ministry can be delivered while their flocks remain in bed or on lockdown. *Candace* is an enthusiastic disciple of the ministry of Joyce Meyer, a charismatic Christian. The messages of the evangelist delivered into the early morning quiet of *Candace*'s prison room, from a woman enhanced by TV's close-up theatricality and who speaks God's word with authority, connects *Candace* to the divine, and so each day's homily becomes particularly meaningful.[8]

"Today [Joyce Meyer] is speaking about the power of words. I have heard her speak on this topic before and I have found it to be very helpful. It makes you think about what you say and why you say it, and the repercussions those words will have in your life, good or bad. I wish I could get all the ladies in this facility to hear and understand this truth." *Candace* embraces God's messages as revealed to her by Joyce Meyer's scriptural interpretations. She notes resignedly that her world would be improved if everyone understood and accepted Meyer's lessons, especially that words, not just actions, have consequences.

Guided by her conversations with God, her devotional readings, and the lessons of Joyce Meyer's ministry, *Candace* strives to empathize with others. She uses the lessons of compassion to re-center herself after unpleasant exchanges. In dealing with "rude guards," for example, she invokes feelings of "compassion . . . more than anger. I feel sorry for them." When she considers an officer's discourtesy, she draws on her lessons in spirituality as she struggles to put these "us" and "them" negative exchanges into positive, self-affirming interactions. *Candace* then destabilizes the "prisoner" and "officer" hierarchy by flipping the relationship and assuming the one-up position by offering the officer compassion. From this ascendant position *Candace* can express kindness and concern for the officer whose discourteous behavior has diminished her as an authority figure and established her as someone worthy of an incarcerated woman's magnanimity. In exchanges akin to these, *Candace* expressly chooses compassion over anger as an act of self-empowerment.

Candace also draws on her devotional practices to ease volatile situations, like those that may arise at any time with her bunkie. The two are "stuck in a small space" together: 6 feet by 10 feet containing two people, one chair, one tabletop affixed to the wall, two stainless-steel bunkbeds also attached to the wall, and a sink.[9] "I try to be as quiet as I can so as not to disturb my roommate. She is a sleeper. Almost every day, she sleeps in until about 12:00 p.m. . . . Normally I don't bring up the subject [of her reclusive behavior], but this behavior has been ongoing for over a month. When this behavior starts to affect my living condition in this small room that we must share, I find clear communication can generally resolve any problems or misunderstandings that we might be having. Unfortunately, because of her history of domestic abuse, she clams up and refuses to confront or acknowledge any of the problems. . . . I begin to pray to God to give her peace and strength to make it through this day and the days to follow."

Candace is not alone in dealing with bunkie "issues" or in asking God for assistance in resolving them. Imprisoned women do not choose the other women with whom they live in close quarters, nor are they allowed to trade places to secure more amenable circumstances. Bunkie assignments are made institutionally, beyond women's control or influence, and they do not include compatibility as a criterion for placement. *Candace's* bunkie escapes her imprisonment through sleep and isolation. But her behavior has consequences for *Candace,* who is locked in place with her. The two must work through the difficulties. Characteristically *Candace* prays for her. Four days after their "clear communication" about her bunkie's reclusive behavior, *Candace's* diary entry reads: "she [bunkie] felt bad about the way she had been treating me. I apologized to her for me allowing myself to become offended at her behavior and not being as understanding as I could have been. So we hugged and she went downstairs to the microwave oven and made us some chicken noodle soup for dinner. I bought a coke out of the soda machine and we split it. God is so good!"

Conclusion

Like many of her peers, *Candace* both organizes her time and immerses herself in religion, spirituality, and devotional practice in an attempt to rehabilitate herself and to self-actualize in place. By carefully routinizing her "free" time and by immersing herself in deeply prayerful practices, *Candace* stabilizes herself emotionally. That she creates the order in her days around prayer and devotional practice admits her into orders of time that work differently than classical clock and calendar time. Her standards of measurement become the informal carceral calculations of "time down" and "time lost," both of which she understands as part of "God's plan."

Candace's time management and devotional routines temporarily remove her from engagement with other incarcerated women and officers as they sometimes also obscure her self-actualizing behavior. Because she mindfully interprets every event as an occasion of praise or thanks to God, nothing is left owing to chance, or wisdom, or (un)happy accidents, or to her own self-efficacy in planning and decision making. "God is my answer" is the response to all her choices and all her hopes, as well as the explanation for her crime and her present life imprisonment. Submission to his authority enables her to become "the person I was truly meant to be."

10

The Way Forward

Policy Solutions

There are no corrections within corrections. *Elizabeth Ashley*

The justice part in here is way off balance. *Sasha Lavan*

We will be treated like this until the government says they [prison administration] need to be liable and accountable for how we're treated. *Lucy Spencer*

It has not been my intent in these pages to present a view of female life imprisonment that would include officer and administrative correctional perspectives. I leave that to other researchers and to the many journals, websites, and governmental entities that serve the correctional career populations. Rather my aim has been to present the experiences of women currently serving life sentences, to help raise their voices to an audible level, and to offer a new terrain through which to fashion a more female-centered criminology.[1] As U.K. feminist criminologist Pat Carlen has suggested, imprisoned women are "seen but darkly through the distorting mirror of male criminality, issues relating to women and punishment have been extremely difficult to extricate from the long shadows cast by the much larger male penal estate. . . . Women are punished as if they *are* men."[2] Yet men and women are distinct in their criminal behaviors and in the ways they "jail."

Women commit different types of crimes than men do, their motivations for criminal behavior are different than men's, the situational factors for violent crime differ between men and women, women's experiences—pre- and postincarceration—are significantly different than men's, and, compared to their male counterparts, women also have more experience with the incarcerations of other family members.[3]

This book is intended to engage the decidedly male-oriented criminal-processing research and practice by filling an ethnographic gap in criminological theorizing about women and by focusing particular attention on the neglected population of women serving life sentences.

The United States is a society that is the world leader in imprisoning its citizens—at rates heretofore unknown anywhere in the world. More than two million men and women are incarcerated on any given day, one out of nine of whom is serving a life sentence, one-third of them without the possibility of parole. Ten thousand of them have been sentenced for nonviolent offenses.[4] All of this is occurring at a time when crime rates have fallen steadily. We have a responsibility to understand the effect of these patterns on the individuals who are caught up in this "imprisonment orgy."[5]

Many Americans support the uncomplicated "do the crime, do the time" individualized solution for the deeply troubling social issues that often precipitate criminal offending.[6] It is a faster and simpler solution than the more difficult work of understanding the social forces driving illegal activity, but it's a solution with socially and individually damaging consequences. For life-serving women in particular, the social forces influencing their illegal activities are significant and complicated. Women sentenced to life imprisonment often already suffer from the extreme health, social, economic, and emotional effects of poverty, addictions, physical and sexual abuse, inadequate educations, delinquent peers, and fragile family constellations.[7] These enervating conditions are compounded by sentences of life imprisonment and the consequent devastating loss of their children.[8]

For those women imprisoned on first- or second-degree homicide charges, murder is often their first and only criminal offense.[9] Many of the women sentenced to life imprisonment were sentenced in felony murder cases where someone else, most often male, was the "do-er," and, as *Kari* asserts, "women who've killed aren't going to do it again. . . . We don't repeat." When the focus is on the criminal deed, or the woman's personal deficits and weaknesses, and not on the more inclusive social forces that contribute to the crime, preventive and punitive attention becomes misdirected.[10] We, as citizens in a mass incarceration nation, fasten onto the individual's inadequacies and immoralities rather than on the adverse contexts within which women are making inadequate, catastrophic decisions. Consequently, we acquiesce to punishment rather than rehabilitation and we agree to the process of consigning women to life terms in prison for their illegal activities, many with 30, 40, 50, 60, or even 70 years yet to live. If, by our silence, we allow these criminal-processing decisions to continue, then minimally we should be informed about the consequences of those decisions. We should be aware of how life sentences are lived. We need to assess the costs—social, economic, and moral—to families and communities when we accede to the imprisonment of mothers, daughters, sisters, grandmothers, and wives for life. Otherwise we remain blindly complicit in judgments that do not offer second chances.

"I'm Valuable": Prison Ironies

Prisons function on the assumption that incarcerated men and women need constant surveillance in order to avoid further offending. Correctional officers and administrators assume that their imprisoned charges are incapable of desisting from criminal activity, as demonstrated by their original offenses, without severe strictures and intense surveillance. In contrast, this book has demonstrated that life-serving women deliberately develop strategies to help themselves to understand and heal from the contextual circumstances within which they made their disastrous choices. *Sheila T.*, for example, shared her process of coming to terms with her tragically flawed decisions: "When I first got here, I was in denial. . . . [I had] the false belief" that "I was going to win my appeal. . . . [I] had a one in a million chance." When her appeal was denied, she "had to come to terms" (with her past decisions and her present circumstances). It took *Sheila T.* "five or six years for me to come to terms . . . [and to understand that] no one else put me here." This study has also illustrated women's concerted efforts to change, to become better women through self-rehabilitation, and to develop the agency to control their change experiences. *Joyce's* words, presented in an earlier chapter, are illustrative of these processes: "The woman I am today mourns the girl I was when I did this."

All of the women in this study reported regretting their crimes; grieving the harms committed against the victims and victims' families; mourning their own losses and the effects of their ruinous choices on their children, family members, and communities; wishing that what was done could be undone; and acknowledging responsibility for carrying the burdens of their crimes for the rest of their lives. *All* also sought to find meaning in the tragedies that resulted from the harms they caused.

In many ways, the prison environment provided scaffolding for the constructions of their life changes.[11] For some women, prison cleared time for recovery, growth, and renewal.[12] Sentenced time offered them opportunities to reflect on and to address personal problems. *Sandy* affirms this positive prison outcome. "One good thing in here is that you can't hide from anything; you have to take responsibility for everything you do." For others, prison provided respite by removing them from toxic environments. *Sheri* contends that being imprisoned "did me good" in the sense that, if she had remained in place, she "probably would've never gotten sober." For *Caren Sue* and some of her peers, carceral conditions helped them to develop empathy. "I think prison has motivated me and mellowed me out a lot. I have more respect for [other] people and for myself." She looks at interactions "differently now. . . . I can understand things better from a different perspective." Others, like *Louise*, learned to challenge others' definitions of them and to appreciate themselves. "I have discovered my strength. I'm valuable. I'm not a piece of trash. I like myself." For some life-serving women, years of imprisonment and arbitrarily assigned bunkies resulted in personal growth. The forced engagement of living intimately with roommates of different races and ethnicities, sexual orientations, class positions, and abilities taught some women lessons about toleration of, adjustment to, and consideration for the needs of others. Of that experience, *Ruth* claims, "We grew, it was a bitter way, but we grew as people." *Doll* echoes other life-serving women's assertions of the slow growth available to self-motivated women by declaring that in prison she had "finally" gained many useful tools for "coping with life wherever I'm at."

But as this book has also shown, life imprisonment is most often corrosive. Prison is an "institution of trauma," and imprisonment for life erodes the scant social capital of women already disadvantaged by the contextual facilitators of crime—disorganized childhoods, inadequate educations, domestic and child abuse, limited employment opportunities, stressed families, and delinquent peers.[13] From outside the walls, without either information or consideration, it is easy to make sweeping ungenerous assumptions about the criminality of aberrant women often highlighted by both law enforcement pronouncements and media headlines. The images of a crime-saturated society that appear frequently in news shows, in magazines, through law enforcement warnings, and in social media promote and perpetuate uncritical pro-prison attitudes.[14] A closer look at the aftermath of those constructions reveals how public support of life sentences actively creates prisons as cemeteries of the living.

"What Is Justice?": Whose Change Is Coming?

"Commentators on both the left and the right are now reacting critically to the incarceration boom, partly out of concern for growing correctional budgets, partly because of questions about the effectiveness of incarceration in reducing crime, and partly out of misgivings about the values that have come to dominate penal policy. [citations omitted] Reform, it appears, is under way. At the state level and in the federal government, many elected officials are supporting initiatives aimed at reducing prison populations and are turning to the research evidence for guidance."[15] These elected officials are not, however, turning to incarcerated men and women for information or suggestions, although they are arguably the people with the most experience of the system at its ground level. Instead, as sociologist Lisa Brush notes, "Policymakers talk *about* rather than *with* disenfranchised or victimized groups."[16]

Brush has argued that impoverished women, like incarcerated women and their families, are among those whose lives are most profoundly shaped by social policy and practice and by the limits of activism.[17] Yet they are the stakeholders repeatedly locked out of policy discussions. Her arguments can also be effectively applied to life-serving women, who are also excluded without consideration from participation in the criminal-processing policy decisions affecting their lives. The omission of imprisoned women as primary stakeholders amplifies the methods of the criminal-processing system in shaping policy and practice and in limiting active consideration of issues such as gender and imprisonment, gender and the provision of health care services, gender and security, gender in sentencing and parole, as well as the diminishing attention paid to the collateral victimization of the families, particularly the children, of life-sentenced women. Yet incarcerated women consistently remain recipients of, but not participators in, public discussions, policy decision making, and critical legislative conversations. There are few, if any, venues for substantive dialogues between policymakers and incarcerated women.

Because of the greater numbers of incarcerated men, the issues relevant to imprisoned females are often overlooked by policymakers.[18] This is not news to incarcerated women. In their focus groups, life-course interviews, and solicited diaries, life-serving women made many suggestions for system improvement. They are, after all, the authorities on the experiences of female imprisonment. Consequently, this chapter will focus on the suggestions of the study participants for both correctional adjustments as well as broader systemic change.

In making their suggestions, these life-serving women accept their incarcerations as legitimate consequences for their wrongdoing. Only one woman in this study claimed to be innocent of the crime for which she was imprisoned. Not a single woman questioned either the morality or the efficacy of societal control through punishment and imprisonment. Every woman, however, questioned both the morality and the efficacy of the inordinate lengths of their sentences. To be effective, sentences for crimes must have meaning. That meaning is lost to life-serving women when punishment is a no-exit banishment that closes off opportunities for remorse, rehabilitation, regret, and restoration. It leaves women, like *Martha,* asking "I have this question for society: What is justice? How am I supposed to do my time?"

"An Eye for an Eye": Current Retribution Solutions

Criminal sentences are intended to serve three social purposes, either exclusively or conjointly.[19] They may aim to prevent further criminality through deterrence and individual incapacitation; they may aim to prevent crimes through rehabilitation of the offender; or they may be intentionally retributory, a kind of "just desserts" for illegal activity. Many advocates of life sentences (and the death penalty), for example, demand individual accountability through intentional retribution: "do the crime, do the time." They often cite the retaliatory "eye for an eye" biblical injunction that supports punishment weighted as equivalent to the harm unleashed by criminal activity (e.g., a life for a life). Such retribution is central in our criminal-processing system. But the Bible is not unitary in retributive messages, nor are the Torah or the Qu'ran, those other sacred texts of Abrahamic traditions that also give testament to forgiveness and second chances. For example:

Genesis 50:15–21 (Torah):
When Joseph's brothers saw that their father was dead, they said, "It may be that Joseph will hate us and pay us back for all the evil that we did to him." So they sent a message to Joseph, saying, "Your father gave this command before he died, 'Say to Joseph, Please forgive the transgression of your brothers and their sin, because they did evil to you.' And now, please forgive the transgression of the servants of the God of your father." Joseph wept when they spoke to him. His brothers also came and fell down before him and said, "Behold, we are your servants." But Joseph said to them, "Do not fear, for am I in the place of God?"

Matthew 18:21–22 (New Testament):
Then Peter came up and said to him, "Lord, how often will my brother sin against me, and I forgive him? As many as seven times?" Jesus said to him, "I do not say to you seven times, but seventy times seven."

Qur'an (Ibn Majah):
The one who repents from sin is like one who has no sin.

Retribution, incapacitation, and deterrence are not the only paths to punishment and "righting the wrongs" of criminal activity. As M. Kay Harris, a scholar of sentencing and alternatives to incarceration, notes, virtually all discussions about change within the criminal-processing system assume that punishment must occur.[20] The consequence is a narrowing of the range of possibilities for change because only rearrangements and reallocations within existing structures can transpire if punishment, and its corollary incapacitation, is the ultimate goal. Prison and crime are not opposites of the same coin and incarceration is not the only means of crime control.[21] Perhaps, as Harris suggests, if we considered *if* we should punish, not just how to punish, we could regain the capacity to recreate relationships and realign deterrence priorities in more secure, effective, and humane ways.[22] A recent National Research Council report, *The Growth of Incarceration in the United States: Exploring Causes and Consequences*, implicitly offers the analogous question for consideration: "*What* is the role of incarceration at a time when *how* we incarcerate achieves little of what we know works to stop reoffending and create stronger people and stronger and safer communities?"[23]

If, as a society, we are not prepared to consider Harris's "if we should punish" question, or the National Research Council's "what is the role of incarceration" question, or the subsequent query "are prisons obsolete" then perhaps we could address the role of incarceration in limiting reoffending and creating safer communities by attending to the suggestions of the life-serving women in this study.[24] While the broader issues of punishment, imprisonment, and prison abolition are being argued in formal and informal venues around the country by policymakers, legislators, lobbyists, prison entrepreneurs, prison abolitionists, criminologists, and legal scholars, there are institutional adjustments identified by these life-serving women that could be enacted now.

System Modifications

Because the lives of female offenders so often include fragmented family histories, physical and/or sexual abuse, significant substance abuse, and multiple physical and mental health problems,[25] life-serving women in this study suggested counseling, programming, and support services, not drugs, to help them heal from these life traumas. The notion that women, especially imprisoned women, are more emotionally and psychologically unstable than men has led to the widespread practice of issuing prescription drugs to promote their easy control and their compliance to institutional orders.[26] Women in this study reported that they "have to" accept medications as a prerequisite to opportunities for individual counseling. Even more disadvantageous was their reported exclusion from group counseling sessions—anger management, domestic violence counseling, assaultive offender programming, and substance abuse counseling—whose spaces were reserved for women returning to civilian life. In the triage of correctional budget prioritizing, because lifers are not expected to leave, correctional administrators tend to allocate resources away from them and toward those women "with years" who are expected to return to civilian life.

"A Wait List That Never Ends": Programming Solutions

Life-serving women want access to programming and educational opportunities often denied them because of their no-exit sentences. *Dennis the Menace* said, "I want to go back [to school] and they won't let me because I'm a lifer. They want me to pay for my GED [from a prison job that pays 15 cents an hour]." As correctional budgets tighten nationwide, life-serving women are often at the "bottom of the list" for programs and education and so must wait for an opening in what one study participant characterized as "a wait list that never ends." Another woman in the study, who works as a clerk in the programs building, affirms that "no lifers will ever get in again [to GED classes]. There literally has to be no waiting list." Seeking to reduce recidivism rates, the administration has determined that the women with early release dates for citizenship reentry, particularly those women under 21 years of age, should get first priority in programming. A life-serving woman under 21 is not an administrative educational priority. Their no-exit sentences and hence their inability to recidivate essentially eliminate life-serving women from institutional program opportunities that might help them heal and stabilize. The consequence is that they are warehoused—without rehabilitative opportunities—for decades. Limited prison resources may create this circumstance, but as Erin George notes, available resources, when allocated equitably, are not wasted on life-serving women. "For the most part, lifers are the women in prison who are most dedicated to improving themselves academically and emotionally."[27]

"Leave Me Alone": Officer Training and Accountability Solutions

In a comparative analysis of women's correctional facilities, feminist criminologist Alana Van Gundy found that facilities function most appropriately and effectively when they are structured to increase companionship, when they provide opportunities for women to socialize, and when they are less rigorously secured by officers.[28] *Merrilee's* pleas capture this feature acknowledged by others: "Let me do my time. Leave me alone." Over and over again the life-serving women in this study affirmed Van Gundy's findings, especially with regard to consistent rule enforcement by officers. *Scarlet*, for example, defines the context, saying, "The daily inconsistencies create stress. There's nothing concrete in the system, even things that are supposed to be [concrete] aren't." Several other women also acknowledged preferring to work with those officers who "let the lifers handle situations" and who respond efficiently and expertly to confusion or disorder without "making it personal." All focus-group participants agreed that they feel less vulnerable when an officer behaves professionally and is "not hittin' people up for every, small thing, like giving a woman a ticket for wearing two earrings in one ear."

Echoing the findings of research literature on women in prison, these life-serving women also had a number of suggestions with regard to correctional officer training and professional behavior. The first and foremost was the importance that women attached to fair and humane treatment by prison staff.[29] As was discussed in chapter 7, correctional personnel consider imprisoned women to be a more difficult population to work with than incarcerated men. Preparing officers to work with women then requires increased knowledge and critical engagement with established cultural notions of the roles and behaviors of both men and women. Officers working in a female facility should be required to have specialized, certified, gender-specific training that includes learning about the consequences to women of early physical, sexual, or emotional trauma; the consequences of their loss of contact with their children; the consequences of the lack of privacy; the consequences of any acute and/or chronic health or reproductive conditions and/or substance abuse; and the consequences of lives lived on the social margins. The training, women suggest, should be recertified yearly so that its importance is reconfirmed. Rather than enmity, life-serving women suggest that officers need to develop "the constructive attitudes and the interpersonal skills necessary for working with women under correctional supervision."[30] *Lynn* echoes the standard, noted in its exceptionalism by other women, when she declares that a good officer "treats you like a human being." *Baby* adds that, when rumors arise as they often do in the "mix," a gender-trained officer would not be "hinting around" and would "instead come to me woman to woman" to ascertain the veracity of the gossiped claims.

THE WAY FORWARD | 249

Inadequate officer training, exacerbated by perceived administrative leniency shown to officers when women "kite" their complaints of officer misconduct, are common complaints of imprisoned men and women and both are frequently cited in literature on imprisonment. Because of the "us" vs. "them" adversarial relationship between incarcerated women and their keepers, and because—as "inmates"—the women's veracity is constantly in question, evidence-gathering techniques, like the 1,400 surveillance cameras that tape in this facility, should be both available and neutrally applied. Yet, when called upon to support a claim about an officer's unprofessional behavior, the evidence is often not obtainable. "I told them to check the tapes, but, of course, 'the camera wasn't working.'" To preserve the authority and integrity of the correctional system, evidentiary information should be available to the women as well as the officers when there is a dispute over claims making.

Additionally life-serving women suggested the implementation of a civilian review, or oversight, board in each facility for contentious claims and as protection, for both officers and imprisoned women, from false claims of assault or seduction. The civilian board would meet with alacrity when women, disputing a ticket or a more serious claim of misconduct or injury by officers, are held in segregation pending investigation. It would otherwise conduct regular investigations of tickets and remands to the segregation unit as well as both suicide attempts and completions. The board would be composed of civilian members of the community.

"My [Now-Grown] Children Have Just Come into My Life":
Solutions That Consider the Children

Because a mother's punishment extends beyond the bars of the prison, the children of incarcerated mothers are an "invisible and voiceless set of victims."[31] So another suggestion necessary to address the gendered nature of imprisonment for women—who are more likely than their male counterparts to be the heads of households for dependent children and who are also likely to be imprisoned far from families and child-care providers[32]—is a 48-hour private visit with children. These private visits could be scheduled on a monthly rotating basis, so that all mothers with dependent children could anticipate, plan, and prepare for their time together.

The visits would also serve as a preventative measure against imposition of the exceptional burden visited upon them by the Adoption and Safe Families Act of 1997. Under the act, parents of children in foster care for 15 of the most recent 22 months can have their parental rights terminated. After termination, parents have no legal relationship to the children and are no longer permitted to have contact. The fragile family support systems of many life-sentenced women make this an especially troubling consequence of the law punishing them further for their lack of family and community resources. Life-serving women understand the intent of the law as protection for children who should not be left to languish in the foster-care system, but they also know the gut-wrenching unintended consequences of the law for imprisoned women and their dependent children. "My [now-grown] children have just come into my life. . . . Eight years ago was the first time I saw my son, but only that one time." Consequently, these life-sentenced women suggest an exclusion from the law so that imprisoned mothers can maintain contact with their children and can assist them, and their caregivers, in making adjustments to their new, challenging life circumstances.

In the remembered past, the facility had provided space for an extended afternoon children's visitation program run by volunteers. Mothers whose children participated could see them on a monthly basis. *Love Evans* remembers her participation and that "they'd sit at a round table and everyone would have a chance to talk." This time together is vital in keeping families connected. The absence of contact weighs heavily on the hearts of life-imprisoned women. *Shequetta Tasha Lynn*, for example, laments, "My mother and my children, I think they've had it worse than I have. I'm not there to help." The unintended consequence to both *Shequetta* and her children is that "you become insignificant to a degree."

Life-imprisoned women identify strongly as involved mothers who are important in the lives of their children. They express remorse over the ways that their incarcerations have affected their children, as few custody arrangements provide children with healthy environments and appropriate guidance.[33] They name maintaining relations with children as a priority, although visits, mail, and phone calls are not easily realized.[34] They continually make decisions on the basis of extended, collective, multiple self-interests (their children's interests, their own, their families', their friends'). They report weighing the needs of their children and close family members as though they were their own. Others' needs become their needs and they are frustrated by delayed participation in problem solving and decision making.[35] "A mother is still a mother to her children, even when she is separated from them by miles and prison walls."[36] *Alexandria*, for example, calls her daughter "everyday, Monday through Friday, to make sure she's up for school and says her prayers before she leaves the house."

A private-visit provision would do much to keep family units intact, keep mothers central in the lives of their children, provide respite to care providers, and assist children in transitions to family or foster care. Visits are also likely to reduce the collateral consequences to children of a mother's imprisonment (e.g., disrupted attachments, school failures, and engaging in antisocial, aggressive, and delinquent behaviors). *Louise* describes her own and other women's current contact with their children, if they are lucky enough to have family or care providers willing to bring the children for visits. Many women are not so fortunate. "You're not there to experience what they're telling you about, and they try to make you feel included, but you're not. It's like kinda, sorta, maybe, but no." Forty-eight hours together once a month would provide sufficient time for both mothers and children to fill in the details of important experiences and lessons and to be included as significant members in one another's lives.

Bus service for the children, the women suggested, could be provided by the state and administered by the Department of Corrections using their transport vehicles (the buses and vans used to move incarcerated men and women from one facility to another). The buses would travel to designated locations around the state with scheduled pickup and return times. All institutional inspections of children—clothing searches, pat-downs, identity checks—would be handled on the bus so that the visits would not upset the children or further burden staff and waste time once the children have arrived at the correctional facility.

Providing services and counseling, educational, and family unification programs is all part of good correctional practice; it is also both a moral responsibility and a rehabilitative imperative.[37] Although these imperatives are visible for women "with years," they are not at all visible for women with life sentences whose participation in program opportunities is exceptional rather than anticipated. This breach in responsibility invites us to confront some of the more difficult and complicated questions about punishment and imprisonment. What is it that we, as a society, are attempting to achieve through life imprisonment? Who is most affected by these sentences? In what ways? Is life imprisonment successful as a deterrent strategy? As retribution? As rehabilitation? What has incarcerating 159,000 men and women for life achieved? As Harris reminds us, "We should recognize that the more we restructure an individual's chances and choices, the greater is the responsibility we assume for protecting that person and preserving his or her personhood."[38]

Structural Change Solutions

Research on prison growth has consistently established the modest deterrent effect of increases in lengthy prison sentences. Because recidivism rates decline markedly with age, lengthy prison sentences, unless they specifically target very high-rate or extremely dangerous offenders, are an inefficient approach to preventing crime by incapacitation.[39]

With bumper-sticker cogency, a conservative Texas representative and businessman from Dallas, Jerry Madden, argues that prisons ought to be prioritized for the people "we're afraid of, [not] the ones we're mad at."[40] In tune with the sentiments of Representative Madden and other national figures, the life-serving women in this study also call for a reexamination of the driving forces in the unprecedented rate of incarceration: mandatory prison sentences, prosecutor "overcharging," felony murder charges, and postrelease limits on opportunities for success, as well as the soul-shattering losses associated, for some, as a result of the Adoption and Safe Families Act of 1997. Some study participants also objected to Michigan's Truth in Sentencing (TIS) law, which mandates that a sentenced individual must serve the entire minimum of years before parole consideration; that means that with a sentence of 25 to 50 years, a woman must serve a full 25 years before she can be considered for parole. *Liberty Flynn* objects to the TIS, saying, "TIS should be abolished. It has ruptured [the Department of Corrections] to the point that they cannot afford to feed us, clothe us, or care for us. The overcrowding is extreme: 4 toilets for over 100 women, 4 showers, 4 sinks. This past winter we were forced to go outside in subzero weather to use porta-johns because they tore up all the bathrooms to put in new showers."

Life-serving women suggest that sentences should not be mandatory but should be proportional to the seriousness of the harms emanating from participation in the criminal actions. The "eye for an eye" life sentence is not proportional, nor is it just. The length of sentenced time should be sufficient, but not greater than is necessary, they argue, to achieve the goals of sentencing policy (e.g., deterrence, incapacitation, retribution, or rehabilitation).[41] Prior to the administration of Governor John Engler in Michigan (1991–2003), a life sentence did not literally mean the rest of one's life. Typically life-sentenced people were released after 10, 15, or 20 years of imprisonment. When Governor Engler reconstituted the parole board under the direct authority of the executive office, the new members adopted the maxim that "life means life," regardless of the severity of the charge (i.e., first-degree murder, parolable life, aiding and abetting). After a lengthy court challenge, the Michigan Supreme Court found in favor of the parole board and the changes remain in effect.[42]

Several of the sentencing judges in the cases of women in this study have publicly stated that they specifically issued life sentences, instead of a lengthy term of years, assuming that the defendants would be released on parole after 10 to 15 years of incarceration. *Esther* is one woman caught in the throes of these political tensions. She served 10 years on a parolable life sentence. She was released from prison on a successful appeal. After several years on the outside, during which *Esther* developed a successful business venture, the prosecutor's appeal challenging her release was heard by the Michigan Supreme Court. The court found in favor of the prosecutor, and *Esther* was brought back to prison to serve the remainder of her life sentence. About the experience, she says, "At first it was a shock to me. I believed in the government, I believed in the law. . . . I was quite shocked. It was quite a shock to me that the government was a lie." At the time of this study, *Esther* remained imprisoned.

"That's Just Not Right": Solutions to Stop Prosecutorial Overcharging

Study participants also suggest that prosecutors should be prohibited from "overcharging" a defendant in order to secure a lengthy, immutable sentence. Many of the life-serving women in this study are incarcerated on multiple charges emanating from a single crime. These charges, entered at prosecutorial discretion, ensure that if a woman's appeal is successful and she is resentenced, her incarceration will continue on the remaining charges. "That's just not right." One woman in the study, for example, has been sentenced for having an unregistered gun (weapons—felony firearm), armed robbery, assault with intent to do great bodily harm less than murder, and homicide in the second degree. While her life sentence for the homicide is in place, the years she was sentenced for the other crimes—all stemming from the single act of a robbery that went very wrong—are concurrent. Should her life sentence be set aside, she would then be required to serve the years she was sentenced for the lesser crimes. Some women have successfully had the additional felonies vacated by the courts under the "double jeopardy" provision when they have been convicted and sentenced for both first-degree felony murder and the underlying felony that led to the murder. Although the lesser charges have been set aside, their life sentences remain in place. As *Jane* emphasizes, "We are *stuck*" (*Jane's* emphasis).

"She Did as She Was Told": Solutions to Revoke Felony Murder Statutes

Many life-imprisoned women, who were sentenced "behind a man" for their complicity in his criminal activity, suggest changes in the felony murder statutes. If a murder occurs during the commission of a felony (e.g., theft, aggravated assault, selling illegal drugs, kidnapping, burglary, etc.), all the persons deemed responsible for the felony can be charged with murder. A felony murder charge does not require a person's intent to kill, only "participation" in the original felony activity. *Raine* says, "That's what happened to me. Aiding and abetting [an armed robbery], where two people were killed." The deaths were unplanned; there was no premeditation. They were the tragic outcome of a robbery gone bad.

Women have been sentenced to life imprisonment for murders committed by their violent boyfriends or abusive husbands. The story of a life-sentenced woman seeking clemency from the governor of Michigan is a case in point. This woman, a study participant, was "beaten, kicked, cut, bitten, burned with cigarettes, spit and urinated on, handcuffed during beatings, raped, locked in closets, and threatened with a loaded gun by her drug addicted boyfriend. She left him several times, but he dragged her back with both promises of change and threats of harm to her family. To her horror, he shot and killed a man who was sitting with them in a truck. Terrified because he threatened to kill her and her parents, she did as she was told and helped him to hide the body to protect her own life."[43] Her actions in assisting him to hide the body resulted in her being charged and sentenced to life imprisonment for first-degree premeditated murder. She was 18 at the time of her sentence; she is 42 now.

"I Don't Want Them to See Me as a Monster": Solutions to End "the Punishments That Keep on Giving"

The final suggestion for change that was a frequent topic of discussion for the life-serving women in the study was an end to "the punishments that keep on giving," that is, a termination of the hundreds of laws and practices that limit the opportunities of men and women who have served their time, "paid their debts to society," and been released or paroled. The women's concern is both altruistic and hopeful.

They worry about their friends, other imprisoned women "with years" who exit prison but who return to the situations and communities that contributed to their original incarcerations and who now must contend with legally imposed obstacles to their successful reentries. Most life-serving women also remain hopeful for their own eventual releases back into society and so are absorbed by the stumbling blocks ahead of them. The most obvious, and most often noted, is the felony checkbox on employment applications. Once a woman is identified as a (former) felon, her skills, experiences, and talents cease to matter to potential employers. She is labeled and discarded. Stories abound, undocumented and anecdotal, about women whose employers overlooked the box or were somehow unaware of their histories of incarceration but eventually found out and fired them precipitously after years of successful employment.

Some study participants who cite "ban the box" as an important system change report feeling connection to and admiration for a former parolable lifer, a woman who was granted parole and who has dedicated her new life to advocacy for reentry people, particularly to "ban the box" initiatives. The women inside are aware of state and national "ban the box" efforts because they follow the activities of their former peer, who now serves as a role model of possibility.

Many states and the federal government have also passed laws prohibiting formerly incarcerated people from securing professional licenses even when their crimes were unrelated to the careers they are seeking. Laws restricting housing options, limiting educational loan opportunities, and accessing public service assistance are additional punishments delivered after "time served." These prohibitions, like life sentences, often continue without endpoints. One section of the Personal Responsibility and Work Opportunity Reconciliation Act of 1996 (PRWORA), signed into law by President Bill Clinton, for example, stipulates that men and women convicted of a state or federal felony offense involving the use or sale of drugs are subject to a lifetime ban on receiving cash assistance and food stamps. *Sheri* is concerned. She wants to be released, yet she knows how she is perceived. "I don't want them to see me as a monster. . . . I'm known as a child molester [aiding and abetting her abusive boyfriend]" and will be a registered sex offender. "I don't want to be defined by that." That's who she was, not who she is now. "I want them [parole board] to see that I'm more." She wants an opportunity to prove that she has "become a person they can let out into the community."

Additionally, many formerly incarcerated people are denied voting rights, the symbol of democracy. Although disenfranchisement is an obstacle to participation in all forms of civic life, according to the National Conference of State Legislatures, an estimated 5.85 million Americans, more than 676,000 of them women, are denied the right to vote because of laws that prohibit voting by people who have felony convictions. Disenfranchisement is not unitary in form; it's more mixed than consistent. In Florida, Iowa, and Kentucky, for example, formerly incarcerated people lose their voting rights permanently, while Maine and Vermont allow their formerly incarcerated citizens to vote. In 13 states, including Michigan, voting rights are restored after a person's release from prison.[44] In 24 states, formerly incarcerated people can vote if they are no longer subject to either probation or parole. In several states, a person released from prison can apply in writing to the state parole board for a certificate/waiver that restores voting rights. In 11 states, legislators are currently considering tightening voting restrictions for people convicted of felonies. Disenfranchisement is the continuation of a punishment for which the individual has already paid the societally prescribed penalty of years of imprisonment. It adds an encumbrance that limits already limited lives and that inhibits successful reintegration into civic and social life.

Under current conditions of life imprisonment, many of the women in this study will never face these legal and social obstacles, but their "sisters with years" will. Nonetheless, they want to be contributors to justice advocacy, even if they personally will not reap the benefits of its successes.

Conclusion

To reduce the "prison leviathan," to stop the forces of mass incarceration, and to return life-imprisoned men and women to their families would require massive social reform, that is, serious political and economic commitment to the strengthening of families and communities, the promotion of economic development in cities and neighborhoods where people have been disproportionately victimized by crime and deleterious social forces, and improvement in the quality and outcomes of K–12 educational experiences, regardless of location.[45] Changes on this scale may not be politically feasible, but we can hold the vision and start demanding justice where we are. That's just one of the lessons that these life-serving women offer to us: Seek justice wherever you are.

The solutions they proffered, borne out of their collective 1,088 years of imprisonment, suggest a way forward. Their solutions are robust and persuasive: Provide rehabilitative programming opportunities that include life-serving women as participants. Require gender training and accountability from officers and prison administrators. Consider the needs of the children of life-serving women. Amend the PRWORA. Imprison only those people whose crimes create fear, not those whose crimes generate anger. Stop prosecutorial overcharging. Revoke assumptions of equitable responsibility in felony murder statutes. End "the punishments that keep on giving." Their suggestions, large and small, simply need the political will to enact them.

The American penchant for mass incarceration and for "natural life" sentences is unsustainable. It is, as a *New York Times* editorial notes, "a moral, legal, social, and economic disaster. It cannot end soon enough."[46]

NOTES

CHAPTER 1. THE LIFE IMPRISONMENT OF WOMEN IN AMERICA

1 National Research Council, *Growth of Incarceration*; Alexander, *New Jim Crow*; Loury and Western, "Challenge of Mass Incarceration"; Walker, *Sense and Non-Sense*, 16; Kruttschnitt, "Paradox"; Kubiac, Hanna, and Balton, " 'I Came to Prison.' "

2 Loury and Western, "Challenge of Mass Incarceration"; Walker, *Sense and Non-Sense*, 16; Alexander, *New Jim Crow*.

3 Loury and Western, "Challenge of Mass Incarceration"; Walker, *Sense and Non-Sense*, 16.

4 Kruttschnitt, "Paradox."

5 Davis, *Are Prisons Obsolete?*; Price and Sokoloff, *Criminal Justice System*; U.S. Department of Justice, *Prisoners in 2010*; Chesney-Lind and Pasko, *Female Offender*; Britton, *Gender of Crime*; Pollock, "Afterword"; Belknap, *Invisible Woman*; Phillips, "Incarcerated Women."

6 Phillips, "Parents in Prison"; U.S. Department of Justice, *Prisoners in 2010*; Mauer, *Changing Racial Dynamics*.

7 Phillips, "Parents in Prison"; U.S. Department of Justice, *Prisoners in 2011*.

8 Adopting the convention initiated by feminist criminologist Joanne Belknap, I refer to the criminal justice system as the "criminal-processing system," because, in many ways for many of these women, the system has not been just. See Belknap, *Invisible Woman*, 1; Phillips, "Incarcerated Women."

9 U.S. Department of Justice, *Prisoners in 2011*; Phillips, "Incarcerated Women."

10 U.S. Department of Justice, *Prisoners in 2011*; Phillips, "Incarcerated Women."

11 Phillips, "Parents in Prison"; Kruttschnitt, "Paradox."

12 National Research Council, *Growth of Incarceration*; Loury, "Crime," 134–142; Walker, *Sense and Non-Sense*, 16; Chesney-Lind and Pasko, *Female Offender*.

13 Petrella and Friedmann, "Slowly Closing the Gates," 1–12.

14 U.S. Department of Justice, *Prisoners in 2011*.

15 Phillips, "Parents in Prison"; U.S. Department of Justice, *Prisoners in 2010*.

16 Chesney-Lind and Pasko, *Female Offender*; Steffensmeier and Schwartz, "Trends in Female Criminality"; Steffensmeier and Schwartz, "Contemporary Explanations."

17 U.S. Department of Justice, *Prisoners in 2011*; Steffensmeier and Schwartz, "Trends in Female Criminality"; Danner, "Three Strikes."

18 Owen, *In the Mix*.

19 Chesney-Lind and Pasko, *Female Offender.*

20 Ibid.; Contreras, "Damn, Yo."

21 Steffensmeier and Schwartz, "Trends in Female Criminality," 101.

22 Nellis, "Throwing Away the Key."

23 Walker, *Sense and Non-Sense,* 16.

24 Nellis and King, *No Exit.*

25 Nellis, "Throwing Away the Key."

26 Michigan Department of Corrections, *2010 Statistical Report.*

27 Wacquant, "Curious Eclipse."

28 Fine et al., *Changing Minds;* Rhodes, "Changing the Subject," 388–411; Gaarder and Belknap, "Tenuous Borders."

29 All study participants chose their own pseudonyms. Some chose only first names; some chose both first and last names; others chose male monikers. I have retained their choices throughout. These are their voices and their names.

30 Rhodes, *Total Confinement,* 10.

31 Davis, "Foreword."

32 Weitzer and Tuch, "Racially Biased Policing."

33 Davis, *Are Prisons Obsolete?*

34 Ibid.; Faith, *Unruly Women.*

35 Goffman, *Stigma.*

36 Chiricos and Eschholz, "Racial and Ethnic Typification"; Dixon, Azocar, and Casas, "Portrayal of Race"; Entman, "Representation and Reality"; Mastro and Robinson, "Cops and Crooks."

37 Dixon, Azocar, and Casas, "Portrayal of Race"; Entman, "Representation and Reality"; Mastro and Robinson, "Cops and Crooks."

38 Faith, *Unruly Women;* Britto et al., "Does 'Special' Mean Young, White and Female?"; Noh, Lee, and Feltey. "Mad, Bad, or Reasonable?"

39 Farr, "Defeminizing," 53; Britto et al., "Does 'Special' Mean Young, White and Female?"

40 Faith, *Unruly Women;* Farr, "Classification for Female Inmates"; Barnett, "Perfect Mother"; Noh, Lee, and Feltey. "Mad, Bad, or Reasonable?"; Danner, "Three Strikes"; Flavin and Desautels, "Feminism and Crime."

41 McCorkel, "Embodied Surveillance"; Britton, *At Work;* Owen, *In the Mix;* Goodstein, "Introduction"; Rafter, *Partial Justice;* Dodge, *Whores and Thieves.*

42 Belknap, *Invisible Woman;* Flavin and Desautels, "Feminism and Crime."

43 Goffman, *Stigma;* Flavin and Desautels, "Feminism and Crime."

44 Barnett, "Perfect Mother."

45 Ibid., 16.

46 Reuss, "Taking a Long Hard Look"; Davis, *Are Prisons Obsolete?*

47 Bosworth, *Engendering Resistance.*

48 Belknap, *Invisible Woman;* Young and Reviere, *Women behind Bars;* Owen, *In the Mix.*

49 Giallombardo, *Society of Women*; Ward and Kassebaum, *Women's Prison*; Heffernan, *Making It in Prison*; Kruttschnitt and Gartner, *Marking Time*; Bosworth, *Engendering Resistance*.

50 McCorkel, *Breaking Women*; Greer, "Changing Nature"; Britton, *At Work*; Belknap, *Invisible Woman*; Price and Sokoloff, *Criminal Justice System*.

51 Goodstein, "Introduction," 1; Chesney-Lind, "Patriarchy, Crime, and Justice."

52 Fili, "Women in Prison"; Carlen, "Introduction"; Mandaraka-Sheppard, *Dynamics of Aggression*; McCorkel, "Embodied Surveillance."

53 Genovese, *Roll Jordan Roll*, 22.

54 Hartsock, "Feminist Standpoint," 157–180; Lennon, "Gender and Knowledge"; Harding, "Comment on Hekman's 'Truth and Method.'"

55 Sweeney, *Story within Us*.

56 Belknap, *Invisible Woman*.

57 Kruttschnitt, "Paradox," 35.

58 National Research Council, *Growth of Incarceration*.

59 Phillips, "Parents in Prison"; Kruttschnitt, "Paradox."

60 Phillips, "Parents in Prison." Numbers exceed 100% because some mothers have multiple dependent children with different caregivers.

61 Dallaire, "Incarcerated Mothers"; Schirmer, Nellis, and Mauer, *Incarcerated Parents*; Siegel, *Disrupted Childhoods*.

62 Siegel, *Disrupted Childhoods*.

63 Ibid.; Schirmer, Nellis, and Mauer, *Incarcerated Parents*; Golden, *War on the Family*.

64 Siegel, *Disrupted Childhoods*; Golden, *War on the Family*.

65 Dallaire, "Incarcerated Mothers."

66 Young and Reviere, *Women behind Bars*; Siegel, *Disrupted Childhoods*.

67 Siegel, *Disrupted Childhoods*, 18.

68 U.S. Department of Justice, *Parents in Prison*.

69 Siegel, *Disrupted Childhoods*.

70 Schirmer, Nellis, and Mauer, *Incarcerated Parents*; Michalson, "Mothers, Children, and Crime"; Belknap, *Invisible Woman*; Pollock, *Women, Prison, and Crime*.

71 George, *Woman Doing Life*, 13.

72 Kruttschnitt, "Paradox."

73 George, *Woman Doing Life*.

74 Logan, "Life and Death."

75 Alexander, *New Jim Crow*, 161.

76 Lempert, Bergeron, and Linker, "Negotiating the Politics."

77 Bosworth, *Engendering Resistance*; Fili, "Women in Prison"; Diaz-Cotto, *Chicana Lives*; Owen, *In the Mix*.

78 Faith, *Unruly Women*, 68.

79 Belknap, *Invisible Woman*; Britton, *At Work*; Owen, *In the Mix*; Goodstein, "Introduction."

80 Belknap, *Invisible Woman*; Britton, *At Work*; Flavin and Desautels, "Feminism and Crime."

81 Ross and Richards, "Introduction"; quotation from T. Irwin, " 'Inside' Story," 513.

82 Thomas, "Gendered Control in Prisons"; Britton, *At Work*; Messerschmidt, "Masculinities and Crime."

83 Loury and Western, "Challenge of Mass Incarceration," 16; Belknap, *Invisible Woman*.

84 Thomas, "Gendered Control in Prisons"; Belknap, *Invisible Woman*; Britton, *At Work*; Flavin and Desautels, "Feminism and Crime."

85 Law, *Resistance behind Bars*.

86 Flavin, *Our Bodies, Our Crimes*; Messerschmidt, "Masculinities and Crime."

87 Siegel, *Disrupted Childhoods*; Young and Reviere, *Women behind Bars*; Belknap, *Invisible Woman*; Mauer, Potler, and Wolf, *Gender and Justice*; Greer, "Changing Nature"; Gaarder and Belknap, "Tenuous Borders"; Owen, *In the Mix*.

88 U.S. Department of Justice, *Prior Abuse*; Renzetti, "Gender and Violent Crime."

89 Ibid.

90 Greer, "Changing Nature"; Steffensmeier and Schwartz, "Contemporary Explanations"; Steffensmeier and Schwartz, "Trends in Female Criminality"; Flavin, *Our Bodies, Our Crimes*.

91 Siegel, *Disrupted Childhoods*; Renzetti, "Gender and Violent Crime."

92 Alexander, "Foreword"; Renzetti, "Gender and Violent Crime."

93 Steffensmeier and Schwartz, "Trends in Female Criminality," 102.

94 U.S. Department of Justice, *Prisoners in 2011*.

95 Steffensmeier and Schwartz, "Trends in Female Criminality," 101.

96 "Felony Murder Doctrine."

97 Jones, *Women Who Kill*.

98 Faith, *Unruly Women*.

99 Ibid.

100 Prejean, "Foreword."

101 Greer, "Changing Nature"; Muraskin, "Disparate Treatment."

102 *Neal v. Michigan Department of Corrections*.

103 Levi and Waldman, "Introduction"; Muraskin, "Disparate Treatment."

104 R. Johnson, "Introduction"; Hassine, *Life without Parole*.

105 Kruttschnitt and Hussemann, "Micropolitics of Race."

106 Bosworth, *Engendering Resistance*, 3.

107 Fili, "Women in Prison."

108 Rowe, "Narratives of Self"; Fili, "Women in Prison."

109 Bosworth, *Engendering Resistance*.

110 Mills, "Situated Actions."

111 Riessman, "Stigma and Everyday Resistance," 113.

112 Fili, "Women in Prison," 3.

113 Kruttschnitt, "Paradox."

114 Comack, "Producing Feminist Knowledge."

115 Gaarder and Belknap, "Tenuous Borders."

116 Morash, "Tackling Key Questions," 1–33.

117 Belknap, *Invisible Woman*; Chesney-Lind and Pasko, *Female Offender;* Pollock, *Women, Prison, and Crime*; Gilfus, "Women's Experiences"; Flavin and Desautels, "Feminism and Crime."

118 Chesney-Lind and Pasko, *Female Offender*; Sokoloff, Price, and Flavin, "Criminal Law and Women," 11–29.

119 Bosworth, *Engendering Resistance.*

120 Jacobsen and Lempert, "Institutional Disparities."

121 Gaarder and Belknap, "Tenuous Borders."

122 Young and Reviere, *Women behind Bars*, 7.

123 Warren, *Deposition.*

124 Michigan Department of Corrections, "About MDOC."

125 Kruttschnitt and Gartner, *Marking Time.*

126 Denizen and Lincoln, *Landscape of Qualitative Research.*

127 Seale, "Quality."

128 Ibid.; Bryant and Charmaz, *Handbook of Grounded Theory.*

129 Krueger and Casey, *Focus Groups.*

130 Hollander, "Social Contexts"; Bryant and Charmaz, *Handbook of Grounded Theory.*

131 Ibid.; Grogan and Richards, "Body Image"; Bryant and Charmaz, *Handbook of Grounded Theory.*

132 Grogan and Richards, "Body Image"; DeVault, "Talking and Listening."

133 Ibid.

134 Abu-Lughod, "Can There Be a Feminist Ethnography?"; Collins, *Black Feminist Thought*; Fine, "Working the Hyphens"; DeVault, *Liberating Method*; Naples, *Feminism and Method*; Smith, *Institutional Ethnography*; Sprague, *Feminist Methodologies*; Hesse-Biber and Leavy, *Feminist Research;* Hesse-Biber, Gilmartin, and Lydenberg, *Feminist Approaches.*

135 Grogan and Richards, "Body Image"; DeVault, "Talking and Listening."

136 Hollander, "Social Contexts."

137 Hanks and Carr, "Lifelines of Women"; Belknap, *Invisible Woman.*

138 Giele, "Homemaker"; Shanahan and Porfeli, "Chance Events in the Life Course"; DeVault, "Talking and Listening."

139 Giordano, Cernkovich, and Rudolph, "Gender"; Shanahan and Porfeli, "Chance Events in the Life Course."

140 Knapik, "Qualitative Research"; Shanahan and Porfeli, "Chance Events in the Life Course."

141 McAdams, "Studying Lives," 251.

142 Tekola, Griffin, and Camfield, "Using Qualitative Methods."

143 Jacelon and Imperio, "Participant Diaries"; Meth, "Using Diaries."

144 Meth, "Using Diaries."

145 Jacelon and Imperio, "Participant Diaries."

146 Tekola, Griffin, and Camfield, "Using Qualitative Methods."

147 Jacelon and Imperio, "Participant Diaries."

148 Meth, "Using Diaries."

149 Glaser and Strauss, *Discovery of Grounded Theory*; Glaser, *Theoretical Sensitivity*; Strauss, *Qualitative Analysis*; Strauss and Corbin, *Basics of Qualitative Research*; Charmaz, *Constructing Grounded Theory*; Bryant and Charmaz, *Handbook of Grounded Theory*; Lempert, "Asking Questions of the Data."

150 Abu-Lughod, "Can There Be a Feminist Ethnography?"; Collins, *Black Feminist Thought*; Fine, "Working the Hyphens"; DeVault. *Liberating Method*; Naples, *Feminism and Method*; Smith, *Institutional Ethnography*; Sprague, *Feminist Methodologies*; Hesse-Biber and Leavy, *Feminist Research;* Hesse-Biber, Gilmartin, and Lydenberg, *Feminist Approaches.*

151 Lempert, "Cross Race."

152 Morash, *Women on Probation.*

153 Giordano, Cernkovich, and Rudolph, "Gender," 993.

154 Thomas, *Doing Critical Ethnography.*

155 Rhodes, "Changing the Subject."

156 Comack, "Producing Feminist Knowledge."

157 Bosworth, *Engendering Resistance*, 3.

158 Fleisher and Krienert, *Myth of Prison Rape*, xii.

159 Faith, *Unruly Women*, xv.

160 Bosworth, *Engendering Resistance.*

161 Ibid.

162 McCorkel, "Going to the Crackhouse."

163 Bosworth, *Engendering Resistance*, 3.

164 Sweeney, *Story within Us.*

165 Owen, *In the Mix.*

166 Thomas, "Gendered Control in Prisons," 7.

CHAPTER 2. CARMELA

1 Gudrais, "Prison Problem."

2 Gaarder and Belknap, "Tenuous Borders."

3 Richie, *Compelled to Crime*, 3. Italics in original.

4 Mills, *Sociological Imagination.*

5 Gaarder and Belknap, "Tenuous Borders."

6 Ibid.

7 Ibid.

8 Perry and Szalavitz, *Boy Who Was Raised as a Dog*, 21.

9 Gaarder and Belknap, "Tenuous Borders."

10 Richie, *Compelled to Crime*; Chesney-Lind and Pasko, *Female Offender*; Chesney-Lind, "Patriarchy, Crime, and Justice"; Belknap, *Invisible Woman*; Pollock, *Women, Prison, and Crime.*

11 Richie, *Compelled to Crime*, 3.

12 Fili, "Women in Prison," 16.

13 Gaarder and Belknap, "Tenuous Borders."

14 DeHart, "Pathways to Prison."

15 Sweeney, *Story within Us.*

CHAPTER 3. BEGINNING THE PRISON JOURNEY

1 R. Johnson, "Introduction."

2 Davis, "Foreword."

3 Britton, *At Work*; Belknap, *Invisible Woman*; Rafter, *Partial Justice.*

4 Wideman, "Doing Time," 17; Giordano, Cernkovich, and Rudolph, "Gender."

5 Gopnik, "Caging of America."

6 Sparks, "Out of the 'Digger.'"

7 Ahearn, "Language and Agency," 112.

8 Morash, "Tackling Key Questions."

9 Ibid.

10 Fili, "Women in Prison."

11 Kruttschnitt, "Paradox."

12 Owen, *In the Mix,* 3.

13 Owen, *In the Mix.*

14 Ibid.

15 Ibid.

16 Ibid.

17 Sparks, "Out of the 'Digger.'"

18 Kruttschnitt, Gartner, and Miller, "Doing Her Own Time?"

19 Belknap, *Invisible Woman*; Owen, *In the Mix.*

20 T. Irwin, " 'Inside' Story."

21 Kruttschnitt and Gartner, "Women's Imprisonment."

22 Chafe, "Sex and Race."

23 Sparks, "Out of the 'Digger'"; Owen, *In the Mix.*

24 Thomas, *Doing Critical Ethnography*; Hassine, *Life without Parole.*

25 Owen, *In the Mix.*

26 McCorkel, "Going to the Crackhouse."

27 Goffman, *Asylums;* Foucault, *Discipline and Punish,* 138; Foucault, *Foucault Reader.*

28 Herrschaft et al., "Gender Differences," 478.

29 Goffman, *Asylums.*

30 Crewe, "Depth, Weight, Tightness."

31 Goffman, *Asylums.*

32 Pollock, *Women, Prison, and Crime.*

33 Goffman, *Asylums.*

34 Ibid.

35 Faith, *Unruly Women,* 59.

36 Goffman, *Asylums.*

37 Opsal, "Women Disrupting."

38 Goffman, *Asylums.*

39 Belknap, *Invisible Woman.*

40 Goffman, *Asylums*, 20.

41 Thomas, "Gendered Control in Prisons."

42 Goffman, *Asylums.*

43 Thomas, "Gendered Control in Prisons."

44 Reuss, "Taking a Long Hard Look," 431.

45 Fleisher and Krienert, *Myth of Prison Rape*, xiii.

46 Lear, *Radical Hope*, 56. Italics in original.

47 Reuss, "Taking a Long Hard Look" (italics added); Nellis, *Lives of Juvenile Lifers;* Leigey, "For the Longest Time."

48 Clear et al., "Value of Religion."

49 Tapia, "Introduction," 1.

50 Goffman, *Asylums.*

51 Reuss, "Taking a Long Hard Look"; Leigey, "For the Longest Time."

52 Reuss, "Taking a Long Hard Look"; Leigey, "For the Longest Time."

53 Belknap, *Invisible Woman.*

54 Toch, *Living in Prison.*

55 Goffman, *Asylums.*

56 Schmid and Jones, "Ambivalent Actions."

57 Ibid.; George, Woman Doing Life.

58 A. Johnson, *Privilege, Power, and Difference, 80.*

59 Pogrebin and Dodge, "Women's Accounts."

60 Owen, *In the Mix.*

61 Schmid and Jones, "Ambivalent Actions."

62 Ibid.

63 Festinger, *Theory of Cognitive Dissonance*; Aronson, "Back to the Future."

64 Thomas, "Gendered Control in Prisons."

65 Giallombardo, *Society of Women*; Ward and Kassebaum, *Women's Prison*; Heffernan, *Making It in Prison*; Greer, "Changing Nature"; Kunzel, *Criminal Intimacy.*

66 George, *Woman Doing Life*, 46.

67 Hassine, *Life without Parole*; Rotter et al., "Personality Disorders"; Rotter et al., "Best Practices"; Trammell, *Enforcing the Convict Code.*

68 Pollock, *Women, Prison, and Crime.*

69 Trammell, *Enforcing the Convict Code*, 40.

70 Hassine, *Life without Parole*; Rotter et al., "Personality Disorders"; Rotter et al., "Best Practices."

71 Pollock, *Women, Prison, and Crime.*

72 Thomas, "Gendered Control in Prisons," 7; Thomas and Thomas, *Child in America.*

73 Pollock, *Women, Prison, and Crime.*

74 Ibid.

75 George, *Woman Doing Life.*

76 Pollock, *Women, Prison, and Crime.*

77 Scarce, "Doing Time," 313.

78 George, *Woman Doing Life.*

79 All of the women spoke about race in dichotomized white/black terms. Even those women who identified themselves as multiracial or Native American categorized themselves, and others, as black or white.

80 Pollock, *Women, Prison, and Crime.*

81 Diaz-Cotto, *Chicana Lives.*

82 Pollock, *Women, Prison, and Crime;* Diaz-Cotto, *Chicana Lives.*

83 A. Johnson, *Privilege, Power, and Difference.*

84 Owen, *In the Mix.*

85 Wise, *Color-Blind.*

86 Ibid.

87 Kruttschnitt and Hussemann, "Micropolitics of Race."

88 Walker, Spohn, and DeLone, *Color of Justice.*

89 Bonilla-Silva, *Racism without Racists.*

90 Ibid.

91 Goffman, *Stigma,* 3.

92 Fleisher and Krienert, *Myth of Prison Rape.*

93 Owen, *In the Mix.*

94 Ibid.

95 J. Irwin and Austin, *It's about Time;* Wideman, "Doing Time"; Kruttschnitt and Gartner, "Women's Imprisonment"; Jiang and Fisher-Giorlando, "Inmate Misconduct"; Thomas, "Gendered Control in Prisons"; J. Irwin and Cressey, "Thieves."

96 Wideman, "Doing Time," 17; Fleisher and Krienert, *Myth of Prison Rape;* Dhami, Ayton, and Loewenstein, "Adaptation to Imprisonment."

97 J. Irwin and Austin, *It's about Time.*

98 Kruttschnitt and Gartner, "Women's Imprisonment"; Fleisher and Krienert, *Myth of Prison Rape.*

99 Owen, *In the Mix.*

100 Toch, *Living in Prison,* 181.

CHAPTER 4. ANN AND CRYSTAL

1 *Miller v. Alabama.*

2 Felony murder law is a rule of criminal statutes that any death that occurs during the commission of a felony is first-degree murder, and all participants in that felony or attempted felony can be charged with and found guilty of murder as aiders and abettors. See "Felony Murder Doctrine."

3 Kruttschnitt and Gartner, "Women's Imprisonment."

4 Owen, *In the Mix.*

5 Ibid.

CHAPTER 5. ACTIVELY DOING LIFE

1 Gopnik, "Caging of America."
2 Bosworth, *Engendering Resistance*, 16.
3 Ibid.
4 Scarce, "Doing Time," 306.
5 Wahidin and Moss, "Women Doing and Making Time."
6 Foucault, *Discipline and Punish*, 138.
7 Bosworth, *Engendering Resistance*.
8 Ibid., 3.
9 Hassine, *Life without Parole*; Hassine, "How I Became a Convict."
10 Toch, *Living in Prison*.
11 Lear, *Radical Hope*.
12 Herrschaft et al., "Gender Differences."
13 Sparks, "Out of the 'Digger.'"
14 Hassine, *Life without Parole*.
15 Nellis, "Throwing Away the Key."
16 Goffman, *Asylums*; Sampson, *Great American City*; Williams and Guerra, "Perceptions."
17 Sweeney, *Story within Us*.
18 Rhodes, "Changing the Subject."
19 Mead, *Mind, Self, and Society*; Goffman, *Stigma*.
20 Bosworth, "Gender, Race and Sexuality."
21 Giordano, Cernkovich, and Rudolph, "Gender."
22 Scarce, "Doing Time."
23 Lear, *Radical Hope*.
24 Giordano, Cernkovich, and Rudolph, "Gender."
25 Toch, *Living in Prison*.
26 McCorkel, *Breaking Women*.
27 Ibid.; Kruttschnitt and Gartner, *Marking Time*.
28 Giordano, Cernkovich, and Rudolph, "Gender."
29 Herrschaft et al., "Gender Differences"; Giordano, Cernkovich, and Rudolph, "Gender."
30 Herrschaft et al., "Gender Differences."
31 Kruttschnitt and Gartner, *Marking Time*.
32 Law, *Resistance behind Bars*.
33 Giordano, Cernkovich, and Rudolph, "Gender."
34 Cooley, *Social Organization*.
35 ^A. Johnson, *Privilege, Power, and Difference*.
36 George, *Woman Doing Life*.
37 Thomas, "Gendered Control in Prisons."
38 Giordano, Cernkovich, and Rudolph, "Gender."
39 Didion, *White Album*, 11.

40 McCorkel, "Going to the Crackhouse"; Sweeney, *Story within Us.*
41 Sweeney, *Story within Us.*
42 Goffman, *Stigma*; Faith, *Unruly Women.*
43 Brush, *Poverty, 86.*
44 Opsal, "Women Disrupting."
45 Kruttschnitt and Gartner, *Marking Time.*
46 Herrschaft et al., "Gender Differences."
47 Giordano, Cernkovich, and Rudolph, "Gender."
48 Rhodes, *Total Confinement*, 126.
49 McAdams, "Studying Lives"; Opsal, "Women Disrupting."
50 Ibid.
51 McAdams, "Studying Lives," 241.
52 Goffman, *Asylums*; Miller, *Warden Wore Pink*; Britton, *At Work.*
53 Bosworth, *Engendering Resistance.*
54 McAdams, *Stories We Live By.*
55 Ibid.
56 Hassine, *Life without Parole.*
57 Owen, *In the Mix*, 4.
58 McCorkel, "Going to the Crackhouse."
59 McAdams, "Studying Lives."
60 Opsal, "Women Disrupting"; McAdams, *Stories We Live By*, 12.
61 Ross and Richards, "Introduction."
62 Gilligan, *In a Different Voice*; Jaggar, "Feminist Ethics"; Ruddick, *Maternal Thinking.*
63 Ibid.
64 Gilligan, *In a Different Voice.*
65 Toch, *Living in Prison.*
66 Butler, "What Are You Looking At?"
67 Greer, "Walking an Emotional Tightrope."
68 Sampson, *Great American City*, 20. Italics in original.
69 Trammell, *Enforcing the Convict Code.*
70 Ibid.
71 Toch, *Living in Prison.*
72 Bosworth, *Engendering Resistance*, 6.
73 Miller, *Warden Wore Pink.*
74 Hochschild, *Managed Heart.*
75 Wahidin and Moss, "Women Doing and Making Time."
76 Scarce, "Doing Time," 303–321.
77 Sweeney, *Story within Us.*
78 Williams and Guerra, "Perceptions"; Sampson, *Great American City.*
79 Rhodes, *Total Confinement.*
80 Williams and Guerra, "Perceptions"; Sampson, *Great American City.*
81 Tapia, "Introduction."

82 Miller, *Warden Wore Pink*; Hassine, *Life without Parole*; Nellis, "Throwing Away the Key."

83 Nellis, "Throwing Away the Key."

84 Fleisher and Krienert, *Myth of Prison Rape.*

85 Miller, *Warden Wore Pink.*

86 Williams and Guerra, "Perceptions"; Sampson, *Great American City.*

87 Belknap, *Invisible Woman*, 214.

88 Chafe, "Sex and Race."

89 Hassine, *Life without Parole.*

90 McAdams, *Stories We Live By.*

91 Sweeney, *Story within Us.*

92 Kruttschnitt, Gartner, and Miller, "Doing Her Own Time?" 681–717.

93 Pollock, *Women, Prison, and Crime.*

94 Lear, *Radical Hope.*

95 Prejean, "Foreword," xxvi. Italics in original.

96 Greer, "Walking an Emotional Tightrope," 124.

97 Sweeney, *Story within Us*, 230.

98 Faith, *Unruly Women.*

99 Giordano, Cernkovich, and Rudolph, "Gender."

CHAPTER 6. *DESIREE*

1 Lempert, Bergeron, and Linker, "Negotiating the Politics."

2 Toussaint and Webb, "Gender Differences."

3 Pecukonis, "Cognitive/Affective Empathy Training Program"; Clark, "Empathy and Sympathy."

4 Toussaint and Webb, "Gender Differences."

5 Michigan Department of Corrections, "Parole Consideration Process."

6 A "flop" is aptly named as it indicates both a heavy ungainly move and a total failure.

7 Wiesel, "I Am Against Fanatics."

8 Lear, *Radical Hope.*

9 Women in this facility do not have kitchen cooking privileges. They "cook" in a microwave that is shared with the 60 other women in the unit.

10 Pecukonis, "Cognitive/Affective Empathy Training Program," 62.

11 Mead, *Mind, Self, and Society.*

12 Barret-Lennard, "Recovery of Empathy."

13 Ibid.

14 Macaskill, Maltby, and Day, "Forgiveness"; Clark, "Empathy and Sympathy."

15 Barret-Lennard, "Recovery of Empathy."

CHAPTER 7. CORRECTIONAL OFFICERS OR "US VS. THEM"

1 Pollock, "Working in Prison"; Gopnik, "Caging of America."

2 Rasche, "Cross-Sex Supervision," 159; Tracy, "Construction of Correctional Officers," 514; Pollock, "Working in Prison"; Faith, *Unruly Women*; George, *Woman*

Doing Life; Goffman, *Stigma*; Vuolo and Kruttschnitt, "Prisoners' Adjustment";
Britton, *At Work*; Miller, *Warden Wore Pink*, 62.

3 Pollock, "Working in Prison."
4 Ibid., 191.
5 Tracy, "Construction of Correctional Officers"; Pollock, "Working in Prison."
6 Bosworth, *Engendering Resistance*.
7 Pollock, "Working in Prison."
8 Ibid.; Gordon, Proulx, and Grant, "Trepidation"; Rasche, "Cross-Sex Supervision";
Britton, *At Work*; Miller, *Warden Wore Pink*, 62.
9 Michigan Department of Corrections, "New Corrections Officer Training."
10 Britton, *At Work*; Pollock, "Working in Prison."
11 Mullendore and Beever, "Sexually Abused Women."
12 Miller, *Warden Wore Pink*.
13 Ibid.
14 Ashenfelter, "ACLU Targets."
15 More than 60 women wrote in protest to the American Civil Liberties Union,
which, with a broad coalition of human rights, health, and religious groups, sent
a letter to the director of the Michigan Department of Corrections, demanding
a change to the search policies. The letter was also published in several Michigan
news outlets. The use of the chair was halted by the warden's order in February
2012, but not before women reported emotionally and psychologically damaging
consequences.
16 Tracy, "Construction of Correctional Officers"; Britton, *At Work*.
17 Rader, "Surrendering Solidarity."
18 Rasche, "Cross-Sex Supervision," 165.
19 Miller, *Warden Wore Pink*.
20 Ibid.
21 Goffman, *Asylums*.
22 Renzetti and Curran, *Living Sociology*; Lindsey and Beach, *Essentials of Sociology*;
Kimmel and Aronson, *Sociology Now*; Ballantine and Roberts, *Our Social World*.
23 Diaz-Cotto, *Chicana Lives*.
24 Dirkzwager and Kruttschnitt, "Prisoners' Perceptions," 405 (italics in original);
Tracy, "Construction of Correctional Officers," 510.
25 Michigan Department of Corrections, "Parole Consideration Process."
26 Mullendore and Beever, "Sexually Abused Women."
27 Michigan Department of Corrections, "Corrections Officers."
28 Trammell, *Enforcing the Convict Code*; Bosworth, "Gender, Race and Sexuality";
Faith, *Unruly Women*.
29 Vuolo and Kruttschnitt, "Prisoners' Adjustment."
30 Bosworth, *Engendering Resistance*.
31 Bordt, "From Angela Davis."
32 Tracy, "Construction of Correctional Officers."
33 Toch, *Living in Prison*.

34 Johnson and Dobrzanska, "Mature Coping."
35 Bosworth, "Gender, Race and Sexuality."
36 Thomas, "Gendered Control in Prisons," 7.
37 Vuolo and Kruttschnitt, "Prisoners' Adjustment."
38 Pollock, *Women, Prison, and Crime.*
39 Genovese, *Roll Jordan Roll.*
40 Tracy, "Construction of Correctional Officers"; Faith, *Unruly Women*; Foucault, *Foucault Reader.*
41 Goffman, *Stigma.*
42 Belknap, *Invisible Woman.*
43 Genovese, *Roll Jordan Roll.*
44 Bosworth, *Engendering Resistance.*
45 Toch, *Living in Prison.*
46 Crewe, "Depth, Weight, Tightness," 513.
47 Ibid.
48 Goffman, *Asylums.*
49 Vuolo and Kruttschnitt, "Prisoners' Adjustment," 331.
50 George, *Woman Doing Life.*
51 Toch, *Living in Prison.*
52 Rasche, "Cross-Sex Supervision."
53 Jiang and Fisher-Giorlando, "Inmate Misconduct."
54 Ibid.
55 Toch, *Living in Prison,* 41.
56 Tracy, "Construction of Correctional Officers"; Owen, *In the Mix.*
57 Tracy, "Construction of Correctional Officers."
58 Goffman, *Asylums*; Britton, *At Work*; Vuolo and Kruttschnitt, "Prisoners' Adjustment."
59 Rasche, "Cross-Sex Supervision."
60 Rafter, *Partial Justice*; Dodge, *Whores and Thieves*; Rasche, "Cross-Sex Supervision"; Britton, *At Work.*
61 Dodge, *Whores and Thieves*; Rasche, "Cross-Sex Supervision."
62 Blackburn et al., "When Boundaries Are Broken."
63 Pogrebin and Dodge, "Women's Accounts," 28–46.
64 Levi and Waldman, "Introduction."
65 Calhoun and Coleman, "Female Inmates' Perspectives," 107.
66 Diaz-Cotto, "Gender, Sexuality and Family."
67 Pogrebin and Dodge, "Women's Accounts."
68 Culley, " 'Judge Didn't Sentence Me.' "
69 Ibid., 208; Kimmel, *Guyland*; Kimmel, *Manhood in America.*
70 Culley, " 'Judge Didn't Sentence Me.' "
71 Ibid., 208; Seidel, "Jury Awarded $15.4 Million."
72 Culley, " 'Judge Didn't Sentence Me,' " 207.
73 Ibid.

74 Culley, " 'Judge Didn't Sentence Me' "; Halcom, "Top Verdicts"; Levy, "Michigan to Pay."
75 Halcom, "Top Verdicts."
76 Culley, " 'Judge Didn't Sentence Me,' " 214.
77 Levi and Waldman, "Introduction."
78 Blackburn et al., "When Boundaries Are Broken."
79 Wise, *Color-Blind*.
80 Pollock, "Working in Prison."
81 Genovese, *Roll Jordan Roll*, 137.
82 Rasche, "Cross-Sex Supervision."
83 Mullendore and Beever, "Sexually Abused Women."
84 Toch, *Living in Prison*.
85 Owen, *In the Mix*.
86 Rhodes, *Total Confinement*.

CHAPTER 8. EATING THE LIFE-SENTENCE ELEPHANT
1 Bosworth, *Engendering Resistance*.
2 Riessman, "Stigma and Everyday Resistance," 122.
3 Ibid.
4 Kubiac, Hanna, and Balton, " 'I Came to Prison,' " 160.
5 Johnson and Dobrzanska, "Mature Coping."
6 Goffman, *Asylums*.
7 Owen, *In the Mix*, 103.
8 Diaz-Cotto, *Chicana Lives*.
9 Ibid.
10 Belknap, *Invisible Woman*.
11 Faith, *Unruly Women*.
12 Johnson and Dobrzanska, "Mature Coping," 8.
13 Ibid.
14 Goffman, *Asylums*.
15 Aday and Krabill, *Women Aging*.
16 Buruma, "Uncaptive Minds"; Davis et al., *Evaluating the Effectiveness*; Reuss, "Prison(er) Education"; Vacca, "Educated Prisoners"; National Center for Education Statistics, *Literacy behind Bars*.
17 Sweeney, *Story within Us*.
18 Ibid.
19 Ibid.
20 George, *Woman Doing Life*, vi.
21 Jacobsen and Lempert, "Institutional Disparities."
22 U.S. Department of Justice, *Federal Habeas Corpus*; Liebman, Fagan, and West, *Broken System*, 32.
23 Toch, *Living in Prison*.
24 Pollock, *Prisons*.

25 Giallombardo, *Society of Women*; Ward and Kassebaum, *Women's Prison*; Heffernan, *Making It in Prison*; Owen, *In the Mix*; Kunzel, *Criminal Intimacy*; Diaz-Cotto, "Gender, Sexuality, and Family."

26 Harner, "Relationships."

27 Owen, *In the Mix*; U.S. Department of Justice, *Federal Habeas Corpus*.

28 Kunzel, *Criminal Intimacy*.

29 Opsal, "Women Disrupting."

30 Kunzel, *Criminal Intimacy*.

31 Riessman, "Stigma and Everyday Resistance."

32 Giallombardo, *Society of Women*; Ward and Kassebaum, *Women's Prison*; Heffernan, *Making It in Prison*; Owen, *In the Mix*.

33 Harner, "Relationships."

34 Foucault, *History of Sexuality*.

35 Kunzel, *Criminal Intimacy*; Pardue, Arrigo, and Murphy, "Sex and Sexuality."

36 Bosworth, *Engendering Resistance*; Kruttschnitt and Gartner, "Women's Imprisonment"; Kruttschnitt and Gartner, *Marking Time*; Fleisher and Krienert, *Myth of Prison Rape*; Tracy, "Construction of Correctional Officers"; Faith, *Unruly Women*.

37 *Neal v. Michigan Department of Corrections*.

38 Ward and Kassebaum, *Women's Prison*; Giallombardo, *Society of Women*; Heffernan, *Making It in Prison*; Owen, *In the Mix*; Kunzel, *Criminal Intimacy*; Diaz-Cotto, "Gender, Sexuality, and Family."

39 Fleisher and Krienert, *Myth of Prison Rape*.

40 Ibid., 66.

41 Foucault, *History of Sexuality*.

42 Koscheski and Hensley, "Inmate Homosexual Behavior."

43 Kunzel, *Criminal Intimacy*; Freedman, "Prison Lesbian."

44 Hensley, Tewksbury, and Koscheski, "Characteristics."

45 Bosworth, *Engendering Resistance*, 137.

46 Ibid.

47 Kruttschnitt and Gartner, *Marking Time*, 92.

48 Belknap, *Invisible Woman*; Kunzel, *Criminal Intimacy*.

49 Kunzel, *Criminal Intimacy*.

50 Potter, " 'Undesirable Relations.' "

51 George, *Woman Doing Life*.

52 Potter, " 'Undesirable Relations.' "

53 Owen, *In the Mix*; Tracy, "Construction of Correctional Officers."

54 Pardue, Arrigo, and Murphy, "Sex and Sexuality"; Kunzel, *Criminal Intimacy*; George, *Woman Doing Life*, 52.

55 Trammell, *Enforcing the Convict Code*, 77.

56 Koscheski and Hensley, "Inmate Homosexual Behavior."

57 Trammell, *Enforcing the Convict Code*.

58 Greer, "Changing Nature."

59 Calhoun and Coleman, "Female Inmates' Perspectives," 108.

60 Pardue, Arrigo, and Murphy, "Sex and Sexuality," 283.

61 George, *Woman Doing Life*, 46.

62 Fleisher and Krienert, *Myth of Prison Rape*.

63 Pogrebin and Dodge, "Women's Accounts."

64 Clear et al., "Value of Religion."

65 Wade, *Faith Instinct*.

66 Ibid.

67 Ibid.

68 Clear et al., "Value of Religion."

69 Ibid., 335.

70 Ibid.

71 Kimmel, "Why Men Should Support," 105.

72 Cherukuri, *Women in Prison*.

CHAPTER 9. CANDACE

1 Scarce, "Doing Time," 305.

2 Clear et al., "Value of Religion."

3 Ibid.

4 Wade, *Faith Instinct*.

5 Ibid.

6 Warner, "Does Empathy Cure?" 137.

7 Ibid., 139.

8 Howley, "Prey TV."

9 The analogy for people on the outside would be sleeping in a bathroom with a sink, toilet, and small desk where the 60-inch tub is situated.

CHAPTER 10. THE WAY FORWARD

1 Comack, "Producing Feminist Knowledge."

2 Carlen, "Introduction," 4. Italics in original.

3 Flavin, *Our Bodies, Our Crimes*; Greer, "Changing Nature."

4 National Research Council, *Growth of Incarceration*; Nellis, "Throwing Away the Key."

5 Walker, *Sense and Non-Sense*, 16.

6 Davis, "Foreword."

7 Carlen, "Introduction"; Faith, *Unruly Women*; Young and Reviere, *Women behind Bars*; Chesney-Lind and Pasko, *Female Offender*.

8 Phillips, "Parents in Prison"; Kruttschnitt, "Paradox."

9 Faith, *Unruly Women*.

10 U.S. Department of Justice, *Prisoners in 2011*.

11 Giordano, Cernkovich, and Rudolph, "Gender."

12 Fine et al., *Changing Minds*; Rowe, "Narratives of Self."

13 Tapia, "Introduction," 2; Loury, "Crime."

14 Davis, "Foreword."

15 National Research Council, *Growth of Incarceration*, 16.

16 Brush, *Poverty*, 86. Italics added.

17 Ibid.

18 Bloom, Owen, and Covington, *Summary of Research*; Pollock, *Women, Prison, and Crime*; Levi and Waldman, "Introduction."

19 National Research Council, *Growth of Incarceration*.

20 Harris, "Moving into the New Millennium."

21 Loury, "Crime."

22 Harris, "Moving into the New Millennium."

23 National Research Council, *Growth of Incarceration* (italics in original); Turner and Wetzel, "Treating Prisoners."

24 Davis, *Are Prisons Obsolete?*

25 Bloom, Owen, and Covington, *Summary of Research*.

26 Davies and Cook, "Sex of Crime."

27 George, *Woman Doing Life*, 32.

28 Van Gundy, "Gender and Corrections."

29 Dirkzwager and Kruttschnitt, "Prisoners' Perceptions."

30 Bloom, Owen, and Covington, *Summary of Research*, 4.

31 Brink, "Other Victims," 262.

32 Phillips, "Parents in Prison"; Kruttschnitt, "Paradox."

33 Opsal, "Women Disrupting."

34 Bordt, "From Angela Davis."

35 Mahoney, "Legal Images."

36 Jabro and Kester-Smith, "Get on the Bus," 68.

37 Muraskin, "Disparate Treatment."

38 Harris, "Moving into the New Millennium," 38.

39 National Research Council, *Growth of Incarceration*, 5.

40 Reddy and Levin, "Conservative Case."

41 National Research Council, *Growth of Incarceration*.

42 For more information, see *Kenneth Foster-Bey et al. v. Rubitschun et al.*, Case No. 05-71318 ["the Foster-Bey Case"], United States District Court, Eastern District of Michigan, Southern Division.

43 Michigan Women's Justice.

44 Sentencing Project, "Felony Disenfranchisement"; National Conference of State Legislatures, "Felon Voting Rights."

45 Loury and Western, "Challenge of Mass Incarceration."

46 *New York Times* Sunday edition, May 25, 2014.

REFERENCES

Abu-Lughod, Lila. "Can There Be a Feminist Ethnography?" *Women and Performance: A Journal of Feminist Theory* 5, no. 1 (1990): 7–27.

Aday, Ronald H., and Jennifer J. Krabill. *Women Aging in Prison: A Neglected Population in the Correctional System.* Boulder, Colo.: Lynne Rienner, 2011.

Adoption and Safe Families Act of 1997. *Govtrack.us.* Accessed October 12, 2011. https://www.govtrack.us/congress/bills/105/hr867.

Ahearn, Laura M. "Language and Agency." *Annual Review of Anthropology* 30 (2001): 109–137.

Alexander, Michelle. "Foreword: Standing without Sweet Company." In *Inside This Place, Not of It: Narratives from Women's Prisons,* edited by Robin Levi and Ayelet Waldman, 9–12. San Francisco: McSweeney's and Voices of Witness, 2011.

———. *The New Jim Crow: Mass Incarceration in the Age of Colorblindness.* New York: New Press, 2012.

Aronson, Elliot. "Back to the Future: Retrospective Review of Leon Festinger's 'A Theory of Cognitive Dissonance.' " *American Journal of Psychology* 110, no. 1 (1997): 127–157.

Ashenfelter, David. "ACLU Targets Strip Searches of Prisoners." *Detroit Free Press.* April 12, 2012.

Ballantine, Jeanne H., and Keith A. Roberts. *Our Social World.* Thousand Oaks, Calif.: Pine Forge, 2009.

Barnett, Barbara. "Perfect Mother or Artist of Obscenity? Narrative and Myth in a Qualitative Analysis of Press Coverage of the Andrea Yates Murders." *Journal of Communication Inquiry* 29, no. 1 (2005): 9–29.

Barrett-Lennard, Godfrey T. "The Recovery of Empathy—Toward Others and Self." In *Empathy Reconsidered: New Directions in Psychotherapy,* edited by Arthur C. Bohart and Leslie S. Greenberg, 103–121. Washington, D.C.: American Psychological Association, 1997.

Belknap, Joanne. *The Invisible Woman: Gender, Crime and Justice.* Belmont, Calif.: Wadsworth Cengage Learning, 2007.

Blackburn, Ashley G., Shannon K. Fowler, Janet L. Mullings, and James W. Marquat. "When Boundaries Are Broken: Inmate Perceptions of Correctional Staff Boundary Violations." *Deviant Behavior* 32, no. 4 (2011): 351–378.

Bloom, Barbara, Barbara Owen, and Stephanie Covington. *A Summary of Research, Practice, and Guiding Principles for Women Offenders.* Washington, D.C.: National Institute of Corrections, 2005.

Bonilla-Silva, Eduardo. *Racism without Racists: Color-Blind Racism and the Persistence of Racial Inequality in America*. Lanham, Md.: Rowman and Littlefield, 2003.

Bordt, Rebecca L. "From Angela Davis to the Long Island Lolita: An Analysis of Contemporary Women's Prison Narratives." *Women and Criminal Justice* 22 (2012): 135–155.

Bosworth, Mary. *Engendering Resistance: Agency and Power in Women's Prisons*. Brookfield, Vt.: Ashgate, 1999.

———. "Gender, Race, and Sexuality in Prison." In *Women in Prison: Gender and Social Control*, edited by Barbara H. Zaitzow and Jim Thomas, 137–155. Boulder, Colo.: Lynne Rienner, 2003.

Brink, Judith. "The Other Victims: The Families of Those Punished by the State." In *Handbook of Restorative Justice*, edited by Dennis Sullivan and Larry Tifft, 261–268. London: Routledge, 2008.

Britto, Sarah, Tycy Hughes, Kurt Saltzman, and Colin Stroh. "Does 'Special' Mean Young, White and Female? Deconstructing the Meaning of 'Special' in *Law and Order: Special Victims Unit*." *Journal of Criminal Justice and Popular Culture* 14, no. 1 (2007): 39–57.

Britton, Dana M. *At Work in the Iron Cage: The Prison as Gendered Organization*. New York: NYU Press, 2003.

———. *The Gender of Crime*. Lanham, Md.: Rowman and Littlefield, 2011.

Brush, Lisa D. *Poverty, Battered Women, and Work in U.S. Public Policy*. New York: Oxford University Press, 2011.

Bryant, Anthony, and Kathy Charmaz. *The Handbook of Grounded Theory*. Thousand Oaks, Calif.: Sage, 2008.

Buruma, Ian. "Uncaptive Minds." *New York Times*. Accessed February 20, 2005. http://www.nytimes.com/2005/02/20/magazine/20prison.htm.

Butler, Michelle. "What Are You Looking At? Prisoner Confrontations and the Search for Respect." *British Journal of Criminology* 48 (2008): 856–873.

Calhoun, Avery J., and Heather D. Coleman. "Female Inmates' Perspectives on Sexual Abuse by Correctional Personnel." *Women and Criminal Justice* 13, no. 2–3 (2008): 101–124.

Carlen, Patricia. "Introduction." In *Women and Punishment: The Struggle for Justice*, edited by Patricia Carlen, 3–20. Cullomopton, Devon, U.K.: Willan, 2002.

Chafe, William. "Sex and Race: The Analogy of Social Control." In *Race, Class, and Gender in the U.S.*, edited by Paula S. Rothenberg, 535–549. New York: Worth, 2001.

Charmaz, Kathy. *Constructing Grounded Theory*. Thousand Oaks, Calif.: Sage, 2006.

Cherukuri, Suvarna. *Women in Prison: An Insight into Captivity and Crime*. New Delhi: Cambridge University Press, 2008.

Chesney-Lind, Meda. 2012. "Patriarchy, Crime and Justice." In *Women and Crime*, edited by Stacey L. Mallicoat, 49–64. Los Angeles: Sage, 2012.

Chesney-Lind, Meda, and Lisa Pasko. *The Female Offender*. Thousand Oaks, Calif.: Sage, 2004.

Chiricos, Ted, and Sarah Eschholz. "The Racial and Ethnic Typification of Crime and the Criminal Typification of Race and Ethnicity in Local Television News." *Journal of Research in Crime and Delinquency* 39, no. 4 (2002): 400–420.

Clark, Arthur J. "Empathy and Sympathy: Therapeutic Distinctions in Counseling." *Journal of Mental Health Counseling* 32, no. 2 (2010): 95–101.

Clear, Todd R., Patricia L Hardyman, Bruce Stout, Karol Lucken, and Harry R. Dammer. "The Value of Religion in Prison." In *Behind Bars: Readings on Prison Culture*, edited by Richard Tewksbury, 329–346. Englewood Cliffs, N.J.: Pearson Prentice Hall, 2006.

Collins, Patricia Hill. *Black Feminist Thought: Knowledge, Consciousness, and the Politics of Empowerment.* 2nd ed. New York: Routledge, 2000.

Comack, Elizabeth. "Producing Feminist Knowledge: Lessons from Women in Trouble." *Theoretical Criminology* 3, no. 3 (1999): 287–306.

Contreras, Randol. "'Damn, Yo—Who's That Girl?' An Ethnographic Analysis of Masculinity in Drug Robberies." *Journal of Contemporary Ethnography* 38, no. 4 (2009): 465–492.

Cooley, Charles Horton. *Social Organization: A Study of the Larger Mind.* 1909. Reprint, New York: Schocken, 1983.

Crewe, Ben. "Depth, Weight, Tightness: Revisiting the Pains of Imprisonment." *Punishment and Society* 13 (2011): 509–529.

Culley, Rachel. 2012. " 'The Judge Didn't Sentence Me to Be Raped': Tracy Neal v. Michigan Department of Corrections: A 15-Year Battle against the Sexual Abuse of Women Inmates in MI." *Women and Criminal Justice* 22, no. 3 (2012): 206–225.

Dallaire, Danielle H. "Incarcerated Mothers and Fathers: A Comparison of Risks for Children and Families." *Family Relations* 56, no. 5 (2007): 440–453.

Danner, Mona J. E. "Three Strikes and It's *Women* Who Are Out: The Hidden Consequences for Women of Criminal Justice Policy Reforms." In *Women and Justice: It's a Crime*, edited by Roslyn Muraskin, 354–364. 5th ed. Boston: Prentice Hall, 2012.

Davies, Suzanne, and Sandy Cook. "The Sex of Crime and Punishment." In *Harsh Punishment: International Experiences of Women's Imprisonment*, edited by Sandy Cook and Suzanne Davies, 53–80. Boston: Northeastern University Press, 1999.

Davis, Angela Y. *Are Prisons Obsolete?* New York: Seven Stories Press, 2003.

———. "Foreword: A World unto Itself: Multiple Invisibilities of Imprisonment." In *Behind the Razor Wire*, edited by Michael Jacobson-Hardy, ix–xvii. New York: NYU Press, 1998.

Davis, Lois M., Robert Bozick, Jennifer L. Steele, Jessica Saunders, and Jeremy N. V. Miles. *Evaluating the Effectiveness of Correctional Education: A Meta-Analysis of Programs That Provide Education to Incarcerated Adults.* Santa Monica, Calif.: Rand Corporation, 2013.

DeHart, Dana D. "Pathways to Prison: Impact of Victimization in the Lives of Incarcerated Women," *Violence against Women* 14, no. 12 (2008): 1362–1381.

Denzin, Norman, and Yvonna Lincoln. *The Landscape of Qualitative Research, Strategies of Qualitative Research, and Collecting and Interpreting Qualitative Materials.* Thousand Oaks, Calif.: Sage, 1998.

DeVault, Marjorie. *Liberating Method: Feminism and Social Research.* Philadelphia: Temple University Press, 1999.

———. "Talking and Listening from Women's Standpoint: Feminist Strategies for Interviewing and Analysis." *Social Problems* 37, no. 1 (1990): 96–116.

Dhami, Mandeep K., Peter Ayton, and George Loewenstein. "Adaptation to Imprisonment: Indigenous or Imported?" *Criminal Justice and Behavior* 34, no. 8 (2007): 1085–1100.

Diaz-Cotto, Juanita. *Chicana Lives and Criminal Justice: Voices from El Barrio.* Austin: University of Texas Press, 2006.

———. "Gender, Sexuality, and Family Kinship Networks." In *Interrupted Life: Experiences of Incarcerated Women in the United States,* edited by Rickie Solinger, Paula C. Johnson, Martha L. Raimon, Tina Reynolds, and Ruby C. Tapia, 131–144. Berkeley: University of California Press, 2010.

Didion, Joan. *The White Album.* 1979. Reprint, New York: Macmillan, 1990.

Dirkzwager, Anja J. E., and Candace Kruttschnitt. "Prisoners' Perceptions of Correctional Officers' Behavior in English and Dutch Prisons." *Journal of Criminal Justice* 40, no. 5 (2012): 404–412.

Dixon, Travis L., Christina L. Azocar, and Michael Casas. "The Portrayal of Race and Crime on Television Network News." *Journal of Broadcasting and Electronic Media* 47, no. 4 (2003): 498–523.

Dodge, L. Mora. *Whores and Thieves of the Worst Kind: A Study of Women, Crime and Prison 1835–2000.* DeKalb: Northern Illinois University Press, 2002.

Entman, Robert M. "Representation and Reality in the Portrayal of Blacks on Network Television News." *Journalism Quarterly* 71, no. 3 (1994): 509–520.

Faith, Karlene. *Unruly Women: The Politics of Confinement and Resistance.* New York: Seven Stories Press, 2011.

Farr, Kathryn Ann. "Classification for Female Inmates: Moving Forward." *Crime and Delinquency* 46, no. 1 (2000): 3–17.

———. "Defeminizing and Dehumanizing Female Murderers: Depictions of Lesbians on Death Row." *Women and Criminal Justice* 11, no. 1 (2008): 49–66.

"Felony Murder Doctrine." *TheFreeDictonary.com.* Accessed January 2, 2013. http://legaldictionary.thefreedictionary.com/felony+murder+doctrine.

Festinger, Leon. *A Theory of Cognitive Dissonance.* Evanston, Ill.: Row Peterson, 1957.

Fili, Andriani. "Women in Prison: Victims or Resisters? Representations of Agency in Women's Prisons in Greece." *Signs: Journal of Women in Culture and Society* 39, no. 1 (2013): 1–26.

Fine, Michelle. "Working the Hyphens: Reinventing Self and Other in Qualitative Research." In *Handbook of Qualitative Research,* edited by N. Denzin and Y. Lincoln. Thousand Oaks, Calif.: Sage, 1994.

Fine, Michelle, Maria Elena Torre, Kathy Boudin, Iris Bowen, Judith Clark, Donna Hylton, Migdalia Martinez, "Missy," Rosemarie A. Roberts, Pamela Smart, and Debora Upegui. *Changing Minds: The Impact of College in a Maximum Security Prison, 2001.* http://static.prisonpolicy.org/scans/changing_minds.pdf.

Flavin, Jeanne. *Our Bodies, Our Crimes.* New York: NYU Press, 2009.

Flavin, Jeanne, and Amy Desautels. "Feminism and Crime." In *Rethinking Gender, Crime, and Justice*, edited by Claire M. Renzetti, Lynne Goodstein, and Susan L. Miller, 11–28. Los Angeles: Roxbury, 2006.

Fleisher, Mark S., and Jessie L. Krienert. *The Myth of Prison Rape: Sexual Culture in American Prisons.* Lanham, Md.: Rowman and Littlefield, 2009.

Foucault, Michel. *Discipline and Punish: The Birth of the Prison.* New York: Vintage, 1977.

———. *The Foucault Reader.* New York: Pantheon, 1984.

———. *The History of Sexuality.* New York: Pantheon, 1978.

Freedman, Estelle B. "The Prison Lesbian: Race, Class, and the Construction of the Aggressive Female Homosexual, 1915–1965." *Feminist Studies* 22, no. 2 (1996): 397–423.

Gaarder, Emily, and Joanne Belknap. "Tenuous Borders: Girls Transferred to Adult Court." In *The Criminal Justice System and Women*, edited by Barbara Raffel Price and Natalie J. Sokoloff, 69–94. New York: McGraw-Hill, 2004.

Genovese, Eugene D. *Roll Jordan Roll: The World the Slaves Made.* New York: Vintage, 1976.

George, Erin. 2010. *A Woman Doing Life: Notes from a Prison for Women.* New York: Oxford University Press, 2010.

Giallombardo, Rose. *Society of Women: A Study of a Women's Prison.* New York: Wiley, 1966.

Giele, Janet Zollinger. "Homemaker or Career Woman: Life Course Factors and Racial Influences among Middle Class Americans." *Journal of Comparative Family Studies* 39, no. 3 (2008): 393–411.

Gilfus, Mary E. "Women's Experiences of Abuse as a Risk Factor for Incarceration." Harrisburg, Pa.: National Resource Center on Domestic Violence/Pennsylvania Coalition against Domestic Violence, 2002. Accessed September 14, 2010. http://www.vawnet.org/applied-research-papers/print-document.php?doc_id=412.

Gilligan, Carol. *In A Different Voice: Psychological Theory and Women's Development.* Cambridge, Mass.: Harvard University Press, 1982.

Giordano, Peggy C., Stephen A. Cernkovich, and Jennifer L. Rudolph. "Gender, Crime, and Desistance: Toward a Theory of Cognitive Transformation." *American Journal of Sociology* 107, no. 11 (2002): 990–1064.

Glaser, Barney G. *Theoretical Sensitivity.* Mill Valley, Calif.: Sociology Press, 1978.

Glaser, Barney G., and Anselm L. Strauss. *The Discovery of Grounded Theory.* New York: Aldine de Gruyter, 1967.

Goffman, Erving. *Asylums.* New York: Anchor, 1961.

———. *Stigma: Notes on the Management of a Spoiled Identity.* New York: Simon and Schuster, 1963.

Golden, Renny. *War on the Family: Mothers in Prison and the Families They Leave Behind.* New York: Routledge, 2005.

Goodstein, Lynne. "Introduction." In *Rethinking Gender, Crime, and Justice: Feminist Readings,* edited by Claire M. Renzetti, Lynne Goodstein, and Susan L. Miller, 1–10. Los Angeles: Roxbury, 2006.

Gopnik, Adam. "The Caging of America." *The New Yorker*, January 30, 2012, 72–77.

Gordon, Jill A., Blythe Proulx, and Patricia H. Grant. "Trepidation among the 'Keepers': Gendered Perceptions of Fear and Risk of Victimization among Correctional Officers." *American Journal of Criminal Justice* 38 (2013): 245–265.

Greer, Kimberly R. "The Changing Nature of Interpersonal Relationships in a Women's Prison." In *Behind Bars: Readings on Prison Culture*, edited by Richard Tewksbury, 110–128. Englewood Cliffs, N.J.: Pearson Prentice Hall, 2006.

———. "Walking an Emotional Tightrope: Managing Emotions in a Women's Prison." *Symbolic Interaction* 25, no. 1 (2002): 117–139.

Grogan, Sarah, and Helen Richards. "Body Image: Focus Groups with Boys and Men." *Men and Masculinities* 4, no. 3 (2002): 219–232.

Gudrais, Elizabeth. "The Prison Problem." *Harvard Magazine.* March-April 2013. Accessed March 7, 2013. http://harvardmagazine.com/2013/03/the-prison-problem.

Halcom, Chad. "Top Verdicts and Settlements: Inmate Abuse. *Tracey Neal et al v. Michigan Department of Corrections.*" *Crain's Detroit Business.* February 28, 2010. http://www.crainsdetroit.com/article/20100228/SUB01/302289985/top-verdicts-and-settlements-inmate-abuse#.

Hanks, Roma Stovall, and Nicole Carr. "Lifelines of Women in Jail as Self-Constructed Visual Probes for Life History Research." *Marriage and Family Review* 42, no. 4 (2008): 105–116.

Harding, Sandra. "Comment on Hekman's 'Truth and Method: Feminist Standpoint Theory Revisited': Whose Standpoint Needs the Regimes of Truth and Reality?" *Signs: Journal of Women and Culture* 22, no. 2 (1997): 382–391.

Harner, Holly M. "Relationships between Incarcerated Women: Moving beyond Stereotypes." *Journal of Psychosocial Nursing and Mental Health Services* 42, no. 1 (2004): 39–46.

Harris, M. Kay. "Moving into the New Millennium: Toward a Feminist Vision of Justice." In *Restorative Justice: Critical Issues,* edited by Eugene McLaughlin, Ross Fergusson, Gordon Hughes, and Louise Westmarland, 31–39. London: Sage and Open University Press, 2004.

Hartsock, Nancy. "The Feminist Standpoint: Developing the Ground for a Specifically Feminist Historical Materialism." In *Feminism and Methodology,* edited by Sandra Harding, 157–180. Bloomington: Indiana University Press, 1987.

Hassine, Victor. "How I Became a Convict." In *Doing Time: 25 Years of Prison Writing,* edited by Bell Gale Chevigny, 7–14. New York: Arcade, 1999.

———. *Life without Parole.* 4th ed. New York: Oxford University Press, 2009.

Heffernan, Esther. *Making It in Prison: The Square, the Cool, and the Life.* New York: John Wiley and Sons, 1972.

Hensley, Christopher, Richard Tewksbury, and Mary Koscheski. "The Characteristics and Motivations behind Female Prison Sex." *Women Criminal Justice* 13, no. 2/3 (2002): 125–139.

Herrschaft, Bryn A., Bonita M. Veysey, Heather R. Tubman-Carbone, and Johnna Christian. "Gender Differences in the Transformation Narrative: Implications for

Revised Reentry Strategies for Female Offenders." *Journal of Offender Rehabilitation* 48 (2009): 463–482.

Hesse-Biber, Sharlene Nagy, and Patricia Lina Leavy. *Feminist Research Practice: A Primer.* Thousand Oaks, Calif.: Sage, 2007.

Hesse-Biber, Sharlene Nagy, Christina Gilmartin, and Robin Lydenberg, eds. *Feminist Approaches to Theory and Methodology: An Interdisciplinary Reader.* New York: Oxford University Press, 1999.

Hochschild, Arlie Russell. *The Managed Heart: The Commercialization of Human Feeling.* Berkeley: University of California Press, 2003.

Hollander, Jocelyn A. "The Social Contexts of Focus Groups." *Journal of Contemporary Ethnography* 33, no. 5 (2004): 602–637.

Howley, Kevin. "Prey TV: Televangelism and Interpellation." *Journal of Film and Video* 53, no. 2/3 (2001): 23–37.

Irwin, John, and James Austin. *It's about Time: America's Imprisonment Binge.* 2nd ed. Belmont, Calif.: Wadsworth, 1997.

Irwin, John, and Donald Cressey. "Thieves, Convicts, and the Inmate Culture." *Social Problems* 10 (1962): 142–155.

Irwin, Tracy. "The 'Inside' Story: Practitioner Perspectives on Teaching in Prison." *Howard Journal* 47, no. 5 (2008): 512–528.

Jabro, Suzanne, and Kelly Kester-Smith. "Get on the Bus: Mobilizing Communities across California to Unite Children with Their Parents in Prison." In *Interrupted Life: Experiences of Incarcerated Women in the United States,* edited by Rickie Solinger, Paula C. Johnson, Martha L. Raimon, Tina Reynolds, and Ruby C. Tapia, 67–70. Berkeley: University of California Press, 2010.

Jacelon, Cynthia S., and Kristal Imperio. "Participant Diaries as a Source of Data in Research with Older Adults." *Qualitative Health Research* 15, no. 7 (2005): 991–997.

Jacobsen, Carol, and Lora Bex Lempert. "Institutional Disparities: Considerations of Gender in the Commutation Process for Incarcerated Women." *Signs: Journal of Women in Culture and Society* 39, no. 1 (2013): 265–289.

Jaggar, Alison M. "Feminist Ethics." In *Encyclopedia of Ethics, edited by* L. Becker and C. Becker, 363–364. New York: Garland, 1992.

Jiang, Shanhe, and Marianne Fisher-Giorlando. "Inmate Misconduct: A Test of the Deprivation, Importation, and Situational Models." In *Behind Bars: Readings on Prison Culture,* edited by Richard Tewksbury, 389–407. Englewood Cliffs, N.J.: Pearson Prentice Hall, 2006.

Johnson, Allan G. *Privilege, Power, and Difference.* 2nd ed. Boston: McGraw-Hill, 2006.

Johnson, Robert. "Introduction." In *A Woman Doing Life* by Erin George, 1–2. New York: Oxford University Press, 2010.

Johnson, Robert, and Ania Dobrzanska. "Mature Coping among Life-Sentenced Inmates: An Exploratory Study of Adjustment Dynamics." *Corrections Compendium* 30, no. 6 (2005): 8–13.

Jones, Ann. *Women Who Kill.* New York: Feminist Press, 2009.

Kimmel, Michael. *Guyland: The Perilous World Where Boys Become Men.* New York: Harper, 2008.

——. *Manhood in America: A Cultural History.* New York: Free Press, 1996.

——. "Why Men Should Support Gender Equity." *Women's Studies Review* Fall (2005): 102–114.

Kimmel, Michael, and Amy Aronson. *Sociology Now.* Boston: Pearson, 2009.

Knapik, Mirjam. "The Qualitative Research Interview: Participants' Responsive Participation in Knowledge Making." *International Journal of Qualitative Methods* 5, no. 3 (2006): 1–13.

Koscheski, Mary, and Christopher Hensley. "Inmate Homosexual Behavior in a Southern Female Correctional Facility." *American Journal of Criminal Justice* 25, no. 2 (2001): 269–277.

Krueger, Richard A., and Mary Anne Casey. *Focus Groups: A Practical Guide for Applied Research.* 3rd ed. Thousand Oaks, Calif.: Sage, 2000.

Kruttschnitt, Candace. "The Paradox of Women's Imprisonment." *Daedalus* 139, no. 3 (2010): 32–42.

Kruttschnitt, Candace, and Rosemary Gartner. *Marking Time in the Golden State: Women's Imprisonment in California.* Cambridge: Cambridge University Press, 2005.

——. "Women's Imprisonment." *Crime and Justice* 30 (2003): 1–81.

Kruttschnitt, Candace, Rosemary Gartner, and Amy Miller. "Doing Her Own Time? Women's Responses to Prison in the Context of the Old and the New Penology." *Criminology* 38 (2000): 681–717.

Kruttschnitt, Candace, and Jeanette Hussemann. "Micropolitics of Race and Ethnicity in Women's Prisons in Two Political Contexts." *British Journal of Sociology* 59, no. 4 (2008): 709–728.

Kubiac, Sheryl Pimlott, Julie Hanna, and Marianne Balton. " 'I Came to Prison to Do My Time—Not to Get Raped': Coping Within the Institutional Setting." *Stress, Trauma, and Crisis* 8 (2005): 157–177.

Kunzel, Regina. *Criminal Intimacy: Prison and the Uneven History of Modern American Sexuality.* Chicago: University of Chicago Press, 2008.

Law, Victoria. *Resistance behind Bars: The Struggles of Incarcerated Women.* Oakland, Calif.: PM Press, 2009.

Lear, Jonathon. *Radical Hope: Ethics in the Face of Cultural Devastation.* Cambridge, Mass.: Harvard University Press, 2006.

Leigey, Margaret E. "For the Longest Time: The Adjustment of Inmates to a Sentence of Life without Parole." *Prison Journal* 90, no. 3 (2010): 247–268.

Lempert, Lora Bex. "Asking Questions of the Data: Memo Writing in Grounded Theory." In *The Handbook of Grounded Theory*, edited by Anthony Bryant and Kathy Charmaz, 245–264. Thousand Oaks, Calif.: Sage, 2008.

——. "Cross Race, Cross Culture, Cross National, Cross Class, but Same Gender: Musings on Research in South Africa." *NWSA Journal* 19, no. 2 (2007): 79–103.

Lempert, Lora Bex, Suzanne Bergeron, and Maureen Linker. "Negotiating the Politics of Space: Teaching Women's Studies in a Women's Prison." *NWSA Journal* 17, no. 2 (2005): 199–207.

Lennon, Kathleen. "Gender and Knowledge." *Journal of Gender Studies* 4, no. 2 (1995): 133–143.

Levi, Robin, and Ayelet Waldman. "Introduction." In *Inside This Place, Not of It: Narratives from Women's Prisons,* edited by Robin Levi and Ayelet Waldman, 15–23. San Francisco: McSweeney's and Voices of Witness, 2011.

Levy, Douglas J. "Michigan to Pay $100M for Inmate Abuse: Settlement Ends 13-Year-Class-Action Suit Asserting Guards' Sexual Assaults, Harassment." *Michigan Lawyers Weekly*, July 27, 2009.

Liebman, James, Jeffrey Fagan, and Valerie West. 2000. *A Broken System: Error Rates in Capital Cases, 1973–1995.* Columbia University Law School Study, June 12, 2000.

Lindsey, Linda L., and Stephen Beach. *Essentials of Sociology.* Upper Saddle River, N.J.: Prentice Hall, 2003.

Logan, John. "Life and Death in the City: Neighborhoods in Context." In *The Contexts Reader,* edited by Jeff Goodwin and James M. Jasper, 437–444. New York: W. W. Norton and American Sociological Association, 2008.

Loury, Glenn C. "Crime, Inequality, and Social Justice." *Daedalus* 139, no. 3 (2010): 134–142.

Loury, Glenn C., and Bruce Western. "The Challenge of Mass Incarceration in America." *Daedalus* 139, no. 3 (2010): 5–7.

Macaskill, Ann, John Maltby, and Liza Day. "Forgiveness of Self and Others and Emotional Empathy." *Journal of Social Psychology* 142 (2002): 663–665.

Mahoney, Martha R. "Legal Images of Battered Women: Redefining the Issue of Separation." In *Domestic Violence Law,* edited by Nancy K. G. Lemon, 16–28. 2nd ed. St. Paul, Minn.: Thomson/West, 1991.

Mandaraka-Sheppard, Alexandra. *The Dynamics of Aggression in Women's Prisons in England.* Aldershot, U.K.: Gower, 1986.

Mastro, Dana, and Amanda L. Robinson. "Cops and Crooks: Images of Minorities on Primetime Television." *Journal of Criminal Justice* 28, no. 5 (2000): 385–396.

Mauer, Marc. *The Changing Racial Dynamics of Women's Incarceration.* Washington, D.C.: Sentencing Project, 2013.

Mauer, Marc, Cathy Potler, and Richard Wolf. *Gender and Justice: Women, Drugs, and Sentencing Policy.* Washington, D.C.: Sentencing Project, 1999.

McAdams, Dan P. *The Stories We Live By: Personal Myths and the Making of the Self.* New York: William Morrow, 1993.

———. "Studying Lives in Time: A Narrative Approach." *Advances in Life Course Research* 10 (2005): 237–258.

McCorkel, Jill A. *Breaking Women: Gender, Race and the New Politics of Imprisonment.* New York: NYU Press, 2013.

———. "Embodied Surveillance and the Gendering of Punishment." *Journal of Contemporary Ethnography* 32, no. 1 (2003): 41–76.

———. "Going to the Crackhouse: Critical Space as a Form of Resistance in Total Institutions and Everyday Life." *Symbolic Interaction* 21, no. 3 (1998): 227–252.

Mead, George Herbert. *Mind, Self, and Society*. 1934. Reprint, Chicago: University of Chicago Press, 1962.

Messerschmidt, James W. "Masculinities and Crime: Beyond a Dualistic Criminology." In *Rethinking Gender, Crime, and Justice*, edited by Claire M. Renzetti, Lynne Goodstein, and Susan L. Miller, 29–43. Los Angeles: Roxbury, 2006.

Meth, Paula. "Using Diaries to Understand Women's Responses to Crime and Violence." *Environment and Urbanization* 16, no. 2 (2004): 153–164.

Michalson, Venezia. "Mothers, Children, and Crime: The Role of Parenting in Women's Desistance after Incarceration." In *Women and Justice: It's a Crime*, edited by Roslyn Muraskin, 69–77. 5th ed. Boston: Prentice Hall, 2012.

Michigan Department of Corrections. "About MDOC." Accessed February 23, 2012. http://www.michigan.gov/corrections.

———. "Corrections Officers as of December 26, 2009." In *2009 Statistical Report*, F-21. http://www.michigan.gov/documents/corrections/2009_MDOC_STATISTICAL_REPORT_319907_7.pdf.

———. "New Corrections Officer Training." Accessed February 23, 2012. http://www.michigan.gov/corrections/0,4551,7-119-1438_28885-5508--,00.html.

———. "Parole Consideration Process." Accessed January 21, 2014. http://www.michigan.gov/corrections/0,4551,7-119-145_11601-22909--,00.html.

———. *2010 Statistical Report*. Modified on February 23, 2012. http://www.michigan.gov/documents/corrections/2011-08-31_-_MDOC_Annual_Stat_Report_-_Vers_1_0_362197_7.pdf.

Michigan Women's Justice and Clemency Project. Accessed June 10, 2014. http://www.umich.edu/~clemency/.

Miller, Tekla Dennison. *The Warden Wore Pink*. Brunswick, Me.: Biddle, 1996.

Miller v. Alabama, 132 S.Ct. 2455, 2464 (2012).

Mills, C. Wright. "Situated Actions and Vocabularies of Motive." *American Sociological Review* 5, no. 6 (1940): 904–913.

———. *The Sociological Imagination*. New York: Oxford University Press, 1959.

Morash, Merry. "Tackling Key Questions about Gender, Crime, and Justice." In *Understanding Gender, Crime, and Justice*, edited by Merry Morash, 1–33. Thousand Oaks, Calif.: Sage, 2006.

———. *Women on Probation and Parole: A Feminist Critique of Community Programs and Services*. Boston: Northeastern University Press, 2010.

Mullendore, Kristine, and Laurie Beever. "Sexually Abused Women in State and Local Correctional Institutions, 1980–2000." In *Women and Girls in the Criminal Justice System: Policy Issues and Practice Strategies*, edited by Russ Immarigeon, 5-1-5-12. Kingston, N.J.: Civic Research Institute, 2006.

Muraskin, Roslyn. "Disparate Treatment in Correctional Facilities: Women Incarcerated." In *Women and Justice: It's a Crime*, edited by Roslyn Muraskin, 329–343. 5th ed. Boston: Prentice Hall, 2012.

Naples, Nancy A. *Feminism and M...* *hy, Discourse Analysis, and Activist*

...*behind Bars: Results from the 2003* ...*rvey*. By Elizabeth Greenberg, ...73. May 10, 2007. http://nces.

...ing Rights." Last modified July 15, ...-campaigns/felon-voting-rights.

...*ion in the United States: Exploring* ...ional Academies Press, 2014.

...aw Circuit Court Case No. ...ss settlement document. July 15,

...*m a National Survey*. Washing-

...fe without Parole Sentences in ...no. 1 (2010): 27–32.

...ing Use of Life Sentences in ...09.

...ltey. "Mad, Bad, or Reasonable? ... Kills." *Gender Issues* 27, no. 3–4

...ntity: Subverting the Parolee ...*y Ethnography* 40, no. 2 (2011):

...*Vomen's Prison*. Albany: State

..."Sex and Sexuality in ...gation." *Prison Journal* 91, no. 3

...raining Program as a Function ...es." *Adolescence* 25, no. 97

... *The Boy Who Was Raised as a Dog: And Other Stories from a Child Psychiatrist's Notebook—What Traumatized Children*. New York: Basic, 2007.

Petrella, Christopher, and Alex Friedmann. "Slowly Closing the Gates: A State-by-State Assessment of Recent Prison Closures." *Prison Legal News* 24, no. 6 (June 2013): 1–12.

Phillips, Susan D. "Incarcerated Women." September 2012. Washington, D.C.: Sentencing Project. http://www.sentencingproject.org/detail/publication.cfm?publication_id=4138&id=136.

——. "Parents in Prison Fact Sheet." September 2012. Washington, D.C.: Sentencing Project. http://www.sentencingproject.org/detail/publication.cfm?publication_id=414&id=136.

Pogrebin, Mark R., and Mary Dodge. "Women's Accounts of Their Prison Experiences: A Retrospective View of Their Subjective Realities." In *Behind Bars: Readings in Prison Culture*, edited by Richard Tewksbury, 28–46. Upper Saddle River, N.J.: Pearson/Prentice Hall, 2006.

Pollock, Joycelyn. "Afterword." In *A Woman Doing Life*, by Erin George, 176–185. New York: Oxford University Press, 2010.

——. *Prisons: Today and Tomorrow*. Ontario: Jones and Bartlett, 2006.

——. *Women, Prison, and Crime*. Belmont, Calif.: Wadsworth, 2002.

——. "Working in Prison: Staff and Administration." In *Women, Prison, and Crime*, edited by Joycelyn M. Pollock, 172–200. Belmont, Calif.: Wadsworth, 2002.

Potter, Sarah. 2004. "'Undesirable Relations': Same-Sex Relationships and the Meaning of Sexual Desire at a Women's Reformatory during the Progressive Era." *Feminist Studies*, 30, no. 2 (2004): 394–415.

Prejean, Sister Helen. "Foreword." In *Doing Time: 25 Years of Prison Writing*, edited by Bell Gale Chevigny, i–xxvi. New York: Arcade, 1999.

Price, Barbara Raffel, and Natalie Sokoloff. *The Criminal Justice System and Women: Offenders, Prisoners, Victims, and Workers*. 3rd ed. New York: McGraw-Hill, 2004.

Rader, Nicole E. "Surrendering Solidarity: Considering the Relationships among Female Correctional Officers." *Women and Criminal Justice* 16, no. 3 (2005): 27–42.

Rafter, Nicole. *Partial Justice: Women in State Prisons*. Boston: Northeastern University Press, 1985.

Rasche, Christine E. "Cross-Sex Supervision of Incarcerated Women and the Dynamics of Staff Sexual Misconduct." In *Gendered Justice: Addressing Female Offenders*, edited by Barbara E. Bloom, 141–172. Durham, N.C.: Carolina Academic Press, 2003.

Reddy, Vikrant P., and Marc Levin. "The Conservative Case against More Prisons." *American Conservative*. March 6, 2013. http://www.theamericanconservative.com/articles/the-conservative-case-against-more-prisons/.

Renzetti, Claire. "Gender and Violent Crime." In *Rethinking Gender, Crime, and Justice*, edited by Claire M. Renzetti, Lynne Goodstein, and Susan L. Miller, 93–106. Los Angeles: Roxbury, 2006.

Renzetti, Claire M., and Daniel J. Curran. *Living Sociology*. Boston: Allyn and Bacon, 2000.

Reuss, Anne. "Prison(er) Education." *Howard Journal* 38, no. 2 (1999): 113–127.

——. "Taking a Long Hard Look at Imprisonment." *Howard Journal* 42, no. 5 (2003): 426–436.

Rhodes, Lorna A. "Changing the Subject: Conversation in Supermax." *Cultural Anthropology* 20, no. 3 (2005): 388–411.

——. *Total Confinement: Madness and Reason in the Maximum Security Prison*. Berkeley: University of California Press, 2004.

Richie, Beth E. *Compelled to Crime: The Gender Entrapment of Battered Black Women.* New York: Routledge, 1996.

Riessman, Catherine Kohler. "Stigma and Everyday Resistance Practices: Childless Women in South India." *Gender and Society* 14, no. 1 (2000): 111–135.

Ross, Jeffrey Ian, and Stephen C. Richards. "Introduction." In *Convict Criminology,* edited by Jeffrey Ian Ross and Stephen C. Richards, 1–13. Belmont, Calif.: Wadsworth, 2003.

Rotter, Merrill, Hunter L. McQuistion, Nehama Broner, and Michael Steinbacher. "Best Practices: The Impact of 'Incarceration Culture' on Re-entry or Adults with Mental Illness: A Training and Group Treatment Model." *Psychiatric Services* 56, no. 3 (2005): 265–267.

Rotter, Merrill, Bruce Way, Michael Steinbacher, Donald Sawyer, and Hal Smith. "Personality Disorders in Prison: Aren't They All Antisocial?" *Psychiatric Quarterly* 73, no. 4 (2002): 337–349.

Rowe, Abigail. "Narratives of Self and Identity in Women's Prisons: Stigma and the Struggle for Self-Definition in Penal Regimes." *Punishment and Society* 13, no. 5 (2011): 571–591.

Ruddick, Sara. *Maternal Thinking: Toward a Politics of Peace.* New York: Ballantine, 1989.

Sampson, Robert J. *Great American City: Chicago and the Enduring Neighborhood Effect.* Chicago: University of Chicago Press, 2012.

———. "The Place of Context: A Theory and Strategy for Criminology's Hard Problems." *Criminology* 51, no. 1 (2013): 1–31.

Scarce, Rik. "Doing Time as an Act of Survival." *Symbolic Interaction* 23, no. 3 (2002): 303–321.

Schirmer, Sarah, Ashley Nellis, and Marc Mauer. *Incarcerated Parents and Their Children: Trends 1991–2007.* Washington, D.C.: Sentencing Project, 2009.

Schmid, Thomas J., and Richard S. Jones. "Ambivalent Actions: Prison Strategies of First-Time, Short-Term Inmates." In *Behind Bars: Readings on Prison Culture,* edited by Richard A. Tewksbury, 3–16. Upper Saddle River, N.J.: Pearson Prentice Hall, 2006.

Seale, Clive. "Quality in Qualitative Research." *Qualitative Inquiry* 5, no. 4 (1999): 465–478.

Seidel, Jeff. "Jury Awarded $15.4 Million to Inmates." *Detroit Free Press,* January 7, 2009. http://www.freep.com/article/20090107/NEWS06/901070395/Jury-awarded-15-4-million-inmates.

Sentencing Project. "Felony Disenfranchisement." Accessed June 17, 2014. http://www.sentencingproject.org/template/page.cfm?id=133.

Shanahan, Michael J., and Erik J. Porfeli. "Chance Events in the Life Course." *Advances in Life Course Research* 11 (2007): 97–119.

Siegel, Jane A. *Disrupted Childhoods: Children of Women in Prison.* New Brunswick, N.J.: Rutgers University Press, 2011.

Smith, Dorothy. *Institutional Ethnography: A Sociology for People.* Walnut Creek, Calif.: AltaMira, 2005.

Sokoloff, Natalie J., Barbara Raffel Price, and Jeanne Flavin. "The Criminal Law and Women." In *The Criminal Justice System and Women,* edited by Barbara Raffel Price and Natalie J. Sokoloff, 11–29. 3rd ed. Boston: McGraw-Hill, 2004.

Sparks, Richard. " 'Out of the 'Digger': The Warrior's Honour and the Guilty Observer." *Ethnography* 3, no. 4 (2002): 556–581.

Sprague, Joey. *Feminist Methodologies for Critical Researchers.* Walnut Creek, Calif.: AltaMira, 2005.

Steffensmeier, Darrell, and Jennifer Schwartz. "Contemporary Explanations of Women's Crime." In *The Criminal Justice System and Women,* edited by Barbara Raffel Price and Natalie J. Sokoloff, 112–126. 3rd ed. Boston: McGraw-Hill, 2004.

———. "Trends in Female Criminality: Is Crime Still a Man's World?" In *The Criminal Justice System and Women,* edited by Barbara Raffel Price and Natalie J. Sokoloff, 95–111. 3rd ed. Boston: McGraw-Hill, 2004.

Strauss, Anselm L. *Qualitative Analysis for Social Scientists.* Cambridge: Cambridge University Press, 1987.

Strauss, Anselm L., and Juliet Corbin. *Basics of Qualitative Research.* Newbury Park, Calif.: Sage, 1990.

Sweeney, Megan, ed. *The Story within Us: Women Prisoners Reflect on Reading.* Urbana: University of Illinois Press, 2012.

Tapia, Ruby C. "Introduction: Certain Failures: Representing the Experiences of Incarcerated Women in the United States." In *Interrupted Life: Experiences of Incarcerated Women in the United States,* edited by Rickie Solinger, Paula C. Johnson, Martha L. Raimon, Tina Reynolds, and Ruby C. Tapia, 1–10. Berkeley: University of California Press, 2010.

Tekola, Bethlehem, Christine Griffin, and Laura Camfield. "Using Qualitative Methods with Poor Children in Urban Ethiopia: Opportunities and Challenges." *Social Indicators Research* 90, no. 1 (2009): 73–87.

Thomas, Jim. *Doing Critical Ethnography.* Newbury Park, Calif.: Sage, 1993.

———. "Gendered Control in Prisons: The Difference Difference Makes." In *Women in Prison: Gender and Social Control,* edited by Barbara H. Zaitzow and Jim Thomas Boulder, 1–20. Boulder, Colo.: Lynne Rienner, 2003.

Thomas, W. I., and Dorothy Swain Thomas. *The Child in America: Behavior Problems and Programs.* New York: Knopf, 1928.

Toch, Hans. *Living in Prison: The Ecology of Survival.* New York: Free Press, 1977.

Toussaint, Loren, and Jon R. Webb. "Gender Differences in the Relationship between Empathy and Forgiveness." *Journal of Social Psychology* 145, no. 6 (2005): 673–685.

Tracy, Sarah J. "The Construction of Correctional Officers: Layers of Emotionality behind Bars." *Qualitative Inquiry* 10, no. 4 (2004): 509–533.

Trammell, Rebecca. *Enforcing the Convict Code: Violence and Prison Culture.* Boulder, Colo.: Lynne Rienner, 2011.

Turner, Nicolas, and John Wetzel. 2014. "Treating Prisoners with Dignity Can Reduce Crime." *National Journal.* Accessed May 22, 2014. http://www.nationaljournal.com/.

U.S. Department of Justice, Bureau of Justice Statistics. *Federal Habeas Corpus Review: Challenging State Court Criminal Convictions.* By Roger A. Hanson and Henry W.K. Daley. NCJ 155504. September 1995.

———. *Incarcerated Parents and Their Children.* By Christopher J. Mumola. NCJ 182335. August 2000. http://bjs.ojp.usdoj.gov/index.cfm?ty=pbdetail&iid=981.

———. *Parents in Prison and Their Minor Children.* By Lauren E. Glaze and Laura M. Maruschak. NCJ 222984. August 2008. http://bjs.ojp.usdoj.gov/index.cfm?ty=pbdetail&iid=823.

———. *Prior Abuse Reported by Inmates and Probationers.* By Caroline Wolf Harlow. NCJ 172879. 1999. http://bjs.ojp.usdoj.gov/index.cfm?ty=pbdetail&iid=637.

———. *Prisoners in 2010.* By Paul Guerino, Paige M. Harrison and William J. Sabol. NCJ 236096. December 15, 2011.

———. *Prisoners in 2011.* By E. Ann Carson and William J. Sabol. NCJ 239808. December 2012.

Vacca, James S. "Educated Prisoners Are Less Likely to Return to Prison." *Journal of Correctional Education* 55, no. 4 (2004): 297–305.

Van Gundy, Alana. "Gender and Corrections: Comparing Facilities and Programs." In *Women and Justice: It's a Crime*, edited by Roslyn Muraskin, 344–353. 5th ed. Boston: Prentice Hall, 2012.

Vuolo, Mike, and Candace Kruttschnitt. "Prisoners' Adjustment, Correctional Officers, and Context: The Foreground and Background of Punishment in Late Modernity." *Law and Society Review* 42, no. 2 (2008): 307–335.

Wacquant, Loïc. "The Curious Eclipse of Prison Ethnography in the Age of Mass Incarceration." *Ethnography* 3, no. 4 (2002): 371–397.

Wade, Nicholas. *The Faith Instinct.* New York: Penguin, 2010.

Wahidin, Azrini, and Dot Moss. "Women Doing and Making Time: Reclaiming Time." *International Journal of Sociology and Social Policy* 24, no. 6 (2004): 76–111.

Walker, Samuel. *Sense and Non-Sense about Crime, Drugs, and Communities.* 7th ed. Belmont, Calif.: Wadsworth Cengage Learning, 2011.

Walker, Samuel, Cassia Spohn, and Miriam DeLone. *The Color of Justice.* Belmont, Calif.: Wadsworth/Thomson, 2004.

Ward, David, and Gene Kassebaum. *Women's Prison: Sex and Social Structure.* Chicago: Aldine, 1965.

Warner, Margaret S. "Does Empathy Cure? A Theoretical Consideration of Empathy, Processing, and Personal Narratives." In *Empathy Reconsidered: New Directions in Psychotherapy*, edited by Arthur C. Bohart and Leslie S. Greenberg, 125–140. Washington, D.C.: American Psychological Association, 1997.

Warren, Millicent D. *Deposition before Timothy Boroski Taken at Women's Huron Valley, October 16, 2012, in Case of Tom Nowacki et al Plaintiffs v. Hon. Archie C. Brown, State of Michigan Department of Corrections.* Case # 11-852-CD. 2012. http://www.fettlaw.com/PSD-motion-brief-Ex-B.pdf.

Weitzer, Ronald, and Steven A. Tuch. "Racially Biased Policing: Determinants of Citizen Perceptions." *Social Forces* 83, no. 3 (2005): 1009–1030.

Wideman, John Edgar. "Doing Time, Marking Race." In *Behind the Razor Wire*, edited by Michael Jacobson-Hardy, 13–17. New York: NYU Press, 1999.

Wiesel, Elie. "I Am Against Fanatics": A Dialogue between Elie Wiesel and Merle Hoffman on Abortion, Love and the Holocaust." *On the Issues,* Spring 1991. http://www.ontheissuesmagazine.com/1991spring/Spring1991_1.php.

Williams, Kirk R., and Nancy G. Guerra. "Perceptions of Collective Efficacy and Bullying Perpetration in Schools." *Social Problems* 58, no. 1 (2011): 126–143.

Wise, Tim. *Color-Blind: The Rise of Post-Racial Politics and the Retreat from Racial Equity.* San Francisco: City Lights, 2010.

Young, Vernetta D., and Rebecca Reviere. *Women behind Bars: Gender and Race in US Prisons.* Boulder, Colo.: Lynne Rienner, 2006.

INDEX

Study participants are *italicized* and filed under the first name of their pseudonym. Page numbers in **bold** indicate tables and figures

prison uniforms, 60–61, 67, 135, 152; stages of (*see* acting at choice points; "becoming a prisoner"; counternarratives; internal compass; navigating the mix; social bonds; stages typology). *See also* "behind a man"; boundaries: "blurred boundaries"; correctional officers (COs); differences, males/females in prison; imprisonment; juvenile lifers; life sentence; religion and a spiritual strategy; "short termers"; social bonds

Yasmeen, **22**, 29–30, 71, 98, 128, 153, 158, 180
Yates, Andrea, 6
Yingling, Isabelle, xi
Young, Vernetta, 9, 24

Z, Officer, 180–81

ABOUT THE AUTHOR

Lora Bex Lempert is Professor Emerita at the University of Michigan–Dearborn. For twelve years, she cosponsored the National Lifers of America chapter at a women's correctional facility and was the coordinator of college-level courses offered at that facility. She also offered the first Inside Out Prison Exchange class in Michigan.